Flip-Flop

Anthropology, Culture and Society

Series Editors:
Professor Vered Amit, Concordia University
and
Professor Christina Garsten, Stockholm University

Recent titles:

Flip-Flop

A Journey Through
Globalisation's Backroads

Caroline Knowles

PlutoPress
www.plutobooks.com

First published 2014 by Pluto Press
345 Archway Road, London N6 5AA

www.plutobooks.com

Distributed in the United States of America exclusively by
Palgrave Macmillan, a division of St. Martin's Press LLC,
175 Fifth Avenue, New York, NY 10010

British Library Cataloguing in Publication Data
A catalogue record for this book is available from the British Library

ISBN   978 0 7453 3412 7   Hardback
ISBN   978 0 7453 3411 0   Paperback
ISBN   978 1 7837 1150 5   PDF eBook
ISBN   978 1 7837 1152 9   Kindle eBook
ISBN   978 1 7837 1151 2   EPUB eBook

Library of Congress Cataloging in Publication Data applied for

This book is printed on paper suitable for recycling and made from fully managed
and sustained forest sources. Logging, pulping and manufacturing processes are
expected to conform to the environmental standards of the country of origin.

10   9   8   7   6   5   4   3   2

Typeset from disk by Stanford DTP Services, Northampton, England
Text design by Melanie Patrick
Simultaneously printed digitally by CPI Antony Rowe, Chippenham, UK
and Edwards Bros in the United States of America

For Jess, Will and Sophie

Contents

Series Preface

Anthropology is a discipline based upon in-depth ethnographic works that deal with wider theoretical issues in the context of particular, local conditions – to paraphrase an important volume from the series: *large issues* explored in *small places*. This series has a particular mission: to publish work that moves away from an old-style descriptive ethnography that is strongly area-studies oriented, and offer genuine theoretical arguments that are of interest to a much wider readership, but which are nevertheless located and grounded in solid ethnographic research. If anthropology is to argue itself a place in the contemporary intellectual world, then it must surely be through such research.

We start from the question: 'What can this ethnographic material tell us about the bigger theoretical issues that concern the social sciences?' rather than 'What can these theoretical ideas tell us about the ethnographic context?' Put this way round, such work becomes *about* large issues, *set in* a (relatively) small place, rather than detailed description of a small place for its own sake. As Clifford Geertz once said, 'Anthropologists don't study villages; they study *in* villages.'

By place, we mean not only geographical locale, but also other types of 'place' – within political, economic, religious or other social systems. We therefore publish work based on ethnography within political and religious movements, occupational or class groups, among youth, development agencies, and nationalist movements; but also work that is more thematically based – on kinship, landscape, the state, violence, corruption, the self. The series publishes four kinds of volume: ethnographic monographs; comparative texts; edited collections; and shorter, polemical essays.

We publish work from all traditions of anthropology, and all parts of the world, which combines theoretical debate with empirical evidence to demonstrate anthropology's unique position in contemporary scholarship and the contemporary world.

Professor Vered Amit
Professor Christina Garsten

Acknowledgements

It's been a long trek and I am indebted to the efforts of many people I have met along the way. First and foremost I would like to thank all of those who contributed their time and their energies to helping me understand their lives and concerns. Ethics and, sometimes, concern for your safety, prevents me naming you, but you know who you are. You may recognise yourself in these pages. My heartfelt thanks are extended to you, my collaborators in Kuwait, Korea, China and Ethiopia. Without you this book could not have been written.

I thank Michael Tan for being my fellow traveller, as well as the photographer, at various points along the trail. The British Academy funded the research on the early parts of the trail. The Leverhulme Trust funded the rest. Clarks Shoes paid for several Ethiopian children to have footballs. I am most grateful for the sponsorship of these funding bodies, and especially for the efforts of Jean Cater. Jane Plastow, Belayneh Abune, Elizabeth Moges, Kibralem Fanta and Daniel Sileshi smoothed the trail through Ethiopia. Fatmah, Mohammed, Samira, Maryam, Quinsan Ciao, Beverly Skeggs, Jeremy Anderson, Abbas Nokhasten, Baker Khundari, Bilal Malkawi, Duncan Brown, Tariq Al Hajji and Geraint Fox helped me navigate Kuwait.

Doonwok Dean Oh, Young Jeon Kim, Miri Song and Susan Choi, helped me understand Korea. Xiuchan explained China to me and introduced me to the right people. He Wenxian, Ms Fan and the students were fabulous. Mohamed Hassan advised on Somalia. Pat Loughrey and Liz Bromley made sure I didn't go there. Francisco Calafate talked rubbish with me. My colleagues at Goldsmiths Centre for Urban and Community Research, especially Carole Keegan, Alison Rooke, Monica Sassetelli, Roger Burrows and Alex Rhys-Taylor all helped in various ways. Bernard Walsh, Noel Dyck and Claire Alexander provided conversation and critical feedback when it was needed. My students at Goldsmiths kept me on track. Friends and family offered much needed distraction when the going got tough. My thanks especially to June and Eric Litton, Patrick and Anne Knowles, Norma and Chris Jones, Kirsten Campbell and Paul Halliday. Bill Schwarz wielded a red pencil over the manuscript and much improved it, as his relentless good humour enhanced my life while I wrote it. Thanks Bill. My children, Jess, Will and Sophie Knowles-Mofford tolerated the absences and inattentions on which they clearly thrive. This book is dedicated to you with my love.

Without the intervention of my friend and colleague, Vered Amit, the manuscript that became this book would have remained in my wastepaper basket. My thanks to you, Vered, for gently suggesting I take it out and have another go at writing it. I would also like to thank the team at Pluto Press, especially David Castle.

Prologue

You might have a pair of flip-flops, perhaps objects you have not given much thought to. I don't think about mine; they sit at the back of a closet, suited only to journeys I don't want to tackle barefoot – to the swimming pool, between the beach and the car park or the terrace – but which don't call for more formal shoes. Flip-flops are an accessory; they are accessory in being unassuming, secondary to more serious footwear in which more significant journeys are undertaken; accessory, as in not the main story, as in just a footnote. *Flip-Flop* follows a footnote through the landscapes, lives and stories in which it is animated; by which I don't just mean small, personal stories, although these are important, but bigger stories too, the kinds of stories which run from place to place. Mobile stories then, stories connecting places; stories which probe, from an unusual angle, the interlacing social fabrics of the twenty-first century on a worldwide scale. This is a book about globalisation; about people and places we have yet to imagine; and it suggests that globalisation may not be what we think it is. And it is a book about plastic, which frankly could be taken more seriously, as *the* material in which our world is fabricated. In a world on the move, what could be more elemental than the shoes in which we anticipate the multiple journeys of our lives? And flip-flops are *the* most elemental of shoes – simple in design, cheap and accessible, worn by more people on the planet than any other shoes. In flip-flops we are all fellow travellers. What follows is a journey of journeys heading in unanticipated directions. Welcome to the flip-flop trail.

1

Navigating the Territories of the Trail

Flip-flops – even shoes – rarely feature as a central character in a book. But unlikely characters provoke new stories. Travelling stories. So fundamental to mobility are shoes that only a minority would venture out without them. In shoes distinctions between object and human are blurred, saturated as they are with bits of skin, DNA and remnants of the ground across which we travel. Flip-flops reveal the world in which we live. Uncounted billions touch more feet (lives) than any other shoe. No other shoe has been to more places on more feet. In them people tackle the epic and mundane journeys of their lives: flip-flops are worn to the bathroom, to the beach, to work, to school, to market, to a new country. They tread all manner of journeys, social scenes and landscapes.

Although designer flip-flops are expensive,[1] flip-flops' popularity lies in their cheapness. They retail for as little as US 40 cents. Thus they have social reach: millionaires and paupers wear them. In the twenty-first century, a billion people walk barefoot.[2] Flip-flops are the first step into the world of shoes. Flip-flops are demographically sensitive: when world population rises so do flip-flop sales. Flip-flops are a shoe with critical mass and mass appeal across social spectrums and continents. They are travelling objects with untapped potential in revealing mobile social worlds of the twenty-first century.

Flip-flops can be made from any materials but today they are made from plastic, connecting them with the mid twentieth century. American mass manufacture of them dates back to 1930s Hawaiian plantations, where they became a substitute for rubber boots – in short supply – copying the design of ninth-century Japanese sandals made in rush and bamboo and brought to the plantations by nineteenth-century Japanese migrants. Flip-flops were popular in the US navy with sailors travelling to Pacific theatres of war, and the period after the Second World War was crucial to their widespread popularity. In the 1950s they appeared in Californian beach and surfer culture and then made their way down the coast to Mexico and into South America, inspiring the term 'slipper foot' applied to the poor.[3] They have different names in different places: 'thongs', 'zoris', 'slaps', 'flaps', 'beach walkers' and 'go-aheads', because it is impossible to walk backwards in them.

Materials are as important as the objects from which they are made and plastic is a thoroughly modernist twentieth-century material: its most common form, polyethylene used in plastic bags, is a thermoplastic polymer created at the junction of the nineteenth and twentieth centuries. Bakelite – a thermosetting plastic that dates from 1909 – was used to fabricate the first telephones and early radios in addition to an array of early twentieth-century household objects. DuPont filed a patent for synthetic rubber in 1931, the first synthetic fibres in 1934 and for ethylene-vinyl acetate (EVA) in 1956.[4] Flip-flops are now made in different kinds of plastic, *the* material of everyday life the world over. Today the world in which we live is literally fabricated in an array of plastics. Plastic is made into spectacle frames, interior car trim, baby seats, electrical wire coating, packaging, buckets, bowls, biro casing, telephones, speakers, computers, telephones, shoes, insoles, light fittings and more: it is injected into fabrics made into clothes. If there is a dominant material in which the contemporary world is made, it is plastic. The objects composing the dominant material fabric of our lives are thus neither precious nor unique but plastic and disposable.

Material and Social Fabrics

Social and material fabrics, social and material worlds, are intimately connected.[5] This book shows this in revealing the mobile fabrics of everyday life. Fabric is used in two (overlapping) ways to refer to materials – in this case plastic – and to social textures – the weave of everyday life. It unpicks both of these fabrics at the same time in order to dramatise *how* plastic and social lives are connected. Objects, rather than materials, have shaped cultural anthropology's[6] exploration of the ways in which lives and objects are entwined, inaugurating new lines of enquiry. In these frameworks circulations of objects and the quiet lives they reveal have become important areas of research.[7] Arjun Appadurai, Daniel Miller and especially Igor Kopytoff have inspired this book. Kopytoff[8] suggests that asking critical questions about the provenance and use of a car in Africa reveals how social worlds work. While he neither applies nor elaborates his example, the car prompts important questions: How was it acquired? Where did the money to buy it come from? What were the relationships between buyer and seller? How was it used? Who drove it? And how was it disposed of? The idea that objects have biographies – life stories – and that exploring them exposes social texture inspired this book. It executes Kopytoff's project while developing a distinctive approach differing from that of Kopytoff and other material anthropologists like Miller and Appadurai by following the entire trail created by the object and unfolding its human and environmental textures along the way.

While Kopytoff reanimated the archaeological methods of Pitt Rivers so that objects (traces) access lost social forms, Miller[9] locates people through their domestic objects, demonstrating both the intimacies of people–object connections and the analytic potential of objects in probing lives. I aspire neither to material cultural analysis nor to the delicious elaboration of lives that comes from juxtaposing people with the aesthetics of the object assemblages with which they cohabit. Instead I use a particular object to explore the vitality and motility of the lives and landscapes connected, in various ways, to its making, transportation, use and disposal. A plastic object is this story's central character and its key investigative tool; it is used to excavate the everyday lives and landscapes it regards as equally significant. Biography and geography, rather than cultures, are the social textures this book explores and which distinguish it from others.

The emphasis on making raises the profile of the material substance of objects and this too distinguishes this book from much material and cultural anthropology. This partly results from the importance placed on fabrication – the making and unmaking of the object – rather than on its end-shape. But it results too from an understanding that materials are more than inert matter moulded into objects. Drawing (selectively) on the idea of 'vibrant matter',[10] I suggest that plastic vibrates with the vitality of the social lives with which it is enmeshed. I hope to show that plastic is animated; that it has flesh and bones and it dances along the road. Activated in the lives it entwines, plastic is mobile and vital. Even landfill sites, full of seemingly disused objects, emit active streams of methane gas as one form of matter becomes another. Plastic's flesh and humanity – its journeys, its circuits, its ways of dwelling in the world – are animated in this book. Flip-flops' material properties, as well as their usefulness and ubiquity make them a worthy protagonist in my book.

I will show how plastic flip-flops make social class, migration, landscape and the multiple translocal social relationships of export, transport and expanding markets. Different types of migratory movement, in particular, come into focus along the trail. As plastic flip-flops create these kinds of social textures so they also make and expose the topographies of their co-production and distribution. Plastic flip-flops make and reveal cities, exurbs, suburbs, borders and zones, the places where people live and travel through on the routine journeys of everyday life. I pay particular attention to these broadly urban forms and to the local and translocal connections composing them. Thus plastic flip-flops are shown to be an ideal object for thinking about the production of topographies and the routes connecting them. Plastic flip-flops are a travelling object, which both makes and reveals translocal worlds: and following the object sequentially through the territories and lives it traverses configures the flip-flop trail.

Trails

Despite the efforts of Kopytoff, and of scholars of material culture that make trails comprehensible, they are not particularly popular in anthropology. They are still less comprehensible in sociology, a discipline whose empirical focus is still conceived in nation-state terms despite the (theoretical) turn to translocality.[11] Trails appeal to a certain kind of vagrant sociologist[12] like myself on account of their methodological challenges and travel requirements. The best examples of trails are interdisciplinary. Deborah Barndt's *Tangled Routes*[13] follows a tomato trail from Mexico to fast food restaurants in Canada, pursuing important questions about environment, global food chains and the lives of the women cashiers and pickers who make them work. James Marriot and Mika Minio-Paluello's *The Oil Road*[14] traces the political cartographies of oil, and the landscapes to which it lays waste, from the Caspian Sea to the City of London.

Trails are increasingly appearing in popular literature in a 'know where your stuff comes from' approach centred on everyday items like tea,[15] fish[16] and underpants.[17] These trails are driven by an imperative to expose a (simplified) global North (consumption)–global South (production) axis and focus on global social justice: these trails show that wages, labour conditions and terms of trade are clearly not 'fair'. The (unstated) intellectual roots of this literature lie in dependency and development theory, and in critiques of uneven terms of trade and the distribution of global wealth and competitive advantage, establishing distinctively uneven playing fields. Driven by moral tale telling rather than by serious investigation of the substance of lives and of the landscapes through which they are lived, this literature focuses on work, not lives in the round nor on the local, national and transnational circumstances in which they are cast. Confined to being workers, the heroes of these tales can only be poor and exploited victims. And while they are certainly poor and exploited they are also much more – active agents, making intelligent decisions about their lives, in particular circumstances.

Adding to the contribution of trail anthropology, the concept of the trail also comes from other routes in the literature exploring 'commodity chains'. These describe articulations of resources – raw materials, manufacturing processes and the logistics of distribution – which imply solid and thoroughly investigated global geographies composed in the connections commodities (not objects) themselves articulate.[18] Jessica Rothenberg-Aalami's Nike chain,[19] following trainers through all stages of production, is a good example. This presents a complex account of global production geographies: a political economy of production, emphasising manufacture and the transport systems of distribution. Still more sophisticated analyses[20] link households, enterprises and states within the territories of global production. But commodity chains are problematic in a number of ways. They are place-blind. Only the narrow scenes of production and their broader political economies are judged relevant, thus their geographies are limited. As in moral tale telling, commodity chain analysis treats people as abstract labour whose life-stories are told in the machinations and sequencing of global production. The opportunity to acknowledge and explore complex and multiply layered lives, and the landscapes through which they are lived, is lost in this abstraction. The priority of commodity chain analysis is the technical operations and economic consequences of the chain, and, in drawing these connections, people are inevitably caricatured and truncated.

I share the concern with production and distribution: with the ways in which things move from place to place. But I am also concerned with the landscapes and lives involved in production, distribution and consumption. Production is explored not for its technical and economic operations alone but for the ways in which such operations are articulated in making people's lives and the territories and spaces in which they live. My narrative seeks out trails in the plural, rather than a single chain. Trails are more than a chain; they are animated by the topographies they cross, by the feet, flesh and lives, living in particular, local, connected worlds.

This story navigates the flip-flop trail, allowing the logics of the trail to shape the book's terrain and scales of engagement. Its scales of spatial analysis are sometimes global, sometimes national or sub-national and sometimes hyper-local: its narrative is organised by different intensities and magnifications, from the microscope to the telescope, in an effort to weave a micro–macro patchwork. It loiters in villages and inside houses, exposing connections between spaces and scales, always illuminating the tension between social textures and lived experience. One of the drawbacks of covering so much ground is that it can work against detailed engagement. Pausing and working more deeply in some places along the trail mitigates this to some degree. Allowing the trail to expose territories, lives and the connections between them turns my narrative into a chronicle of uncertain journeys, into a travel story across unimagined micro landscapes as the object itself unfolds. My concern lies with the globally networked uncertainties which wash through specific located neighbourhoods: more of this later.

Mobilities

Trails embed the movement which both constitutes them and which provides a method for their investigation. The reframing of the social in mobile terms belongs to a shift in thinking which admits the intertwining of human and physical worlds networked in dynamic open structures across a globalised civil society.[21] It is not just that social and material forms are restlessly on the move: they are themselves *generated* through movement and thus form its social substance.[22] In attending to the social textures of mobility it becomes apparent that the 'mobilities thinking' of many contemporary social theorists, such as John Urry and colleagues, which also inspires this book, is deficient. It is over-theorised and under empirically demonstrated. Specifically, mobility thinking supports two serious deficiencies. The first is evident in the use of terms like 'scape' and 'flow'[23] to establish force fields in which movement is part of the architecture of space. Flow conveys an unreal ease with which people and things move from place to place. On the contrary, I will argue that movement is achieved with difficulty and the application of complex skills in (social) navigation. There is no force field, no scape, with embedded inevitabilities of motion: instead we have a fragile shifting set of trails which bend this way and then another way with the exigencies of circumstances and human effort. The second deficiency extends from the first. Mobility thinking erases the social textures of travel in calling movement flow. Where people and objects travel, how they travel and the knowledge with which they travel matters: making lives through the journeys in which they are cast.

Driven by empirical investigation, this book contests these versions of mobility. I demonstrate that people and objects do not flow and that the social substance of travel matters. Rather than flow, people and objects bump awkwardly along the pathways they create as they go. They grate against each other, dodge, stop and go, negotiate obstacles, backtrack and move off in new directions, propelled by different intersecting logics. The tangles of mobilities composing the social world have their own trajectories, geographies and connections, and they move at different velocities propelled by discordant logics. Differences in velocity, shifting trajectories and fuzzy and emerging logics and logistics expose the very shape (the morphology) of social worlds connected along the trail, revealing the ways in which they are (dis) organised. Mobile thinking, on the contrary, erases important information in the textures of shifting, contingent connectivity that form the core business of social research. It does not reveal how shape-shifting, multiply interconnected substances of the social in individual and collective life – and the dynamics between these and the inanimate substances with which they are intertwined – actually work. This book does. It explores the uncertainties, fragilities and contingencies of life as people and things shuffle and dance along the trail.

Journeys

Apprehending mobility for its social texture demands better thinking tools than the abstracted scapes and flows proffered in much existing mobility thinking. Journeys provide this improved thinking tool. In elaborating a useable version of journeys I am indebted to Tim Ingold,[24] Walter Benjamin[25] and Raja Shehadeh's[26] (divergent) conceptions of walking; to Michel de Certeau's idea that spatial practices structure everyday life[27] and to Henri Lefebvre's[28] conception that space is socially produced, elaborated to describe urban landscapes so effectively by Doreen Massey.[29] Journeys are temporally defined episodic and continuous sequences of movement. Evidently belonging to the general category of travel, journeys ground specifics – who, what, where, how and why – and in this lies their value in revealing the operation of social worlds. Journeys equally describe the trajectories of the materials and objects with which people travel, as well as the travel of unaccompanied objects and materials propelled by the efforts of drivers, sailors, loaders and others. Journeys thus articulate the travel routes of intertwined human and inanimate materials/objects, hence their value as a thinking tool with which to make sense of a world on the move. The elaboration of the concept of journeys which follows reveals their value in exposing the social textures of the trail and describes their explanatory potential.

The concept of journeys describes the matrix of people's coming and going in ways that lend them to cartography. Journeys, in other words, draw people's maps and in so doing provide a way of thinking about them. Working from the ground up these are individual comings and goings: daily journeys around a neighbourhood, a workplace or a home. Sometimes, in the case of (internal or international) migrants, local journeys are interspersed with longer ones to other places either in the same country or in other countries. Thus journeys provide a way of understanding the maps people live by, at the same time offer a way of making sense of their lives. Put simply: people are where they go. Of course, people are more than a collection of journeys. But journeys provide a powerful analytical tool for thinking about people in a world on the move – where and how do they go, and why?

This book maps people's journeys in tandem with flip-flop journeys: it maps the journeys of people whose lives, livelihoods and neighbourhoods the flip-flops travel across and co-constitute. Journeys equally describe the movements of objects and materials. Like all maps these are not *just* maps: they are social fabrics to be explored, with journeys offering a point of departure in excavating individual lives on the move. Thus journeys bring configurations of people and objects in motion into analytic focus. Their existential properties aside, journeys are rarely individual but shared with others: grasping one person's cartographies implicates others who travel similar routes in similar circumstances – fellow travellers. Although the travelling stories in this book illuminate individual lives, they have broader resonance in placing the lives of fellow travellers in the analytic frame.

The journeys people and objects travel map places as well as lives. This thinking is consistent with contemporary urban geographies and landscape theories which conceptualise people, dwelling and places as co-produced. Landscape – and its subcategory of places – is thus the enactment of mobile dwelling itself[30] rather than a surface on which dwelling *takes place*. This book adds to existing frameworks the idea that journeys[31] are key mechanisms in the social creation of places. Additionally, drawing on Tim Ingold, in this book places are understood as deep surfaces – textured by people and matter in motion – making them rich sites for investigation and for imagination. As people journey through the deep surfaces of their everyday lives, and through the sporadic routines of long-haul travel, they map and connect otherwise disparate places. These journeys and the terrains they map describe particular geographies as surely as they describe the lives that co-create them. Thus the journeys that cross or converge upon a place offer a means of thinking about place itself as a matrix of connections, maps drawn in the trajectories of people and objects. Thus journeys draw the cartographies of local and translocal movement in revealing connections; they display cross-cutting directions of travel and different types of traffic – who and what goes where and different routes and methods of travel, at differing scales from the neighbourhood to the global highways. Journeys map, and maps describe and summarise, the comings and goings of a world on the move, revealing directions, velocities and volumes of travel, and the tangible ways in which the world is actually connected: all of which is concealed in the idea of flow.

Journeys reveal and describe different scales of movement. Journeys making translocal connections – migration, multiple travel practices and the routes of commodity chains – are sometimes prioritised over local ones without this being acknowledged.[32] These, of course, are important journeys and this book traces them. But equally important in revealing the social textures of lives and places are the short-haul, everyday routine journeys around the locales people inhabit. These might be simple circularities – journeys between work, home, family and friends. The description of journeys has the added advantage of revealing topographical, social, personal and political landscapes. Journeys are an effective way of thinking about people engaged in the long- and short-haul mobilities of their routine lives: they display rhythms of settlement and unsettlement as well as the local and translocal places in which they are lived. This book treats journeys of any scale as equally relevant: it avoids the conceptual distinction between internal and international movement which prevails in migration studies. This makes it possible to trace journeys near and far, and to note the connections between them while lingering along the trail to dig deeper into its surfaces. Placing long- and short-haul journeys in the same frame poses critical questions about the character of places and about the lives they sustain. It compels us to ask who goes where, and why?[33]

Journeys prompt consideration of methods and speeds of travel too. Thinking of travel in terms of combinations of planes, trains, ships, private cars, scooters, bicycles, taxis, trucks, buses and walking implicitly disturbs notions of flow and emphasises the human effort of travel in the traction between the sole of the shoe on the one hand and the ground/accelerator/ truck floor/first class lounge, on the other. Here, in the specifics of travel's technologies and human effort, lies a world of different speeds, different access to travel technologies and social differences raising important questions about who lives in the fast/slow lane and how the temporalities of differing routes are navigated.

How should we think about the place-and-people-making journeys outlined above? Are they planned and organised? Are they random? Do they follow maps or make them? Variation, I argue, is decisive. Some journeys are planned and executed according to plan. In some, plans go awry and have to be abandoned or adapted. Some journeys embed itineraries which are so routinised that no one thinks about them. Algorithms drive object journeys organised by logistics software, but not always. Journeys may embed an intention which is/not realised. Journeys are best understood as unfolding possibilities, involving speculative way-finding and serendipity.[34] And, while some journeys follow maps, maps are more an outcome than an instrument of navigation. Maps are made in the enactment of journeys rather than the other way around, making them rich sites for social enquiry.

Journeys embed and reveal navigational skills, deepening our understanding of people through their practical grasp of the landscapes they travel. Navigation is ordinary way-finding, improvised exploratory movement, and skill is compressed knowledge about the world and about how to operate in it.[35] Journeys thus make transparent the navigational skills they embed, providing clues about navigators and the terrains navigated. This makes it possible to ask: what skills are required to navigate a particular path, to live a particular life, to live along a particular trail?

In some respects we might conclude that people are the sum of their journeys: people are *where* they go – and *how* they go. I am suggesting that journeys not only place people in interactive mobile social scenes but also provide a useful way of thinking about the social itself. Lives are lived and narrated through journeys,[36] as sequences of places connected by the traveller: a here and then, a here and there: physical enactments of biography.[37]

In short, journeys – people and things on the move – matter, and they make matter in flesh and stone as they weave (in)substantial connections between otherwise seemingly disconnected peoples. How the world walks and rides is how the world works. Journeys are epic and mundane; sometimes they are both at the same time. They constitute and expose the operation of the social world on local and translocal scales. Journeys are the key to social fabrics: to assemblages of objects, people and places. The social world is fabricated in journeys and studying them reveals key elements in the composition of the social world. Journeys themselves are a critical thinking tool in apprehending the modern world on the move. Journeys, in this book, provide powerful intersections from which to observe and ask questions. Journeys are a more effective tool to think with than flows.

Globalisation

Trails and journeys provide a distinctive ground–up approach to globalisation. This places my own account at odds with classic globalisation studies,[38] which, in common with mobilities studies, are over-theorised and under-substantiated empirically. Notions of globalisation as 'entrenched and enduring patterns of worldwide connectedness'[39] prevail: the stability of connections, and not randomness, shapes this classic formulation. This book, on the other hand, shows that the translocal connections of globalisation – through the flip-flop trails composing it – are anything but enduring and stable. Quite the contrary. The stretching and intensification of social relations, in which the local is shaped by, and in turn shapes, distant social forms,[40] is an important interjection in globalisation studies dominated by economic and business thinking.[41] Rather than starting out from high theory, as much current globalisation theory does, I begin from empirical observation: from social life on the flip-flop trail. What can be concluded from this direction of travel cannot be known in advance.

In tune with its economic bias, a concern with multinational business, technology, information, brands, mediatised imagery and similar flows dominates theories of globalisation.[42] These biases are rarely balanced with consideration of the social relationships, with the lives and geographies lived around the economic–business axis. In this regard, too, this book is unusual. Among the objects considered worthy of globalisation theorists' attention, cheap plastic shoes usually would not qualify, despite their ubiquity. The flip-flop trail is not one of the 'landing places of network value'[43] and this places it beyond the consideration of contemporary theorists of the global. Even the literature on global risk[44] does not address the lives lived along the flip-flop trail. These are explored here, where risk and precarity constitute the practical knowledge guiding navigation.

Even the more sophisticated analyses of globalisation, which admit the instabilities of its core networks, underestimate people's everyday resilience. Manuel Castells[45] claims that 'the human matter on which the network was living cannot so easily [as the network] mutate. It becomes trapped, devalued or wasted '. My research shows that it does not. On the contrary 'human matter' finds new routes, new strategies and new places in which to live.

My story adds to a small ethnographic literature on globalisation as objects and trails, as opposed to the ubiquitous literature exploring migration as one of globalisation's constituting forces. It builds on Anna Lowenhaupt Tsing's[46] account of environmental struggles in Indonesia, which suggests that ethnographic methods challenge the telling of universal 'truths' about globalisation, and, usefully, offers friction as a counterpoint to conventional theories of flow. It adds to MacGaffey and Bazenguissa-Ganga's[47] graphic portraits of Central African traders in Paris and Brussels, who move objects back and forth, showing the complex circularities of trails directed from the margins. It adds an understanding of the instabilities and the fragilities of lives beyond the production of global food supplies to Deborah Barndt's[48] excellent account of the tomato trail from Mexico to Toronto. And it adds to James Marriot and Mika Minio-Paluello's story of the oil road from the Caspian Sea to London[49] another set of oil routes – those which trail into plastics, inaugurating new networks which criss-cross modern lives and animate the social world.

My narrative grounds overarching macro-geographies of connection, exploring the hyper-local microcosms revealed in the flip-flop trail, unpacking social and material landscapes to see how they 'work' and 'walk'. It is not written to illustrate a theory, but holds existing theories of globalisation to account and adapts them in the light of new evidence. Unlike the high-profile trails of global finance, of dominant brands or mediatised images, the flip-flop trail meanders the quiet back roads of globalisation, roads that, unseen, are alive with traffic. This book tells hitherto untold stories about quiet lives and overlooked topographies, plodding along off-beat routes and discovering how globalisation works and walks along the back roads. Yet these are the trails which make the world in which we live. As (almost) everyone has a pair of flip-flops we are all connected to these trails, though we may well have never given it a thought. As we follow the flip-flop trail from the oil wells from which plastics originate, to the garbage dumps on the edge of cities to which they are finally consigned, my hope is that – through the larger resonance of a small object – the human dimensions of 'the global', which so easily trips off the tongues of social commentators and theorists alike, will slowly enter our field of vision.

Uncertainty is a key concept underwriting my analysis. This refers to the topographies of the trail, which are constantly mutating, as well as to the local and distant circumstances and ways of living which do not easily settle into the commanding matrix of globalisation theorists. These routes and circumstances co-produce lives and the conditions in which they can be lived. Uncertainty brings temporariness, and new kinds of unreliability, in understanding the way things are and the way they might work, constantly undermining the navigational skills through which lives, and the myriad routes concocting them, are navigated. It develops the idea that lives and landscapes, and the routes connecting them, are always emergent, that topographies and the social landscapes they co-produce are restless, improvised, makeshift, constantly calling forth new versions of resilience[50] and knowledge,[51] enabling people to get by. Resilience is about people's ability to adapt to conditions generated by different tempos of social change,[52] conditions which create ever-new forms of social fragility.[53] The concept of uncertainty develops 'the provisionally stitched together, jigged up intersections of bodies and materials upon which things are both moved and caught'[54] – the textured surface on which *contemporary* life is lived. Uncertainty is thus both concept and descriptor of our time: alerting us to the ways of being and the moving surfaces through which we live.

The flip-flop trail proffers a version of globalisation that is less neat, finished, predictable, settled and routed than the familiar theorists suggest. Instead it is messy, stitched together, improvised,[55] rigged together from whatever is at hand, made[56] and remade as the trail develops. This is a version of globalisation which emerges as the trail proceeds; it crosses many borders, some of them difficult to anticipate; it connects with an extensive set of concerns at a larger scale in the geopolitics of our time: back-road globalisation branches off that major highway, providing the connective tissue of globalisation.

Travelling Methods

This book chases big issues through small places,[57] learning from and extending discussion of global and multi-sited ethnography.[58] Following a travelling object, allowing the object to draw the route, demands travelling methods. The travelling methods I used, like the trail itself, were rigged together: an ad hoc patchwork of pragmatics reinvented at several junctures in order to address the problems which confronted me as

I myself took to the trail. In my methods toolkit were techniques familiar to micro-sociologists and anthropologists. Photography, for one. On large parts of the trail I worked with Singapore artist Michael Tan, but otherwise took my own photographs, displayed in a website that accompanies this book. In interviews on the hoof, sometimes called 'go-alongs', I walked informants' habitual landscapes with them, tracing the journeys of their everyday lives. I mapped long- and short-haul journeys, turning lives – the sum of their journeys – into maps and representing them visually and topographically. I spent many hours observing local life – recorded in notes, sketches and photographs. Photographs evoked and recorded fieldwork scenes for later analysis. They caught people in the scenes of their everyday life and in the material and environmental contexts in which they lived, capturing crucial intersections between people and places along the trail. Like other forms of data, photographs are part record and part theorisation; they involve selection with the lens (framing) and selection already creates a story within a conceptual framework. Urban landscape and photography – both layered repositories of multiple truths – are always duplicitous. The question is how to unravel their multiplicity and duplicity and get a sharper view of them, and how to see things that lie unnoticed in the textured surfaces of the world. As John Berger[59] rightly says, the relationship between what we see and what we know is never settled. The biggest methodological challenge I faced was not in applying these methods, but in applying them *on the move* in order to explore a trail which constantly moved on to places I had not anticipated. While I could figure out the macro-contours of the trail, its details – the small places it actually passed through – posed constant challenges.

   Only at the end of it did the trail become knowable. I followed it while it was being made, although I had a sense of where it might go. Trails pose a number of methodological problems. Because they are continuous I had to create places to stop and investigate – vantage-points from which I could log the traffic which moved along it. I think of these as viewing platforms. The selection of viewing platforms was pragmatic: they must provide a good vantage-point into the core activities I was chasing along the trail; and they had to be reachable by standard methods of transport, primarily by air and road. Actually travelling with the raw materials and, later, with the flip-flops themselves, was impractical if not impossible as I could not fold myself into containers, ships and trucks. Thus I was forced to generate parallel trails in order to catch up with the flip-flops. Sometimes simply picking up the trail was difficult. International flights are inevitably routed through key cities and I would have to search out the trail from unpromising starting-points.

The cities on the trail – cross-cut by multiple intersecting trails of people and objects[60] – were both omnipresent and slippery and this posed another set of methodological problems. Often the viewing platforms I selected looked, from a distance, as if they were in cities; but closer examination often proved otherwise. Thus city visits strayed into urban zones, exurbs, suburbs, and borders between nation-states into zones of unregulated activity. In each case, guided by flip-flops, I had to figure out if there was a relationship between these platforms and adjacent cities, and if so what it consisted of. Whole cities are always un-researchable, and so in dealing with cities I chose small junction points – where flip-flops passed through – as viewing platforms. Working in city neighbourhoods, I found trails to distant rural villages from the people who moved along them. Sometimes close to the centre of a city I discovered that the people who lived there considered their neighbourhood a village: such understanding articulates recent patterns of urban expansion and migration. The trail thus passed through villages which looked like urban neighbourhoods and villages which looked like industrial landscapes. Visual apprehension and reading of landscape is always problematic, always provisional. Thus following the trail – applying mobile methods of investigation – demanded flexibility and respect for both temporality and mutability, especially in grasping the trails which ran through, and around cities, which grounded a matrix of intersecting routes.

A third set of methodological problems arose around the routes the trail created. At all points the trail splintered and moved off in many directions. I could only follow one of them. Thus even in following a single object there are uncountable potential trails to take into account in reckoning the working of globalisation on the ground. Of course, flip-flop routes run all over the world. The trail I followed was mostly a calculation of volumes and significance: where do most things go? This was partly about the biggest production sites for plastics and flip-flops, as well as about the biggest emerging markets. Along a largely insignificant route I was tracing significance where possible. Occasionally this bent around expediency: some routes had impenetrable platforms and had on account of this to be ruled out. Sometimes impenetrability was about access; sometimes it was about dangerousness, propriety or feasibility. Even the route I followed, which presented the fewest practical obstacles, I came up against no-go areas; small parts of the trail were missing for reasons which will become clear.

Because of these methodological difficulties, because of the character of trail research itself as well, I ended up in places I could never have anticipated.

This leads to a further set of difficulties, which extend beyond methods and are to do with time and expertise. First, time. Fitting this research around university commitments and personal obligations meant that I could not tackle the trail in a single arc. Thus it was spread over six years, finishing in 2013. During this time a good deal of backtracking and updating became necessary and, when it came to access to key parts of the trail I lived on anxiety and hope. I was denied permission to access several platforms along the trail but went anyway and my optimism paid off. Much of this was due to luck and to local negotiations in which I put my case face to face instead of at a distance. For information deriving from these platforms, as well as elsewhere on the trail, I am indebted to the generosity and goodwill of informants and interlocutors.

Second, expertise. While I felt the comfort of a methodological expertise developed over decades, I was challenged in applying this expertise in the travelling circumstances of the trail. On the trail I was forced to relinquish all presumption of expertise and work entirely beyond my intellectual and linguistic comfort zone. The landscapes, situations and people I met on the trail were barely intelligible. I had no expertise in the geographies of the trail and had to supplement my ethnography from secondary sources so that I could think about a trail which passed through microcosms of five different countries. Not only did this demand local knowledge I didn't have, it demanded language skills I didn't have too. Thus on most of the platforms along the trail the information I gathered from interviews passed through the ears and understanding of interpreters, and I have to accept that filters amounting to a case of Chinese whispers may apply to my data. Social researchers often write about the power geometries of expertise. Translocal social research is inevitably semi-skilled labour on account of its scope, its scale and the lack of control by researchers over the research process. It is thus appropriately tackled with imagination and due humility, as well as the stamina necessary to follow the trail when the going gets tough.

Ultimately the test of a method lies in the stories and insights it generates, matters best left for readers to judge. This book follows where the flip-flop trail leads, from oil wells to a city landfill site. It traces the connections flip-flops forge, unfolding their scenes of material production, factory production of objects from materials, use and disposal – the fabrics of material and social co-production; unfolding unseen lives and landscapes and the translocal matrix of connections between them along the trail. On to the flip-flop trail!

2

Oil – Maps Beneath the Sand

God has given us so much: as long as Burgan is pumping we are rich.
(Ashan, Indian oil geologist)

I'm not lazy I'm Kuwaiti. (Kuwait City t-shirt)

Plastics are made from oil, and oil, hidden beneath the deserts of the
Middle East, runs through Abdullah's life. Along with the call to prayer
from Kuwait's 1320 mosques,[1] oil shapes the rituals and journeys of his life.
An oil geologist, his mental maps reveal the black liquid beneath the sand.
A Muslim moral compass dictates his social obligations and the way he
lives them. Small, slender and bearded, Abdullah scrambles into his jeans
and t-shirt, ready to drive his youngest daughter, Zafera, to school. Alem,
the family's Ethiopian maid, makes breakfast. His wife, Suad, is leaving in
her Hummer for the hospital where she works as a doctor. Their driver,
employed to wash, rather than drive their cars, because they don't need a
driver, is late again. The family leave in unwashed cars. Their large house
in a quiet tree-lined street near the centre of Kuwait City falls silent as they
leave Alem to tidy and make the lunch they will eat in the early afternoon
after work. Another day in Kuwait City.

Finding the Beginning of the Trail

The flip-flop trail has many beginnings. My plan to follow the largest
volumes of traffic points to Saudi Arabia, which holds the world's largest
oil reserves and supplies centres of plastic production. But researching
the (male) world of oil in Saudi poses problems of propriety, dress and
mobility for a female researcher, ruling it out.[2] Oil reserves in Venezuela
and Canada follow Saudi's[3] and both are potential research sites. But oil
from these regions, like oil from the Russian Federation and former Soviet
bloc countries, also key producers, does not flow towards the epicentres of
plastic production which make flip-flops. This is the wrong oil. I needed to
find a workable research site with the right oil geographies. Oil geographies
are partly a matrix of pipelines, tanker-routes and proximity to markets,
which are, anyway, materialisations of past geographies. They are shaped
by complex, shifting, geopolitical calculations expressing and generating
tensions between regimes. Oil security and diplomacy are interlaced, as

oil purchasing and producing nations favour some alliances over others, and this, too, directs where oil flows.

There are new expediencies too. The Cold War still runs through oil. Russia seeks to trade it for influence in bordering regimes. Sanctions against Iranian exports means finding new sources. America secures its recently won oil-independence with Canadian supplies, reducing its reliance on the Middle East,[4] and the tectonic plates of geopolitics shift once more as oil redraws world maps. The dystopian scenario in which the oil runs out and we live by other means is once more avoided.[5] Iran and Iraq's oil reserves place them after Canada, but Iran is difficult to access while sanctions limit exports, ruling it out as a research site. Oddly, Iraq is accessible to researchers[6] but, as a recent theatre of war, its everyday security is poor. I ruled it out.

And so the flip-flop trail begins in Kuwait. Kuwait is a major oil producer in its own right and part of a significant oil-producing region in the Middle East. Kuwait exports 87 per cent of its oil and favours Asia's growing (plastic producing) markets. This is the right oil and it flows in the right direction. Oil *makes* Kuwait: makes its impressive GDP (gross domestic product); accounts for 95 per cent of its export earnings and for 95 per cent of the government revenues on which its citizens depend, as we will see. Over half of its oil comes from the Burgan Field – the world's second largest oil field. While securing stable oil supplies is problematic for those countries without it – the early twenty-first century is (still) a carbon economy and a road economy – societies and economies shaped by oil production have their own problems. The source of Kuwait's wealth is also a source of fragility and insecurity, as will become apparent.[7]

Kuwait is also a pragmatic choice. Oilfields are inaccessible to the public. Middle Eastern governments generally control their oil as sole producers. Consequently I had only one access-opportunity in each of the Gulf countries and this usually involved clearance at ministerial level. Failing repeatedly in my formal approaches to oil companies and ministries I searched for personal connections. A neighbour who works in the oil industry explained that oil companies are anxious about letting researchers in: was I an environmental activist? No. I followed three potential leads through ever more distant social networks. I made phone calls to people who promised to speak to other people on my behalf. All proved to be dead ends paved with generous intentions.

Trying another route, I discovered from my university's International Office (IO) that we have four Kuwaiti students. The IO offered to email these students with my details. One replied. Her dad worked in oil. A difficult correspondence followed in which I reassured him that my research was not intended as an *exposé* of the oil industry. Trust and personal connections are important: but so too is research integrity. Until I arrived in Kuwait City and spent the first day talking to the student's dad, I wasn't certain I could access Kuwait's only oil company. An intelligent and generous soul, he spent hours explaining Kuwait to me and introduced me to his contacts in the Kuwait Oil Company. Responding to a request, this time from *inside* of the company, the Minister of the Interior approved my visit. This gave me access to the company, the informal gatherings of oilmen and, to my amazement, one of the drilling sites, once the Health and Safety Officer had located a pair of steel-capped boots that were small enough. Equally unanticipated, I was absorbed into the warmth, generosity and hospitality of the student's family and, especially, its women, who introduced me to their friends, offering me a special, if specific, vantage-point onto life in Kuwait.

Oil Globalisation

Oil is not just central to globalisation, a fundamental, if fragile, vector of translocal connection, it literally constitutes it. To say that oil *is* globalisation is not an overstatement. Oil is fundamental because it makes globalisation possible. Providing the energy that transports people and objects around the world, oil is responsible for the time-space compressions that define globalisation. Global politics is shaped by the scramble to secure oil and distribute it around a shifting matrix of regimes. This central constituent of globalisation is also fragile, as we will see; it generates and transmits new uncertainties. Growing militancy in the Middle East, also the location of the world's largest remaining oil deposits, disperses local sources of uncertainty globally. The rapid industrialisation of China and India, making them oil-hungry on an unprecedented scale, upsets existing calculations of global oil demand. Fluctuations in oil prices and supplies up end delicately balanced subsistence in the global South, by raising the price of basic foods, and transportation, impacting balances of payments, while securing record profits in oil-producing countries. Oil constitutes the substance of globalisation itself. Political and economic calculations prioritise it and its connection with theatres of war is not coincidental. The destruction of Kuwaiti oilfields ignited by retreating

Iraqi forces in the 1990 invasion of Kuwait generated images that have become part of the iconography of war.[8]

The Wildcat

A senior geologist and supervisor in the Kuwait Oil Company's (KOC) exploration department, Abdullah is heading in his SUV land cruiser for a wildcat – rig 776 – in the desert just north of Kuwait City. Wildcats are multi-million dollar speculative drilling operations;[9] the ultimate test of the geological data he compiles. Only the wildcat determines if the predicted oil really exists beneath the sand. Wildcats have a high hit rate in Kuwait because large reserves of oil lie buried in the desert. Wildcats make it possible to build a production profile: a story about the amount of oil that lies beneath the sand, and, most importantly, how much of it is recoverable. A convincing story will move the development department at the KOC to put the well into production. A lot hangs on rig 776.

The wildcat is the result of two years' work for Abdullah and a multi-disciplinary team of geologists, geophysicists, petroleum engineers, reservoir engineers and petro-physicists gathering data to justify the cost of drilling. The technologies of oil prediction develop continually: two-, three- and now four-dimensional seismic mapping surveys – in which speed and sound changes read the rock densities to identify oil-bearing formations underground – are now used routinely. New CT scans provide minutely detailed information instantly from rock core analysis. Building geophysical models of seismic sections, geologists develop maps of rock formations. The team is classically looking for a dome-rock formation with gas at the top, oil beneath the gas, and water beneath the oil. Only the wildcat, which drills from what the team gauges to be the peak of the dome, can verify the putative maps. If no oil is found, they will plug the wildcat and leave. If oil is found, a number of delineation wells will be drilled to establish the size of the oilfield, making it possible to estimate the total amount of oil and the reserves – the amount of oil that can be recovered – 60–70 per cent is considered a high recovery rate.

As he approaches rig 776, Abdullah passes a large flock of goats guarded by a Bangladeshi migrant working for a Bedouin. Meat is big business but not as big as oil. The open desert is flat and golden brown: sand and electricity pylons, like whacky sculptures, stretch into the distance. Ali Al Salem Air Force Base, the Kuwait defence facility near the Iraq border, and a base for US and allied troops operating in Iraq theatres of war, is nearby. Kuwait City Airport, a short land journey from southern Iraq, is a landing and departure point for troops. Abdullah passes teams of Filipino workers laying pipes across the desert to carry the oil from the new wells to the gathering centres and then to storage tanks. As he enters the rig site Abdullah smiles at the wildcat: a tall metal structure rising high above the sand next to a generator working the pumps. Bags of cement and mud lie around its base. The site is unfenced but guarded by security cameras. He walks to row of gleaming white, heat-reflecting portacabins. Metal walkways connect them, raised above the sand. Summer temperatures soar above 50° Celsius. The noise of the drilling and the generator are deafening.

Abdullah walks into the portacabin office of the (KOC) 'company man', an Indian migrant from Goa called Lazar, who is employed through a KOC service company dealing with security and logistics called OSCO. As he is in overall control of the drill site Lazar must be there 24/7. His bedsit is connected to his office via a bathroom. Both are fiercely chilled by air-conditioning. After checking in with Lazar, Abdullah moves down the chain of command to 'operations' in the adjacent portacabin.

He greets the 'tool pusher', Chuck, a large man with an accent from the deep American South. Chuck is in overall charge of the drilling and, like Lazar, has living quarters attached his office so that he can be onsite at all times. Drilling is contracted-out to specialist drilling companies through a highly regulated tendering process, in which the entire operation is minutely detailed in legal documents. Chuck works for Weatherford International, a multinational oil industry service company operating in over 100 countries, headquartered in Switzerland. Drilling contractors provide labour and equipment in addition to their expertise, gained in drilling all over the world. Chuck is eating a late breakfast at his desk. A problem with the rig had him up most of the night and wildcats, because they are exploratory, don't always have a 'night pusher'.

Abdullah moves on to the next portacabin and Kim, the Goan Health and Safety Officer, who issues him with a safety helmet, goggles and steel-capped boots. Gas explosions, hazardous chemicals, cranes and forklifts make drill-sites dangerous. Just moving around the site takes skill and practice. Abdullah climbs into the lift and is hoisted to the top of the rig. Rigs do only two things. They are a hoisting system and a pumping system. But, on account of their scale, the number of activities going on at any time, and the deafening noise, they can seem intimidating.

At the top of the rig Abdullah greets the (Egyptian) driller, Adjo, who is drilling the hole from the drill console next to his 'office' called the doghouse. The lexicon of oil is American and used worldwide. Adjo, who controls the well, the rig staff and the equipment, is monitoring the pressure and the vibration on the drill console. Occasionally there is a 'kick', a small gas explosion, and he must decide whether it is serious enough for the men to abandon the rig. An assistant driller takes over when he needs a break. Two derrick men sit in the monkey house, just above the drill console, feeding pipe casings into the well. The casings, which provide the architecture of the well, will be secured with cement to make sure the well doesn't collapse. A couple of juniors, called roustabouts, are cleaning the floor. No one is allowed to sit down on the job, there is always cleaning and maintenance to be done: 'think of it as a ship' says Adjo. The roustabouts, juniors on the rig floor, will eventually be promoted to roughnecks, senior staff, who break out the pipes with spanners under the supervision of the derrick men. Mechanics and electricians support the drilling operation. Roustabouts can take this promotion route too.

Back-office support services – safety is king and that means paperwork, equipment and briefings – administer the drilling, making sure equipment and supplies are available when they are needed. Rig 776 has 85 employees split over two shifts, 19 of whom support the camp where the men live with catering and cleaning. Kuwaiti drilling is semi-automated. Laying down and picking up pipes is done mechanically, because more fully automated hydraulic systems run the risk of seizing up if sand gets into them.

Abdullah has come to the wildcat to ensure that his calculations are working in practice. Geologists direct the drilling plan, choosing the casing points for the pipes being fed down the well by the derrick men. Different rock formations have different hydrostatic pressures, and a change in pressure signals a change in the rock. As the well gets deeper new casing pipe is cemented in with each change in (rock) pressure down to the oil reservoir. Rig 776 is not at this point yet, but when it is the oil reservoir will be perforated to release the oil and a thin pipe will connect the production zone to the surface, and something that looks like a Christmas tree. This controls the flow of oil. Meanwhile, mud circulates out of the well for analysis by mud loggers, who work near the rig bottom weighing the mud and shouting out the weight. The mud loggers work for another subcontracted company based in Italy. Mud, mixed with chemicals to the right texture, is pumped into the well to stabilise it, or it can blow. The use of mud is a finely calculated balancing act. If rig 776 produces oil, the area will be enclosed with high security fencing and holding stations where gas, oil and water are separated will be constructed.

At midday the rig crew shift changes. Crews work from midnight to midday when they are replaced by a second shift working from midday to midnight. Drilling rigs are too expensive to stand idle. A bus takes the off-duty crew to their camp, which also consists of white air-conditioned portacabins, a safe distance from the rig – a safety precaution in case of explosions – where they will eat in the canteen, watch TV and sleep until it is time to work again. The drill site is like a military camp, but it could also be at sea. Offshore drilling clearly provides the template organising the site, but a sea of sand, rather than water, surrounds it. The site is an entirely male domain. The handful of women mud loggers who work for a service company, leave at the end of their shift. The rig workers will not leave the camp until the end of their 28-day (senior staff) or 56-day (junior staff) shift. They are then driven to the airport where they fly home to different parts of the Persian Gulf, returning at the end of their 28-day break. More of these shift-worker migrants later in this chapter.

Abdullah must return to KOC headquarters, but first he gets the driller to give him a rock core taken from the hollow centre of the drill, carefully labelling it with the well number and depth at which the sample was taken. While the wildcat piques his geological imagination, it is only one of the 90 rigs currently operating in Kuwait. He drives south, towards Kuwait City, and on towards the Saudi border to the south of Kuwait, turning off the highway at Al Hammadi, where the KOC is headquartered.

Oil HQ

The KOC is responsible for fabricating Al Hammadi's buildings, its streets and the lives of the people who live there. Most of the town's residents work for the KOC, and thus for the government, or one of its contractors. Al Hammadi is deeply embedded in Abdullah's biography, in how his life is saturated with oil. He drives past the junior staff housing where he and his 13 siblings grew up and went to the local school, before he studied geology at Kuwait University. Al Hammadi's housing is an architectural version of the company's hierarchical structure. It is divided by size into 'senior', 'middle' and 'junior' staff housing. The KOC owns the leisure facilities and the hospitals. Abdullah's dad was a southern Iranian migrant who worked as a water and gas pipefitter. Abdullah, four of his brothers and his sister (a nurse) are second-generation KOC employees. A third generation will enter the business when Abdullah's son returns from studying petrochemical engineering in the US. The KOC is the family firm, as well as the government firm. It generates the maps logging the journeys composing Abdullah's life.

Al Hammadi's past is announced in its architecture too. Its low white bungalows, with red corrugated roofs, set in tree-lined streets, are a planning and architectural style repeated throughout areas of British colonial administration, as far apart as Nigeria and India; often referred to as Government Residential Areas. In the past senior staff residents were British. Now they are Kuwaiti. Kuwait was a British protectorate from 1899 to 1961. Britain supervised defence, foreign policy and, later, the exploitation of oil reserves. In return, the authority of the ruling family and the integrity of Kuwait's borders against the expansionist ambition of its neighbours, were secured.[10] When oil was discovered, the (British) Anglo Persian Oil Company (later BP) and the (American) Gulf Oil Company explored it and put it into production.[11] Following its oil interests, the British administration moved to Al Hammadi, setting up the KOC in 1934. Oil exploration, the British protectorate and Al Hammadi are interwoven.[12]

The KOC's history in providing the rationale for the British Protectorate, and the nationalisation of its oil fields in 1975, still shapes Kuwait's relationship with the commanding heights of globalisation, as it is routed through oil. The government of Kuwait owns and controls all development in the oil sector: non-Kuwaiti contractors must have Kuwaiti interlocutors. In fact, Kuwait's constitution prohibits foreign ownership of Kuwait's natural resources and this rules out product sharing agreements that incentivise foreign investment. Kuwait's international interests are pursued through the Kuwait Foreign Petroleum Exploration Co. (KUFPEC). Government control is supervised at the highest level by the Supreme Petroleum Council (SPC) – which sets policy – headed by the Prime Minister and a Council of Ministers and representatives from the private sector, all selected by the Emir. Kuwait is a constitutional Emirate. The Ministry of Petroleum supervises all policy implementation in upstream (drilling) and downstream (refineries) operations. The Kuwait Petroleum Company (KPC) is the parent company managing all domestic and foreign oil investment. The KOC is the KPC's upstream subsidiary and the Kuwait National Petroleum Company (KNPC) controls the downstream operations and exports.[13] Thus the KOC is both an arm of the Kuwaiti government and a key part of its oil matrix.

The Kuwaiti government-controlled oil matrix – the KPC, KNPC and KOC – with its enclosed campuses, often split over several sites of low-rise blocks and well-tended gardens, dominates the Al Hammadi landscape. The KOC alone employs 8000 workers, in professional and back-office support capacities, on several campuses, secured by guards, fencing and security passes. This massive bureaucracy creates torturously slow paperwork chains, and it takes months, or even years, to produce decisions or buildings. For external and foreign companies, securing contracts takes years; and this favours the big multinational companies with KOC-experience and sufficient finance to be patient. The multinational Halliburton, for example, is a major beneficiary of KOC contracts. The oil matrix connects a vast, shifting, transnational network of expertise and technology supplying companies and oil customers. Behind the drilling operations in the desert is a vast, complex, global-local bureaucratic government job creation scheme, which dominates Al Hammadi's physical and social landscape.

The oil matrix has turned Al Hammadi into a vast industrial landscape strewn with pipes and other bits of discarded oil hardware. Large tracts of land are occupied by holding tanks, where oil sits waiting to be shipped, as well as petro-chemical plants processing it. Oil is geologically embedded, extracted, and then re-embedded in the landscape's sequestered architectural forms. Al Hammadi lies at the centre of a giant transnational web of circulating workers, contractors, expertise and technologies, linking it with other oil cities like Calgary, Aberdeen, Stavanger and Houston, as well as cities across Saudi Arabia and other parts of the Middle East. The transnational geographies of oil are further extended by the operation of contractors supplying technical services, such as the Italian mud logging company and the Swiss multinational, Weatherford, employing Texans and South Indians drilling at the wildcat.

Reading the Rocks

Parking next to the exploration department, Abdullah takes his new rock to the core store. This vast warehouse, where 300,000 metres of cylindrical rock in fibreglass sleeves, inside long metal containers, is stored for further analysis, is his favourite place. Geology is literally a core part of the oil business and cores – a multi-million dollar industry worldwide – are central to geology. Core analysis is on the advancing technical frontier of the oil industry. CT scanning, providing fast, accurate, analysis of cores every 5 millimetres, is the latest technology for revealing rocks' structures and properties. The cores in the store come from active wells, they log changes in the wells as oil is pumped from them. As wells are pumped, their geology reveals what lies deep beneath the earth's surface: the location of the next pool of oil, its accessibility, and the viability of extraction given current technology and extraction costs. Drilling requires ongoing geological analysis – reading the rocks – because wells change as they mature. Cores expose the porosity and permeability of rocks revealing to geologists how oil and water will behave inside them, information necessary for guiding further drilling. The lab where small sections of rock are prepared for microscopic analysis is next to the core store. Geology is a visual practice, as much art as a science, and under a microscope a piece of sandstone looks like a shiny jewelled white (sand) and black (oil) brooch.

Abdullah's office in the exploration department has colourful charts on the walls and computer-generated 'sections' of the desert's rock formations. On his computer he reviews models of the data compiled by the multi-disciplinary team. Bottles with oil and mud samples are tangled up with piles of paper – 'well logs' – recording other readings of the properties of the rocks, through wire logging, rather than core analysis. Oil reacts to the pressure of the rock formation which in turn shows where the oil lies and how recoverable it is. These calculations are intended to optimise, rather than maximise, oil production, keeping the oil flowing over time. As Abdullah says: 'The oil in the ground is safe. Convert it into paper money and you don't know what will happen to it.' He is referring to the sovereign wealth fund, the size, location and administration of which is opaque.

Most analysts agree that the oil economy is in its final phase.[14] The era of the super-fields, like the Greater Burgan, is over and Kuwait knows the extent of its oil, although it has yet to fully explore its offshore reserves. These large fields were easy to discover and exploit. But small, complicated, oil fields mark the current era. The oil game worldwide is not now about new discoveries, but better exploiting old ones for less accessible deposits. Exploration is now more complex. Shifts in knowledge and technology make it possible to recover previously unrecoverable oil. New geological mapping and drilling technologies make it possible to drill deeper, and horizontally, to recover what is called 'tight oil' and shale gas. These developments are responsible for reconfiguring the global oil geographies mentioned earlier.

Oil City

Thursday afternoon is the beginning of the weekend. Abdullah drives north from Al Hammadi along the highway heading for his home in Kuwait City and lunch with his family. Because it is a beautiful, cool, winter's day he picks up his wife and youngest daughter and heads for the Corniche at Salmiya; a luxury beach development which runs alongside the Persian Gulf, just south of the city. Here, families and the young smart set gather in beachside restaurants, in upscale malls, or just cruise up and down the road in luxury convertibles and motorbikes, as bored rich young people do. Kuwait City un-self-consciously displays its wealth in stores, on bodies, on wheels and keels. With no real need to be industrious, most finish work by mid afternoon.

Kuwait is highly urbanised, 98 per cent of its (2.3 million) population lives in Kuwait City. Its GDP per capita is US$41,700 making it 18th in the world. It is a constitutional Emirate with a periodically difficult relationship between Parliament and the Emir, and 2011 and 2012 saw large-scale protests against corruption and the electoral changes proposed by the Emir. Politically concerned Kuwaitis are annoyed with the Emir. His frequent absences – in Bosnia falcon racing, in Mongolia, or relaxing in Morocco – create the feeling that no one is running the country. Abdullah says Kuwait is 'a rug in need of a good shake' to get rid of its cronyism, its leaving work early, its not doing very much while at work but waiting to leave. Kuwait, he says, is not Dubai or Qatar, by which he means a modern, successful Middle Eastern country run with imagination and enterprise, but ticking along, not diversifying fast enough, nor anticipating what will replace oil when it runs out. The state that feeds everyone stifles initiative. The oil city's wealth and high living standards conceal deep fragilities, which cannot be drowned out by the roar of hummers and land cruisers and the call to prayer that form its soundtrack. Abdullah's iPhone app tells him it is time to pray.

Kuwait City's architecture reveals its insecurities. The prestigious National Museum, and parts of the city's traditional market, both destroyed in the Iraqi invasion in 1990,[15] have not been rebuilt despite UN funding. The city still wears the scars of invasion, keeping it alive in the fabric of the city and in people's memories and stories. For Abdullah, who vividly recalls his part in the resistance guarding the hospital where his wife attended to the injured, the invasion was another chapter in the book of government ineptitude and abandonment. A failure to listen to the advice of the army and station troops in northern Kuwait on the Iraq border was compounded by a failure to announce the invasion once it was under way. Kuwaitis first heard of it from friends and family in the US, who heard of it on the news. Kuwait's royal family fled over the Saudi border, leaving citizens to deal with the invaders. Kuwait's oil strength became its vulnerability as Iraqi troops entered the KOC and removed the oil logs, before setting file to the wells as they retreated under UN coalition bombardment in the winter of 1991. A central and most dramatic part of the KOC exhibition narrating the nation's oil story is devoted to the invasion, more than 20 years later.

Domestic versions of invasion stories reverberate around the city too. Suad's mother describes the daily struggle to secure bread, the difficulty of washing the black residues of burning oil from carpets and curtains, and tactics for dealing with house-visits by occupying Iraqi soldiers on looting sprees, which could result in summary execution. Suad's father bought a large framed photo of Saddam from an Iraqi soldier and hung it prominently in the lounge. When soldiers came to the house they looked startled to find Saddam supporters, saluted the photograph, and left as quickly as they had arrived. Families still reference their martyrs, captured for resistance, taken to Iraq and punished with execution.

The reasons these stories still circulate lie in Kuwait's anxious relationship with bordering countries. Iraq and Iran are difficult neighbours. Iraq has shown recent disregard for Kuwait sovereignty. Dwarfed by Saudi Arabia, at various times increasing its territory to the detriment of southern Kuwait, Kuwait feels to its middle-class, politically savvy citizens like a small strip of desert bordering the Persian Gulf with an uncertain future. It has a political elite who cannot be trusted to act beyond their own interests, inattentive and largely absent rulers, and no feasible plans for when the oil runs out. How does Kuwait fit into the conversations about the 'new Middle East' and the strategic arc of American influence following the protracted occupation of Iraq? Kuwait, says Abdullah, is a rented house you dare not settle in, just in case it turns out to be temporary.

Gathering in the Desert

Kuwait's current political circumstances, the micro oil politics of the KOC and the oil matrix beyond, and global oil politics, all surface in the conversation of the Friday night gathering of oilmen in the desert. For the last ten years of Fridays Abdullah has joined his oil friends at Hamad's chalet, 18 km north of the Saudi border. He drives south along the highway from Kuwait City. Thousands of tents, belonging to extended families taking advantage of the cooler weather to go winter camping in the desert, line the road. The winter camping season is from December to March; at other times it is too hot to camp. Abdullah pulls off the highway when he sees the giant yellow arches of MacDonald's and goes straight to the other M to offer prayers. Traders are selling kites from the back of four-wheel-drive vehicles to parents who want to help the maid entertain their children. An atmosphere of expectation of a weekend of family gathering and conviviality prevails.

The chalet is painted outside in heat-reflecting white. Its air-conditioning makes it useable through the summer. It has interconnecting rooms containing sofas and bunk beds anticipating (extended) family arrivals. The chalet is set on an artificially created inlet, which provides swimming from the deck at the back of the chalet. The front-yard is already filling up with land cruisers as the oilmen arrive. Because it is still cool they gather in a large tent in front of the chalet. This is the *diwani*, a place intended for receiving visitors, where the men and the older boys gather to discuss the things that concern them. Gatherings are often gender segregated, and women and children typically gather in the main room of the house. The tent has carpets on the floor and cushions around its canvas walls. Men sit cross-legged snacking on dates, sweets, mint tea and cardamom coffee. By dinner time 20 men and 2 teenage boys are exchanging news. The principle of the gathering is that people can ask to join and will be added to the dinner roster. The men are all professionals – geologists, petrochemical engineers, drilling contractors; some are highly influential in the KOC and in other parts of the (local) oil matrix. The men each take turns to provide dinner for the group. Sometimes this means their wives packing cooked food for (male) servants to reheat and serve, but tonight the food is brought from a Chinese restaurant in Kuwait City. It is set out in a separate building from the main chalet and the tent, on plastic tablecloths, on the floor. Over dinner the men tell each other jokes; a team of servants serve food and clear up. After dinner the oilmen return to the tent and read poetry from sites accessed on their iPhones.

Chitchat about work-level oil politics soon gives way to the bigger issues. A discussion of Gulf politics and the 'new Middle East', by which the men refer to the instabilities in Syria and Egypt following the 'new mood' of the Arab Spring, as well as new American strategising in the Gulf, ensues. The oilmen suspect that America is playing a new game in encouraging Middle Eastern countries to turn on each other as a substitute for American intervention. In this scenario the old plot of US dominance is secured through new means. In their conversation, America is still a superpower and China a set of business interests. They suspect that America doesn't mind Iraq being divided, as the oil then falls into more hands, making it less centralised. Iraqi oilfields are vast and yet to be fully exploited. Thus in their version, the new Middle East is balkanised. The discussion moves on to local politics and the corruption that prevents the benefits of oil being fully extended to the people. Then it turns to migrants and the question of whether Kuwait really needs them, as the fragrant coffee and sweets continue to circulate and elaborate deserts, brought from the city's elegant patisseries, are served.

The oilmen know that control of the benefits of oil eludes the oil-producing countries, even those, like Kuwait, organised in OPEC (Organization of Petroleum Exporting Countries). This brings particular insecurities to bear on the country's situation. This concern is amplified through another route on the globalisation superhighway. The oilmen know that the price of oil is not just about supply and demand, nor the geopolitical deals cut with oil-producing nations, nor yet the wielding of American superpower influence. Oil is a speculative commodity trading on global futures markets, and this financialisation of oil, brings particular forms of fragility to Kuwait. The oil futures market guarantees an oil price at a predefined date. But futures traders come in two types. There are hedgers who, for example, protect airlines' fuel prices, and there are speculators who, in fact, dominate futures trading. Less than 3 per cent of transactions result in actually taking possession of the oil: this is paper oil.[16] Oil is not only something geologists find, and drillers bring to the surface; oil is a speculative commodity.[17] At a 2012 OPEC meeting a bundle of intersecting sources of insecurities were aired. These included the fragility of the global economy, the instabilities in the Eurozone, the increase in oil speculation on commodities markets and geopolitical tensions, including demands for regime accountability and greater social justice.[18] The oilmen know that Kuwait must live alongside these globally calibrated fragilities, and it makes them anxious.

Around midnight the men depart for the city in their land cruisers and hummers. Tomorrow Hamad's extended family will arrive and the space will be transformed by a different kind of weekend gathering that includes women and small children.

Family Gathering

Gathering is a Kuwaiti skill practised at the weekends, and during festivals and holidays. Gathering is not about activity, although there is plenty of activity embedded in their staging – preparing food for example. Gathering is about inactivity, sitting, being, listening and talking: spending time with family, friends and, as we saw with the oilmen in the desert, wider social networks. A Saturday lunchtime gathering is a weekly feature at Abdullah's dad's house in Al Hammadi. His dad's house is vast. It easily absorbs 25 women and children, who can be accommodated on 9 large sofas in the main basement drawing room, as well as 15 men in the *diwani*. Upstairs a dozen maids, each brought to the gathering by her employing household in order to help with the work, take care of the smaller children, who cruise up and down the stairs to the basement.

The women's dress ranges from smart jeans and tops, to dresses and black robes (*beshts*). Some cover their faces and others don't. The robed and covered remove outer clothes in the absence of men. Beneath their robes they are elegantly and fashionably dressed. These educated women, all high achievers in science-related fields, work in science, dentistry, computing and medicine. One is a well-known hospital consultant. Headscarves and robes are matters of individual custom. Suad wears a scarf but not a *besht* and she does not cover her face. One of her friends comes from a secular family too, but wears a scarf to fit in with her husband's family's traditions. She adds a black miniskirt, tights and ankle boots to express hers. Suad has single professional women friends. While marriage is the norm, it is certainly not obligatory. Kuwait is liberal in these matters, as well as in matters of dress.

Migrants

Different types of migrants co-construct the oil city. Alem has come from Addis Ababa on a two-year visa permitting her to work in domestic service. So too has the tardy driver from Sri Lanka who is tasked with washing the family's cars. The drilling and support staff from the wildcat work one- or two-month shifts. Abdullah's professional migrant colleagues at the KOC are long-settled in Kuwait. Suad's Syrian friend is married to a Kuwaiti. These migrants have different visa arrangements with the Kuwaiti authorities; they stay for different lengths of time and for different reasons.

Although Abdullah is descended from Iranian migrants, because his father came to Kuwait in the 1930s and he was born here, he thinks of himself as Kuwaiti. This tiny country has a long history of shifting populations and borders which configure the calculation of migrant status.

Migrants outnumber Kuwaitis, who form a minority (45 per cent) population in their own country. In 2012 the population of Kuwait was 2,646,314, more than half of which are non-nationals. Other Arabs, by far the largest migrant group and the result of long-term mobility around the Gulf, constitute 35 per cent of the Kuwait population, South Asians 9 per cent, Iranians 4 per cent and other migrants 7 per cent. Non-Kuwaitis compose 60 per cent of Kuwait's workforce.[19] Kuwait runs on migrant labour, much of it unnecessary, according to the oilmen, who agreed that they don't need drivers and servants. Ending Kuwaiti dependence on the domestic labour of what are perceived to be unskilled migrants would redress the population and labour force imbalance while increasing the domestic duties of Kuwaiti women.

This Kuwaiti sense of being outnumbered targets particular migrants. Abdullah experiences this feeling at the KOC where, he says, Egyptians and Palestinians give jobs to their fellow countrymen, and keep Kuwaitis out, by losing their job applications and by not passing on vital job information. Abdullah also has many migrant friends. He judges migrants in terms of their efforts at integration and how far they maintain connections with their countries of origin. His friend Ahmed, a long-term migrant from Yemen who studied at the University of Kuwait and a KOC professional, is in Abdullah's judgement, an ideal migrant. Ahmed stayed during the invasion, demonstrating beyond question his commitment to Kuwait. Abdullah judges more harshly the intentions of those who have strong external connections and who see Kuwait in instrumental terms, as a place to earn money or in other ways advance themselves while maintaining lives elsewhere. His judgements are shaped by class and migrant status. The 'integrated' are permanent employees. Their visa arrangements do not require them to rotate in and out of Kuwait, but allow them to stay and build connections.

Rig workers are contractually denied continuous connection by the terms of their employment, which are brokered through multinational drilling companies. Even Lazar, who is a mechanical engineer employed by OSCO as the company man on rig 776, is a rotating migrant shift worker who must return to Goa after his 28-day shift. Rig workers see little of Kuwait except the airport and the rig and this, too, limits their connection.

They are not allowed to leave the drilling site unless they need to deal with personal business, in which case a company driver escorts them to the nearest town. Most drilling sites are in the desert so there is nowhere to go and no transport. Thais, Filipinos, Indians, Egyptians and Syrians constitute the rig workforce. Senior staff work a 28-day shift followed by 28 days' rest in their own country. Juniors work a 56-day shift and return home for 28 days. Although a handful of Kuwaitis work on rigs, 12-hour shifts in intense heat are considered to be arduous. Kuwaitis anyway have access to easier jobs and regard rig work as incompatible with family life. Working conditions on the rig support long-distance, episodic, family lives, and this makes rig work a migrant job in most Kuwaitis calculations. Drilling companies provide everything: medical care, tickets home, food and accommodation in the camp, transport between the rig and the camp. Conditions are tough but salaries are high compared to those in the migrants' home countries. Junior rig staff earn US$500–$1000 a month, and up to US$10,000 is paid to seniors. Pay scales in the oil industry are calculated internationally and wage bands reflect risk. In hostile areas workers are paid multiples of these salaries, with parts of Iraq paying the highest salaries.

Ako, an Egyptian roustabout junior on rig 776 has worked in Kuwait for a year on the rig catwalk, helping out wherever he is needed and learning the job. He is eager to learn new things and advance. Living near Alexandria with his parents, he is just back from a field-break where he had a 'complete rest, made my mind clear; met some friends.... We are paid in Kuwaiti dinar. When I go home I take all my money with me. I am saving it to get married.' He says there is no work in Egypt, and even if there were the salary would be lower. His brother, who also works in drilling, helped Ayo to get the job. His fellow roustabout, a Syrian, Asu, who is 30, sends all of his money back to Syria to feed his wife and three young children. Syria is engulfed in civil war. He says things are not good there but it's a big country and he tries to avoid the conflict, which many of his family are swept up in, when he returns.

When Asu and Ako are not working they watch TV and sleep. It is hard for them to get enough rest to get them through the next day. They live for their field-breaks, but seem contented with the prospects and pay offered by the rig. Not all migrants are so content. Joki, a Goan tug master who dredges one of the ports and cleans up oil spills, says that some Kuwaitis are kind but others, especially the young, are rude. He says he dare not step out of his house without his ID card or his passport, as the police check all the time. Like the other migrants who are permitted to roam the city, with ID cards at the ready, he travels the city by bus, and this too distinguishes him from Kuwaitis, who travel in private cars, sometimes with drivers, or in taxis driven by migrants.

Migrants navigate different routes through the oil city. The leisured lives of Kuwaitis rely on them. Migrants clean the city and the houses. They serve in shops, they have stalls in the market, they look after Kuwaiti children, they drill oil, they do professional jobs, they start businesses and they do the hard physical labour. The everyday lives of Kuwaitis are organised by migrants. Migrants are simultaneously evidence of Kuwait's wealth and a source of anxiety for the dependencies they sustain.

Dock Traffic

A visit to Shuwaikh Port – secured with rolls of barbed wire, CCTV and guards – reveals further fragilities. Kuwait makes and grows none of the goods needed to sustain the (luxury) standards of consumption evident throughout the city. Even water supplies are precarious, and rely on two desalination plants. Given this situation, ports are a vital supply line. Hundreds of containers labelled Maersk, PIL, China Shipping and so on, arrive at the docks to be unloaded onto a fleet of trucks distributing goods all over the city. The dock labour force – gantry crane operators, dredgers, port handling and tug masters – belongs to the Port Workers' Union, and through the union to the International Trade Union Federation. This acts as an authority of last resort in union dealings with the port authorities. The unloading operation occupies 120 men and 4 women in three-hour shifts. Between shifts the labour force manages the flow of trucks and containers. The dock migrant labour force is declining as efforts to Kuwaiti-ise it are stepped up.

Oil is Kuwait's only export apart from the used oil pipes which are cleaned and returned for reuse. The oil leaves, unseen, from a secure port near Al Hammadi. It has travelled across the desert from the drilling rigs in pipes which pass through the gathering centres nearby. Here, oil, gas and water are separated before being piped to storage tanks in Al Hammadi. Kuwait keeps a fraction of its oil for domestic use and for its petrochemical industry. Most is exported, and Chinese and Korean petrochemical industries are important customers. Only small oil tankers can draw up to the piers. The Persian Gulf is not deep enough for super tankers. For the oil to reach these it must be pumped first to the offshore mooring terminal.

Moving on

Kuwaiti oil is exported all over the world. But the oil on the flip-flop trail moves towards the centres of plastic production. There are many of these and at this point the trail could be followed in any number of directions, along a shifting matrix of routes. But the oil we are following moves from the sea terminal in the Persian Gulf, southward through the narrow Straits of Hormuz between Oman and Iran. This 21 nautical mile chokepoint, described by Cyrus Vance[20] as the 'jugular vein' of the global economy, is, perhaps, the world's most critical energy nexus: 35 per cent of all crude oil carried in tankers passes here. At this point the oil is exposed to an Iran with plummeting oil exports as a result of sanctions. In July 2010 a mysterious explosion on the M Star super tanker from Mitsui OSK Lines in the straits raised anxieties to the extent that the Kuwait Tanker Company was prompted to station armed guards on its ships. Saudi Arabia invested billions in pipelines circumventing the straits, and NATO patrols were deployed to secure the passage of oil through the straits which stand between Kuwait and Asian markets.

Clearing Hormuz the oil tanker, guided by its Filipino and Indian crew, heads south into the Arabian Sea. From here it rounds the southern tip of India and moves into the Bay of Bengal, and onwards to the south-east and Singapore. Singapore is an important Kuwaiti oil customer too, but the oil on the flip-flop trail moves on, turning northward, past Hong Kong and into the South China Sea. Heading north along the China coast past Shanghai, the tanker could release its oil into the Chinese market. Here, burgeoning private car ownership and petrochemical industries making plastics demand ever-increasing volumes of oil. But it doesn't. Instead it continues northwards until it reaches the Korean peninsula to the east and the oil ports of Daesan's petrochemical plants on the west coast of Korea, 120 km south-west of Seoul. The oil it carries is part of a vibrating, mobile, tapestry of uncertainties organising the lives of Kuwaiti citizens and migrant workers.

3
Choreographies of Petrochemistry

As the oil tanker from Kuwait approaches the coast of South Korea at Daesan, corporate Korea rises up to meet it. Oil refineries and petrochemical plants sequester much of this north-west coastline around the Yellow Sea. The jetty fingers of the giant corporations of the Korean chaebols[1] – Hyundai Oil Bank, Samsung Total, LG and the Lotte Daesan Petrochemical Corporation – suck the oil ashore. Daesan, 120 km south-west of Seoul, is a well-located petrochemical platform.[2] It is closer to Middle Eastern oil supplies than Ulsan – the bigger petrochemical cluster on the south-east shore of South Korea – and only 400 nautical miles from the China coast and the burgeoning markets for oil and plastics.[3] The oil is piped from the tanker, in the deep harbour, into the giant round holding tanks of the Hyundai Oil Bank Refinery. At this junction on the trail, the oil industry ends and the world of petrochemicals lies before us. In the Hyundai Oil Bank Refinery naphtha cracking plant, Kuwaiti oil is broken down into the chemical components in which it enters the petrochemical industry. It is then piped to the vast LG Chemical Plant next to Hyundai.

As the petrochemicals arrive at the LG (Lucky Gold Star) plant the workforce marches in step to meet them – theirs is a collective journey – and the choreographies of petrochemicals commence. A white bus with 20 uniformed men, in various states of wakefulness, arrives from the LG apartments nearby and drives through the checkpoint at the main gate. As the bus passes, the security guard stands to attention and raises a white-gloved hand in respectful salute. The men are dropped off at the 15 sub-plants where they work. These are divided into monomers and polymers, and then by the different materials made there. Those travelling by other means join the arrivals. A line of cars, carrying car-pooling team-mates, waits in line at the checkpoint. A trickle of cyclists pauses while the guard checks their security passes. Those arriving on foot, or on the number 900 bus from the nearby city of Seosan, which stops outside the gate, pass through the automatic gates by placing their security pass on the reader. The working day begins and ends as workers move in and out of the plant and the day shift replaces the night shift. The same bus will transport the men coming off the night shift to the LG apartments, a five-minute drive away, for their breakfast.[4]

The LG plant is where the bus from Seosan dropped me, and my Korean student assistant, whom I had met up with in Seoul before boarding the bus to Seosan. The airline having lost my luggage on the flight from London explains why I was standing, freezing, outside of a petrochemical plant in temperatures of minus 15° Celsius in shoes which slipped on the ice. We were *outside* because all efforts at gaining access from London and, later, from California, when the (Berkeley-based) Korean student began making calls on my behalf, had failed. Having been refused entry at every petrochemical company in South Korea, we agreed to turn up anyway. The fall-back plan was to work from one of the cafés near the plant with workers coming on and off shift.

The security guard at the main LG gate refused us entry too. He also refused to tell us from whom we should seek permission to enter. Hearing our exchange with the guard, a subcontracted engineer, going into the plant to repair a machine, told us to wait until he got back, saying 'there is always a way'. When he returned he gave us a lift to our hotel and some information, offering to try to get us into the Samsung plant a few days later, where he was to do another repair. While he was helpful, he didn't, in the end, have the authority to get us in. The next day we returned to the LG gates and the café opposite in the hope of making contacts. It was lunchtime and the café was full of uniformed LG men taking a break. Spotting an older, distinguished-looking man I thought might be senior, my assistant agreed to follow him when he left the café. He joined him outside for a cigarette, explaining our interest in the plant. He seemed sympathetic but offered no advice. Back in the cafe, a call came through for us. It was the older man we later learned was Mr Kwon, saying he would phone security and authorise our access. Minutes later we were inside the plant. There we spoke with Mr Kwon and his staff; we were given a tour of the plant and told how it worked. Through Mr Kwon and his colleagues we were invited to workers' homes, had dinners hosted for us and further trips around the plant. While its official countenance may not be welcoming, the personal face of corporate Korea is warm and generous.

Chemicals and Plastics

The Daesan LG petrochemical plant is vast and empty. Its automation has reduced the number of workers needed to 800 – a workforce largely confined to computer terminals with only occasional human–machine interface. Hyundai built this plant in 1989. LG bought it in 2005 when the petrochemical industry in South Korea was restructured. On this January morning the plant looms in monochrome greys and whites: a bitterly cold wind blows through its vast open spaces. Giant (grey) silos and vast pipe structures belt out white smoke. Long warehouse-like sheds the size of multiple football pitches house clusters of noisy machines. Even the office buildings, from where production is organised and monitored, have the same warehouse aesthetic.

In the (polymer) polyethylene (PE) section of the plant the Production Department offices are on the first floor of a warehouse building. On the ground floor below, stand a row of silver bicycles bearing the LG logo. These provide the fastest way to get around the site. Upstairs, the production team are going about their tasks for the day in a large open-plan office with two workstations occupied by women at one end, and a table for team project meetings at the other. The PE production team move around their office with the practiced familiarity that comes from spending many years as co-workers: theirs is a well-rehearsed group dance in which each knows the movements expected of them. The team, including the women, are identically dressed in mid grey mandarin-collared jackets, with a subtle narrow dark red trim, on which each has their name embroidered. They wear black casual-smart trousers and, anticipating long journeys around the plant on foot, black leather shoes with thick soles. Their collective mission is to keep the PE plant running, efficiently producing the right amount of PE, at the right time.

PE is a staple in the world of plastics and, along with EVA – a co-polymer product of ethylene adjusted with the chemical vinyl acetate – provides the material substance of flip-flops. These plastics are made in the arrangement of carbon and hydrogen, derived from the cracking of crude oil into the naphtha that comes from the Hyundai Oil Bank Refinery next door. Cracking takes large hydrocarbons and breaks them down into smaller ones. In other parts of the LG plant, naphtha is further cracked into a group of primary petrochemicals, monomers, such as ethylene and propylene (called olefins).[5] Monomers are molecules with a single chemical bond, which can be combined into polymer chains. In this way a primary chemical like ethylene, for example, becomes polyethylene. Carbon, a natural material derived from oil, forms the spine of the polymer chain and bonds with hydrogen. Other elements are added to this basic polymer chain, such as chlorine, nitrogen and sulphur.[6] PVC (polyvinylchloride), for example, contains chlorine and is commonly used to make flip-flop straps. These plastics emerge from reactors as a raw material that can be subjected to additional treatments with additives – like antioxidants and colorants – which further change their physical and chemical properties. As a material it is, well, plastic, easily made into different shapes, colours and densities, and available for a range of uses.

PE, EVA and PVC are thermoplastic resins: combinations of hydrogen and carbon altered through heat and pressure.[7] Plastics divide into two groups. Thermosets are plastics in which the molecules are cross-linked. These cannot be reheated, remoulded or recycled. Car seats, mattresses, lacquer and electrical wire coating, are examples of thermosets, for which LG supplies the raw materials. Thermoplastics, the second group, are more malleable. Having weak secondary molecular bonds, they can be reheated, reformed and recycled. These are softened by heat and harden upon cooling. They are shaped by extrusion, moulding or pressing, as will become apparent further along the trail. Thermoplastics are supplied by LG to flip-flop factories around the world as tiny coloured granules.

Production Team

Seo-yeon, a slim married woman in her mid 30s, sits at her desk in the open-plan office. She does the support work for the team, filing papers, photocopying, ensuring that they don't run out of office supplies. Mr Kwon arranged her (part-time) hours to fit in with the care of her school-aged children, when she returned to the company four months ago, after 12 years at home. She has been up since 6.30am to make sure her husband and children have their breakfast before they leave: only then does she make her way to the plant.

The team leader and senior operator, Mr Kwon, reports to the PE plant manager. Mr Kwon is a distinguished-looking man in his early 50s. He has been with the company 25 years and is highly respected by his fellow workers. Mr Kwon arrives early to make sure the team is running well. He has been up since 6am, allowing time for a run along the beach outside of the LG apartments. He drives to work after eating the breakfast his wife makes. Mr Kwon no longer operates machines himself, but checks instead on the operators in his team. He gathers data on current PE production, and he plans and budgets future production. While his working day officially ends at 6pm, he is often at his desk until 8pm, occasionally working on Saturdays, even though he is not contracted to. He believes in the importance of hard work as part of the collective effort to secure national, as well as personal, prosperity, so that, 'when we are older we don't depend on others'.

Young-soo is a chemical engineer in his early 40s and a 'part leader' in the production team, placing him directly below Mr Kwon. He joined

LG 17 years ago, straight from university, and has worked in LG's Yeosu plant too. Young-soo has been up since 4.30am because he attends an early church service with his family. After church his wife makes the family breakfast and his three children head off to different schools. His wife walks the youngest child to school before tackling her domestic and church duties. Engineers form 20 per cent of the LG workforce. The work of production falls on operators, who, under Young-soo's supervision, have lower rank in the company hierarchy. Young-soo also believes in the value of hard work and self-advancement. As an engineer, he is more mobile than the operators, and is keen to further develop his skills by working for LG in China.

It is Jung-ho, the operator below Young-soo, who actually makes the PE, although in this automated world, he does this at a distance. Unlike those in the team above him, he and his work-group (of five operators) are shift workers. On site for the start of the 7am shift, and preferring the car pool to the bus, they drive to work together in one car, and they return to the LG apartments together when their shift ends at 3pm. Three shifts a day keeps the plant in continuous production. After four days, operators take a day off, and then the pattern repeats. In his mid 30s, he is married to Seo-yeon, who runs their home and family as well as working part-time in the office. Jung-ho and his work team-mates sit in front of their computer screens most of the day monitoring the machines. Sometimes the machines freeze or break down and he will call the maintenance division who will arrange for a contractor to fix them. He checks that the right quantities of chemicals go into the PE mix and that the small white granules that come out are of the right composition.

These small routine tasks compose a giant global enterprise. Petrochemicals shape the world in which we live. A new and ever expanding world of chemicals is injected into our food, our clothing, our objects, our shelter and our leisure.[8] The Second World War advanced the remit of petrochemicals, expediting a search for synthetic materials to replace expensive natural ones. These new synthetic fabrics and the modern world were co-produced. Today petrochemicals are made into soap, detergent, solvents, paints, drugs, fertilisers, pesticides, explosives, synthetic fibres and rubbers, flooring, and insulation, in addition to plastics. Our cars, our clothing, our homes, our electrical equipment, our furniture and more, are made from petrochemicals. Without petrochemicals the world as we know it could not exist. Their significance, in addition to the scale on which petrochemicals are produced, makes them a constituent part of the global mainstream. Jung-ho's PE finds its way into blue plastic carrier bags – the most ubiquitous object of our time – as well as into a plethora of objects composing the fabrics of everyday life the world over. Jung-ho's small routine world could not have wider significance.

Jung-ho is a field operator. In additions to sitting at his monitor he makes two physical inspections of his machinery every day, to verify computer information on how they are working, and to listen for unusual sounds. He and his field officer teammate divide their PE plant and inspect half each: this takes an hour and a half. When he walks around the plant he traces manually, instead of from his computer, the large grey pipes into which the chemicals are fed and turned into granules, and the large silos to where the granules are blown. Otherwise, from his computer terminal in the control room, he checks whether the right amount of heat and pressure is applied in combining hydrogen and carbon molecules to make the PE granules, which are then stored in giant silos until they are needed. At this point machines pack them into 500 kg plastic sacks stamped 'LG Chemical'. After packing they are moved (mechanically) onto pallets and then onto small driverless train carriages that run around the plant. The plastic sacks are moved to a vast storage area where they are loaded, by subcontracted loaders, finally touched by hands, into shipping containers labelled MEARSK and PIL.

So-yeon, who is in her early 30s, has worked at LG for ten years and is one of only 20[9] full-time women workers in the company workforce of 800. Her wages are half those of male workers who are often younger. Like the other women at LG, she does office support work, filing drawings, monitoring the budget and recording the men's working hours and holidays. Officially she works from 9am to 6pm and she car-pools with some of the other women who live, as she does, on the second floor of the 'singles' LG apartment block – men occupy floors 3–15 – but she often arrives early too, after her breakfast in the company restaurant downstairs from her apartment.

Mr Kwon runs his team like a benevolent father: manoeuvring work around their personal circumstances when necessary, and taking an interest in their welfare. The company 'values' are posted on the office wall, and allude to morality, ethics, fair competition and honesty. Being able to adjust to the work environment of the plant is as important as qualifications and operators – who typically have four years of college education as well as having completed their military service – are carefully selected through personality tests. Selection favours those in rude health:

hard work and optimism are prized. New recruits are drawn into the circuits of company supervision and rising pay scales linked to years of service (unless they are women). Long service is rewarded with pay rises and this militates against moving, connecting workers to LG for the duration of their working lives.

These workers are well-paid. As an operator with 20 years of service at LG, Yung-ho is paid the equivalent of US$100,000 a year. Mr Kwon is considerably more highly rewarded than this for his 25 years of service. Young-soo, as an engineer, has higher status than Yung-ho, but earns a little less because he is not a shift worker. Combined with low rates of income tax and substantial company benefits, such as accommodation, part-paid utility bills and transport, these are substantial salaries by any standard. The men form a highly rewarded cohesive team. Work regarded as unskilled, described by Mr Kwon as 'simple labour' – security, catering, distribution – is less secure, less well-paid and allocated to subcontractors.

These circumstances scale-up countrywide. Excellent employment conditions and pay in petrochemical and other major industries run by key corporations come at the expense of poorer conditions in other industries and subcontracted work in major companies. In the mid 2000s 14.6 per cent of the Korean population lived in relative poverty, defined as less than 50 per cent of median income. The Korean Development Institute reported absolute poverty among 17.6 per cent of its population. The biggest social divisions are between those in regular and those in irregular (informal) work, and between those in full-time and those in part-time work. This disproportionately disadvantages women. Among construction workers, 8 per cent are irregularly, informally employed, many of them foreign migrants. An elite, highly paid, workforce with stable conditions of employment in core industries coupled with substantial benefits, means casualisation and subcontracting for others, producing a system of social disparities. A staggering 40 per cent of Korean employees do not have regular employment. This is coupled with a youth unemployment rate of over 8 per cent (in 2010) and minimal social welfare provision.[10] The salaries of core petrochemical workers come at a cost borne by other workers.

Oyster Dinner

Team drinks and dinners are weekly activities everyone is expected to attend, except Seo-yeon, who is expected to go home and look after her children. Tonight, Mr Kwon has booked a simple oyster restaurant near the main gate of the plant for his team. Fifteen men and So-yeon arrive in uniform, in four cars, and arrange themselves around two trestle tables that hold large steaming ramen pots. Mr Kwon bought, from an elderly couple of seafood diggers at Samgilpo, just along the coast, two carrier bags of oysters and a large bag of a seafood-delicacy called 'bird fish', for the restaurant to cook. The team are all professionals, and the dinner is an acknowledgement of social status: only people with money eat with friends in restaurants. The dinner extends Mr Kwon's position as the team leader and senior worker to the table: he presides, orders and pays. He smokes, while the younger men, out of respect for their elders, leave to smoke outside. Jung-ho, the operator, eagerly joins the conversation and toasting. Young-soo, the engineer, joins in without drinking the milky white rice wine and *soju* that circulates throughout the dinner. His religious faith forbids the alcohol that fuels the event his social codes and team spirit take him to.

The conversation is wide-ranging and the alcohol flows. Drinking (for men) is a vital part of the evening and an expectation from which only Young-soo is exempted. As more and more food arrives, belts are unfastened and the national predicament debated. Will South and North Korea ever be united? Should they be? Will Psy's 'Gangnam Style' YouTube hit be repeated? Jun describes how he left LG to work for another corporation in another city, but came back because he missed his colleagues. The moral of the story: there isn't another life to be lived elsewhere, there is only life at LG, and it is a good life. Their lives, they suggest, are ordinary and similar to each other. The repetition in their lives makes it boring as well as comfortable. Korea, they concur, is overpopulated and limited in the experiences it offers. It is better to live outside Korea than inside, especially in the US. It is better to travel than to stay in Korea, but it is necessary to speak English in order to do this. They are all proficient at passing English-language tests, because work promotion demands it: but this is different from speaking English well enough to travel, they explain. So-yeon has travelled to China and Thailand and intends to travel further. The only woman at the table, she is teased about having once been Jun's girlfriend. She takes this in good humour. The team are well educated and have a sense of the wider world through TV and news coverage. Food keeps arriving.

Drinking, all agree, is an important activity for men. Guys are drinking friends and people who don't drink are outsiders immersed in their families, although they concur that a 'good Korean' puts his family before his work team. Drinking is listed as a top leisure activity. Only unmarried women, like So-yeon, can go out drinking with workmates but social activities are gender segregated for married women. Ironically, the election of Park Geun-hye (2012), Korea's first woman president – and the daughter of the man who seized power in a military coup in 1961, and was assassinated in 1979, leaving a legacy of human rights abuses – coincides with the highest level of gender inequality in the world.[11]

As the evening progresses, and the rice wine flows, talk turns to politics. Politicians are corrupt: not all are happy with Park Geun-hye's election. It is complicated being Korean. 'District feeling' guides the political map, and, through this the development of Korea, as national politicians favour their own regions by directing investment towards them. Park Chung-hee, Guen-hye's father, came from the south-east. This explains the factories and ports around Ulsan and the twin poles of Korean growth in Ulsan and, more recently, in the Seosan–Daesan area, as industrial magnets. Do businessmen turned politicians have the right political skill to run Korea? Is running a country significantly different from running a company? In the production of its political class, as in the dominance of the chaebols and their paternalistic reach into (some) workers' lives, Korea is aptly described as corporate.

It is still early in the evening when this concentrated burst of eating and drinking comes to an end with many of the major issues of the day unresolved. The happy team drift off home in their car-pools, thanking Mr Kwon for his hospitality, and pausing to smoke one more cigarette outside of the restaurant.

Company Lives

The men (and So-yeon) move in step in the work–home–socialising choreographies of day and evening. The entire work team live in the LG apartments, just a five-minute drive from the plant and the oyster restaurant. Ninety per cent of LG of workers live in the LG apartments: the remainder live in Seosan and Seoul, usually for family reasons, which reference children's education as priorities. Mothers supervise where these distant family forms are practised; 'wild goose' fathers join families in Seoul at the weekends. The LG apartments form a cluster of 15-storey blocks with the company logo on the top. Families are given spacious, three-bedroomed apartments, some with sea views. Singles have studio apartments. Communal facilities include a table tennis hall, a 'Happy Centre' for yoga, a couple of restaurants, a bar and a few shops, including a convenience store. On one level, these lives are lived as collective journeys, making them more like 'package tours' than individual journeys. Mr Kwon's repetition of the mantra of the oyster dinner – 'we lead similar lives' – in response to my request to speak to team members about their lives, confirms this. The concept of a standard company life, in many ways replicates the military model of their (compulsory) army experiences: wearing uniforms; socialising in groups organised by the rationale of the job; collective living in the LG barracks. But this standardisation is only on the surface. The corporatisation of lives extends only so far into individual biographies. Beyond this point the journeys (and lives) of this group of LG workers displays many differences.

So-yeon and a couple of the younger men from the team live in the singles block. Her bed-sitting room, with a separate bathroom, is painted in light colours chosen by the company. It is spacious and sparsely furnished (by the company) with a bed, desk, sofa and flat-screen TV. She likes living on her own now that she is used to it, although she is pressured to marry and have children. Families as well as corporations encourage the standard fabrication of lives. Born in Incheon – part of the hyper-developed south-west corridor connecting Seoul to its modern airport – her family moved to Seosan when she was a teenager to look after her grandma when her grandpa died. Her parents and younger brother still live there. She left the family home two years ago to avoid the two-hour daily commute to LG and her parents' scrutiny. She says Korean parents don't like to see older children around the house, and at her age she should be married with children: 'I want to get married: people ask when I am getting married – I would get married right now if there was a guy I liked … someone I can respect; someone who is able to support the family.' Korean women meet potential husbands at work – or out clubbing, which she has only done once – and most of the men she works with are already married, or much younger than her. She speculates on lowering her age-limits: someone five, maybe six years younger than her would be acceptable.

She socialises with friends from high school in Seosan, but most of them are married. She has to endure the Facebook pictures of them holding new babies, and listen to her parents talking about the importance of marriage. But she also knows that marriage brings less freedom. She won't be able to socialise with her male team-mates; she won't be able to go skiing with her girlfriends, as she will tomorrow; she may not even be able to continue working. Although these things are slowly changing, there is still the presumption that men, rather than women, work: although this is shifting with the rising cost of living, especially with the financial burdens of educating children. Modern, educated, Koreans are more likely to share the financial burdens of family life. In this context, women's earning capacity and professional status become assets in negotiating marriage. So-yeon thinks that life at LG, and Korea more generally, favours men.

So-yeon also socialises with a small group of 30–40-year-old single women who work at LG and meet for drinks after work. Their conversations often consider whether to marry, and how to arrange this, now that they are substantially older than available men. Another conversation ruminates on their position at LG – also a nudge towards marriage. Mostly clerical and office support workers, the women are not unionised like the men. There are no prospects of promotion, or of the kinds of pay increases available to men. So-yeon says that each worker is set a goal, and while men are judged on their own efforts, and anyway rewarded for the length of time in the company, women are judged on the work team grade, rather than on individual merit. Sidelined into support work, LG women get small annual rises: So-yeon earns the equivalent of US$30,000 a year with bonus. This is less than half the salary a man of her age and experience earns. At least marriage, with all of its restrictions, would give access to a male wage and the prospect of time out to raise children.

I am very dissatisfied with how men dominate in Korea, if I worked 20 years I would stay at the same level. Women used to make coffee and copy papers in the past but now it has improved a bit. Women work more and harder but stay the same. When we go for a drink we complain about it. I have been here for 12 years. I know women of 40 who have not married who just want to live by themselves.… Women in Korea do not have equal opportunities.… All of the women workers think this is bad. Maybe in 10, 20 or 30 years it will change but now it's very male-dominated. In ten years I will be focusing on family life and married. (So-yeon)

So-yeon calls a girlfriend to confirm that she is driving the four women on the ski trip near Seoul tomorrow – her day off. She says guys cuss girl drivers, but she doesn't care, she shows them that she can drive as well as a man.

When Mr Kwon returns to their spacious, three-bedroomed, family apartment overlooking the Yellow Sea from the twelfth floor of one of the LG blocks, his wife is pleased to see him. Mrs Kwon has not worked since they married 20 years ago. In her early 50s, she doesn't think it proper for women to work, and she doesn't need to as Mr Kwon's salary meets current family needs and allows them to plan for the time when they will need to buy somewhere to live. All company benefits end at retirement. Mrs Kwon put her energies into their two sons, aged 19 and 15, instead and with good results. The 19-year-old is studying chemical engineering at a good university in Seoul. She knows it would better serve his future job prospects if he studied in the US, but this is more expensive and has higher English-language requirements. He could only meet these with the aid of an English-language education outside of Korea, preferably in the US, but this is prohibitively expensive. A cheaper alternative is offered in international schools in Thailand. She expects that his Seoul university degree, combined with his father's contacts at LG, will position him well for the future. Like everything else in Korea, education is strictly hierarchised. It is also a major family investment.

Now that her younger son is 15, Mrs Kwon has more time for herself. She plays golf with her women friends, meets at their houses for tea or goes shopping in Seosan. LG runs buses to Seosan and to Seoul for family members: the company provides everything. Their son arrived home, from his afterschool schooling, with more homework, even later than Mr Kwon. He shut himself in his room, not finishing until 10pm. The Korean education system is very demanding of its students and educational success is highly valued for its promise of future success and for developing family prosperity.

When Jung-ho arrives at their identical three-bedroomed apartment, Seo-yeon is still supervising the children's homework in the living room.[12] Their daughter, aged 8, now walks to and from the elementary school with her friends, arriving home at 1pm to spend time reading and doing homework with her mother. Their son, aged 11, arrives later because he goes to Taekwondo after school. When he goes to high school he will catch the company school bus. At 5pm the tutor arrives to teach the children English. Seo-yeon says: 'this is the most important thing. They have piano lessons too and art.' Education, at the centre of the family project, is displayed in the living room in bookcases full of children's books, educational games, toys and art materials. When the tutor leaves at 7.30, Seo-yeong has another set of homework, this time set by the tutor, to check. She says:

> From 10 to 1pm [when the children are at school] I think I am wasting my time and have done for ten years so I prefer to work. It is a minority of women who work. It is different for each women, I have no thoughts on women who do not work. There are not many jobs here, so there are not many places to work. Younger women may envy me but older women who don't work like Mrs Kwon are satisfied with their lives. Older women have more time so they can go golfing and walking in the mountain nearby. Some people value leisure time more and they don't want to work. People get paid well compared to others so they can enjoy their leisure time. I don't want to work full-time, I like my life the way it is. I am happy. It is really important as a mother to raise children until the age of 20. In ten years I will still be here because in Korea the women follow the men. (Seo-yeong)

Seo-yeong is happy to give her children opportunities she did not have. Born near Seosan, only an hour away, her parents were garlic farmers and all seven daughters had to help with the crop and the housework. Family resources were focused on the only boy, who was excused farming and domestic labour. After leaving school Seo-yeong commuted from the family home to the LG plant, leaving both when she married Jung-ho, who still helps his parents on the farm. When he is not at team dinners Jung-ho comes home to be with the family; some evenings he organises the table tennis league or goes for a drink with his neighbour-colleagues. On days off he likes to go fishing or treat himself to a game of golf. He says:

> It's an ordinary life.... No it is different.... There are many conversations within the family, which makes it different from other families.... We talk about things such as school life and friends.... In ten years' time I will be here working at LG.... Until I retire ... I don't have specific plans.... We may go back to where I grew up.... We are just saving money with no purpose right now. I have 20 more years to work so there is plenty of time. It's the best company, LG makes workers feel like they are home, it makes them smile, and the environment is good.... We are treated nicely there is no class [difference] between us so they respect the lower people who are working under them, even the employer treats them nicely ...

Seo-yeong reads while Jung-ho watches television: by 10pm the entire family are in bed with the children's homework checked.

On the eighth floor, Young-soo enters an identical apartment, having sat with a glass of cola all night: a serene atmosphere prevails. His wife Mi-kyung sits cross-legged on the floor with two of their three children. The elder son, aged 14, is in his room doing his afterschool homework. Their 10-year-old son is finishing his with his mother's help, while she reads to her 5-year-old daughter. Their apartment, too, is furnished with child learning. Young-soo says of their lives as evangelical Methodists, 'We lead a sacred life.' His wife, Mi-kyung, was a Japanese teacher before they married. Her dad was a driver at Korean Electronics in the 1970s and thus better placed than Young-soo's dad, who did casual work to support his family. They are one generation removed from South Korea's social and economic struggles and its mass rural-to-urban migration. She says:

> I have always been interested in foreign languages. In high school I learned English and Spanish but I though there were better opportunities in Japanese. I stopped working when we got married. We met at a church in Yeosu.... I don't want to start work again for the money. I do church work because I am a Christian. It is an evangelical church so I like to bring other people to the church.... I spend time in the day doing church work.... It is a happy life.... It is different from others' lives because of our faith. The purpose of living is different.... What we value is different from others.... Korean people are different ... ordinary Korean families just work for money and try to save money so that they can support themselves when they get older, so this would be their final goal. But for us we work hard and want to show other people the benefits of worshipping God.

Young-soo and Mi-kyung, both in their mid 40s, are the first generation in their families to have secure, well-rewarded employment. Incorporating their spiritual values, their journeys are distinctive. They are also more expansive, migrating, as they have, from the south-east industrial pole in Ulsan and in wanting to move to China. While remaining in the LG family, they navigate distinctive routes from others.

In this small group biography of team lives are many similarities. These are organised in the ways in which corporate Korea supplies the fabric of everyday life, in a tightly hierarchised structure of employment, reward, transport, housing and leisure facilities. These petrochemical lives are lived in step, in small journeys from the same apartment complex to the same plant, to the company ping pong tables, to its yoga facilities, to the same bars and to the same restaurants. These short, repetitive, journeys, composing the fabrics of daily life, are lived in the expectation that they will endure. But inside the choreographies of team journeys marched in step, inside identical apartments, are small but significant differences in the ways in which people think about, and live, their lives. There are variations in the journeys they tackle and anticipate. Women show these differences in the minutiae, around work and child-care, where variation is possible. Even when they work, women do not move in step with men because their lives are shaped by different expectations.

Petrochemical Landscapes

Petrochemicals landscape – and landscape is here used as a verb – the area, as well as the journeys and the lives it sustains. Around the fenced and entry-controlled LG plant are scattered traces of the people inside and the purposes they pursue. A van selling one-piece industrial work suits in navy, blues and muted reds, announces a casual workforce needing industrial clothing. Several cafes sell bowls of noodles; there are simple bars, hotels and hostels, which accommodate the seasonal, foreign migrant, casual construction workforce. There is no doubt about what happens in this area. It is littered with the oil refineries and petrochemical plants of the giant corporations. Plants belching white smoke dominate the countryside, plants which can only be seen at a distance through the security fences and razor wire that protect them from public gaze and casual encounter. Lit up at night they look eerily beautiful. Mr Kwon says that plants are dangerous places. Intruders can cause damage and shut down production. There are concerns about piracy and competition too. Between plants is a sub-industrial wasteland cluttered with the detritus of heavy industry: bits of pipe, large metal containers, abandoned safety helmets. Petrochemicals dominate the coastal area and its hinterland. No other activity in the area inscribes the landscape as emphatically.

Just along the coast, east of the enclosed petrochemical harbours, in the little fishing village of Samgilpo, it seems as if the influence of petrochemicals has finally run out and a different kind of world holds sway. Samgilpo attracts weekend visitors from Seoul, who might stay at the Sea and Tel Pension, or one of the other small hotels. The modern glass construction of the village, contrasts with the bleak calmness of the Yellow Sea beyond. Samgilpo's restaurants, with their tanks of seafood and fresh fish, served raw, do brisk business at the weekend. Old wooden boats lie moored off the jetties. These lead to the fish holding tanks in the sea where live fish are stored. A weather-beaten couple, with raw red hands, prepare the cockles they rose at dawn to dig, from their van, mobile-shop and resting place. They grumble that the causeway that links the area to the petrochemical plants has reduced the fish stocks, extending petrochemical influence further than it appears. Aged 80 (him) and 72 (her), they sell seafood because they don't want to be a burden to their son – a hairdresser who must support a family of his own. While the old couple don't want to compete with their grandchildren's education for family resources, they have neither pensions nor savings. They belong to an ageing precariat, like Sun-Ja, who admits to being over 80 and cleans the guestrooms at the Sea and Tel Pension. Sun-Ja rents out her ancient rusting Toyota to tourists (and passing researchers) grounded by the lack of public transport. She also drives it herself, providing an unofficial taxi and a truly terrifying experience for her passengers. Those who lived through Korea's difficult past and remain outside of its corporate largess can look forward to an old age of casual employment.

Petrochemicals forge the landscape beyond Daesan and Samgilpo. Korea's two growth poles are closely interconnected with the petrochemical subdivisions of the big chaebols, and with Korea's megacity, Seoul. Discussion at the oyster dinner suggested that the petrochemical poles of Ulsan (south-east) and Daesan (north-west)[13] reflect the geographic origins and cronyism of national politicians. This, in turn, shapes the development of petrochemical industries, and distributes population along urban and suburban corridors of socioeconomic activity and residence. Ulsan and Daesan are connected to Seoul by corporate head offices, inaugurating the movement of labour and expertise connecting administrative and production centres.

Seoul is the centre of South Korean economic activity and financial assets piled high in city architecture, accumulated first from a large industrial base to which petrochemicals contributed and then from a burgeoning service sector. Seoul is a megacity with a population of 10 million, now losing population to the suburbs in response to rising real estate values.[14] Over 22 million people live in Greater Seoul, making it the world's third largest city after Tokyo and Jakarta.[15] The capital area, Seoul, Incheon and Gyeonggi-do account for almost half of Korea's GDP, half of its (50 million) population, as well as half of its companies and jobs.[16] The corridor from Seoul to the Daesan growth pole passes through Incheon and the airport and continues south-west. Along it is a massive development of suburbs and replicated city centres, creating a fractal urban arc. South Korea has less than a million foreign workers – below 2 per cent of population and low among OECD countries – to offset its low birth rate and ageing population. Foreign workers are concentrated in the capital area in low-paid service sector (restaurant) jobs, construction and manufacturing.[17] Contemporary journeys around South Korea are not, as in other parts of the trail, the movements of rural-to-urban migrants. This was over by 1980. Nor, except on a small scale, are they the journeys of foreign migrants. Korea's migrants are from China, Vietnam, the Philippines, Indonesia, Mongolia and refugees from North Korea. Public policy focuses on 'foreign brides' and the integration of North Koreans.

Like the rest of South Korea, Seoul was shaped through central government direction. The story of its development is the story of the nation's relentless and successful pursuit of a state-directed industrialisation. Resonances of South Korea's centralisation and state direction ripple through Korean lives, and this makes sense of the team biography in Daesan.

Korea was a Cold War compromise. It emerged from the Second World War and Japanese occupation (1910–45) to be occupied in the north by the Soviet Union and in the south by the US. This escalated into a war that ended in 1953 with a border drawn between north and south on the thirty-eighth parallel. There are still 35,000 US troops stationed in Seoul, monitoring North Korea, internationally branded as a rogue state and destabilising force in the region. South of the thirty-eighth parallel, a country decimated by war and poverty was organised through a series of military dictatorships (1961 to 1987), which were crucial in the development towards prosperity of this highly centralised nation and its capital. Military dictatorships enforced a hybrid version of urban and industrial planning, and collaboration between state and private industry. This late state-led industrialisation generated the chaebols, the big business conglomerates, which were directed where and how to invest by successive authoritarian governments. In return they received state approval and support in securing their own development, becoming Korea's multinational corporations.[18] Korea's industrial success was driven by an aggressive export-oriented manufacturing sector.[19] Although neoliberal private enterprise is the favoured model, substantial state involvement still underpins it and Korea still runs on government interference on a large scale. The new ideas and entrepreneurs that could refresh its deeply entrenched hierarchical corporate structures experience difficulty in finding their way against the influence of the chaebols. Thus, the basis of Korea's success is also the source of its fragility.

In the context of the head start for the key corporations that led Korean development, it is now difficult for new enterprise to establish itself against the might of the chaebols, with their historic advantage. Most of the big corporations – Hyundai, LG and so on – have widely spread business interests, combining electrics, petrochemicals, automobiles, real estate, store chains and finance. The tentacles of the chaebols extend into most lucrative forms of business. LG, for example, runs an electric manufacture and battery business as well as petrochemicals. Lotte runs department stores and hotels, as well as the production of petrochemicals.

Petrochemicals are one of the key engines of growth, (selectively) sustaining living standards, which, along with differences in political regime, separate North from South Korea. The Korean National Oil Corporation (KNOC) was founded in 1979 to secure stable supplies of oil[20] because South Korea has no oil and no pipeline, making it vulnerable to fluctuating supplies and oil prices, particularly as it is the ninth largest consumer of oil in the world. This inevitably draws Korea into oil geopolitics. Seventy-five per cent of Korean oil comes from the Gulf region; it is one of Iran's biggest customers and, controversially, resumed imports from Iran in 2012 despite EU sanctions. Half of its imported oil is fed into the petrochemical industry. It has three of the world's ten largest refineries.[21] Without oil there is no petrochemical industry. Disruption in supply would decimate it. Large oil price rises would erode petrochemical profitability.

Koreans' lives are thus delicately balanced around the fragilities that come with being a major purchaser and processor of oil. Albeit in the context of the (apparent) stabilities of large, robust, multinational corporations, which themselves selectively expose workers to insecurities, as we have seen. Resilience and appropriate navigational skills secure the survival of Korean women, part-time and contract workers, and the elderly. Korea has the highest suicide rate among the 34 OECD countries.[22] This is skewed towards men aged over 64,[23] facing retirements that are not secured through social benefits and, although we should not read too much into suicide rates, they often log social and individual stress.

Petrochemicals and authoritarian government shaped urban development too. Korea's successful industrialisation precipitated a rapid redistribution of population from rural to urban areas from 1960 to 1980. This produced Seoul's informal squatter settlements, later demolished in large-scale urban renewal and the formalisation of the city. The government led this, selling land to private developers. This bulldozer phase shaped the city. It relocated workers around the factories in low-income housing.[24] The chaebols, which consolidated themselves during this period through connections with central government, along with those governments, remain the main players in urban land speculation. The central government Ministry of Home Affairs controls local governments. Quasi-governmental organisations, the Korean Land Development Corporation and the Korean National Housing Corporation, collaborated with the big construction firms, building Seoul in its current form. Through these arrangements central government led urban development with local government and planners doing the administrative and technical work, significantly, using profits from land speculation to build urban infrastructure.

By the late 1980s Korea had one of the highest rates of urbanisation (80 per cent) in the world and a rapidly emerging urban civil society. This, including the broad-based student-led protests, unleashed the political momentum that dismissed authoritarian military rule in 1987, clearing the way for democratic elections. The 1990s brought prosperity and political stability. GDP was growing at a rate of 10 per cent annually, although it has since slowed to 6 per cent, and GDP per capita was over US$24,000 by 2012.[25] South Korea today is a wealthy, highly educated and developed country with a well-developed service sector.

Petrochemicals shape the personal landscapes of the production team as earlier sections in this chapter show. Koreans are affluent and acutely status-conscious, and they exercise the discernment that arises from this across multiple domains of consumption and competition. The hierarchies displayed in the team at the Daesan plant resonate throughout the country. These landscapes demand appropriate navigational skills in upward and onward journeys. Resources and maternal attention poured into education configure competition for the most prestigious schools and universities (worldwide). Everything is ranked. There is an expectation that educations, alongside personal networks, are leveraged on job markets. Big companies like Samsung, LG and so on, are prized employers on account of the lifelong benefits and securities they bring to a minority of the workforce. Those less well placed will work in lower positions, in less prestigious companies, for lower wages. Or they will take less secure contract work.

To competition over education and jobs must be added a third source of competition, as young Koreans search for marriages that lift family circumstances. The affluent Seoul neighbourhood of Gangnam, which Psy sings about in his YouTube hit, has a plastic surgeon's office on every street corner. Here women's appearance and marriage prospects can be improved. Such enhancements are visible on the streets in a standardisation of (perfect) facial features among young women. In the more affluent parts of Seoul, women display the dual status symbols of a designer handbag and a bandaged face.

Global Highways and Side Streets

The KNOC has 189 exploration projects in 36 countries in an effort to exert control over the supplies on which petrochemical industries depend. Like oil, petrochemicals constitute globalisation's mainstream, funnelled through subdivisions of transnational giants like LG, Hyundai, Lotte and so on. LG, for example, manufactures and distributes appliances and electronic equipment worldwide. Its chemical operation alone employs 10,000 people worldwide and has sales of just less than 14 billion Wan,[26] making petrochemicals important global businesses reaching into every continent.

I suggested earlier that petrochemicals supply the materials from which the objects composing so many areas of everyday life are fabricated. Companies like LG focus on high-end, high-value materials, like synthetic rubbers that make car bumpers, seals and so on. Car bumpers and rigid plastics made from high-density pellets generate higher profits. LG also sells the material from which to make these high-end products to other manufacturers, particularly in China. Alongside these mainstream routes are minor trails too. Along them, travel low-value plastic pellets used to manufacture cheaper objects, like flip-flops, from polyethylene and EVA.

At this point the flip-flop trail once more splinters into thousands of routes, along which minor, low-grade, low-value materials travel. These materials contribute less to the profits of global corporations in the mainstream. China, but other places too, like Vietnam and Sudan, buy these pellets to make flip-flops. As China develops its own petrochemical industry so Korea will lose business: and this fragile shifting connection is easily moved elsewhere.

After the small white pellets of EVA and PE are poured into 500 kg bags at the LG plant, they are loaded into the large ships that pull in at the pier inside the plant compound. From here they reverse the last part of the journey taken by the oil, as they head towards the eastern coast of China. The small white pellets bear fragments of the Korean petrochemical lives in Daesan, which they shape.

4

Plastic City

The city must never be confused with the words that describe it. (Italo Calvino, *Invisible Cities*, 1997: 61)

On this part of the trail, at this junction between the material and the object, the book's protagonist is in a transitional form. In transition from its chemical arrangements to its business arrangements, the flip-flop itself is rather elusive. In this interstitial state between the material and the thing, a set of business opportunities that may or may not be realised, the shoe is continually slipping around a corner at the end of the street, disappearing out of sight as I catch up with it. It is leading me on a dance through the city, in a search for the place where it is made. I know that the plastic factories are there, but I can't locate them. Alongside the flip-flop, a second character in the dramas of the quest, the plastic city, becomes a constituent of the trail: the plastic shoe and the city produce each other. The SE China seaboard city of Fuzhou is the city in question. It is fabricated in the fragmented business of plastics. In addition to being a central character on the trail, the city is also an expressive form.[1] What it expresses are the movement of people, materials and objects that give it shape.

In contrast to previous chapters, which cover much ground at speed, this and the following two chapters, work at a greater intensity and magnification. This makes it possible to explore flip-flops' Chinese production centre in some depth. Flip-flops produce urban and peri-urban forms, at the same time as they make social forms like lives and class, as you will see. Most importantly, flip-flops make contemporary China, writ small.

Plastic granules, loaded on to bulky container ships, navigate the China Sea on journeys south-westwards from Korea, to the eastern seaboard city of Fuzhou. This epicentre of plastic manufacture is created in the journeys of materials, objects, and people on plastic business, criss-crossing it. In China, where materials are transformed into objects, plastic moves through the port twice, once as a material and a second time as objects, when they are shifted onto world markets. Viewed through the lens of manufacture, China is a plastic, metal, wood, ceramics factory to which Fuzhou gives local object-and-urban form. The vibrancy, the animation, the social agency of objects; their capacity to matter, and to make social-and-material-matter enacted in people's journeys, lives and social arrangements, takes over from the agency of materials on this part of the trail. Thus the term 'plastic' here refers, not to the material alone but to its many object forms.

The Korean plastic granules join materials from all over the world to dock at Mawei Port, located at the mouth of the Min River. One of China's ten major container ports, Mawei has 13 10,000-ton docks, including three container docks. Fifteen million tons of cargo, in which manufactured goods predominate, are distributed annually to over 40 countries worldwide.[2] This makes it a significant junction in particular global circuits. The Min River creates a natural corridor from the port and the technical and industrial zone in the south-east, stretching north-westwards to the commercial centre of the city. This river corridor is lined with attractively designed high-rise apartment buildings, some 50 storeys high, and evidence of a vibrant real estate market.

At the port, the plastic enters a twenty-first-century urban transport nexus. Like most eastern Chinese cities, Fuzhou has been adjusted, if not originally designed, for connection. Its bridges, its roads, its tunnels, its port and its airport, transport people, objects and materials around and beyond the city, forging its footprint[3] in multiple material-and-object circulations. The port is connected to the 104 State Highway to Beijing, and to China's highly developed eastern coastal corridor, which links to the national highway network.[4] Buses, trucks and cars run these routes. Railways connect the port and the city to all parts of China, linking manufactured goods and domestic markets. China's biggest markets are its own. Fuzhou's international airport deals with 6.5 million passengers and 200,000 tons of air cargo annually. It connects 40 domestic and international routes through more than 260 flights a week.[5]

Zones

Along the eastern seaboard, the zones bring new vitality to cities. The Fuzhou Economic and Technical Development Zone, the urban edge-land and the fulcrum of transport networks next to Mawei Port, like other zones along the coast, stands apart from the commercial centre of the city. The Fuzhou Economic and Technical Development Zone was established in 1985 as part of the Deng Xiaoping economic reforms,[6] and it took off in the 1990s as the pace at which private enterprise developed accelerated. The zone comprises 23 square km of industrial development, a financial climate supporting foreign investment in manufacture, and a high-tech industrial park. Investment from 30 different countries, and big transnational companies, have secured high-tech industries in electronics, photo-electronics, machinery, biochemicals, pharmaceuticals, metallurgy, building materials, textiles and a range of light industries, including footwear. Zones attract foreign direct investment with favourable tax regimes and low offshore production costs. Zones are technologically advanced industrial-export-oriented dynamic hubs, fuelled by leading-edge technology intended to leapfrog over older technologies and stages of development, launching China into rapid economic (and social) development. Following the failure of the Great Leap Forward (1958) to modernise Chinese industry, zones invert traditional development theory, challenging chronological conceptions of time by refusing to build sequentially from fundamentals,[7] refusing to accept, for example, that copper wire precedes fibre optics: jumping straight to the most advanced technologies instead. Zones are the great leap forward the Great Leap Forward failed to deliver. Zones develop the entrepreneurial *Zeitgeist* of China's socialist market system, briefly reined in by Mao's collectivisation. The zones promote new possibility, unhindered by traditional obligations of cities and architecture. The zones support new Chinese ambition.[8]

Zones are also attempts to contain this new ambition. Outside of the structures of urban and municipal governance that regulate cities, administrative committees run zones. Their authority extends over the management and the approval of overseas-funded projects.[9] Crucially, zones are beyond the authority of the central government. This partition of economic and commercial interests from broader political concerns, maintains the central authority of the Chinese state, in parallel with a climate attracting foreign direct investment. Governed more flexibly and autonomously than the rest of China, zones embrace the logics of capital accumulation, while formally maintaining the sovereignty of Chinese socialism. China is a unitary state under the central government of the Chinese Communist Party. Elections only take place at a local village level. Article 1 of the (2004) amended 1982 Constitution says:

> The People's Republic of China is a Socialist state under the people's democratic dictatorship led by the working class and based on the alliance of workers and peasants. The Socialist system is the basic system of the People's Republic of China ...[10]

This political form remains strong and secures popular participation. Chinese Communist Party membership is over 70 million and membership of the Communist Youth League is over 68 million. There is 'permissible private speech', but speaking publicly against the regime carries heavy penalties.[11] There are few channels for formal political protest and many forms of censorship. While the zones provide a mechanism for the formal coexistence of divergent systems, and they are distinctive in the scale of their ambition and organisational structures, the social and economic transformations they have unleashed, the loose patchwork of labour practices they inaugurate, seep into all areas of Chinese life as we will see.

Zones drive economic growth. Between 1980 and 1995 this averaged 10 per cent each year, but it is unevenly distributed to the east and to the urban areas. In the same period, China had the highest rate of growth in GDP in Asia. China doubles its output and its personal incomes every ten years.[12] It is the world's second biggest economy. Average incomes have risen by 7 per cent per year so that per capita income in 2006 was US$1700 dollars per annum.[13] This new prosperity is industry (46 per cent of GDP) and tertiary trade (40 per cent of GDP) generated, inevitably displacing agriculture (13 per cent of GDP).[14] The social impact of this growth in prosperity has both lowered rates of poverty and increased social inequalities.

China has 18 per cent of the world's poor,[15] with 200 million people living below the poverty line, defined by the World Bank as US$1 a day. China is caught in a race between the growth of GDP catalysed by the zones and a population with rising expectations. Its 1.3 billion people produce 10 million extra mouths to feed each year, from a land area in transition from agriculture to industry. The zones simultaneously reduce the volume of agricultural land and provide the economic growth to reduce poverty. China accounts for three-quarters of all the people in the world lifted out of abject poverty between 1979 and 2006, with the number subsisting on US$1 a day having fallen from 490 million (1981) to 88 million (2006).[16] The Chinese Communist Party is betting on the social impact of cutting-edge innovation in the zones outstripping the social problems they create.[17]

This increase in prosperity inaugurated broad-ranging structural changes with important social consequences. Small businesses thrived, but in the inefficient and insufficient state enterprises 28 million workers lost their jobs and the social benefits that came with them, including health care, housing, education and pensions. While the government is setting up a social security system that is not based on work units to replace some of the social benefits lost to industrial-economic development,[18] people all over China are struggling to pay for education, housing and health care. The World Bank suggests that the last 25 years have changed China from one of the most equitable systems of income distribution in the world to one of the most inequitable. Income inequalities resonate through lives and accumulate to produce profound social differences and more inequitable social structures.

Zones have driven further wide-ranging social transformation throughout China, reformulating cities. In attracting farmers to the new opportunities provided by factories, zones have generated rural-to-urban migration on a massive scale. This opens new routes to cities for rural populations, and makes urban residents out of those whose land is engulfed by cities as they expand. Some people move to the cities and others have cities move to them. Zones transform cities and create dynamic, improvised urbanism where markets take priority over central planning, and chaos management has replaced ideology in the calculations of the formally communist regime.[19] In cities, rural migrants live beyond the household registration and identity card system that tie people to places of long-term family residence. While household registration systems are breaking down with the sheer scale and speed of urbanisation, they sustain informal residence and a lack of rights to the city.[20] Vagrancy and prostitution[21] are rife in cities, where needs exceed municipal governments' ability to provide basic services like sanitation and water. As one commentator put it, Chinese society is an unstable stew of hope, ambition, fear, misinformation and politics. Only chaos-theory can provide meaningful organisation.[22]

Zones fundamentally redraw urban landscape. The Shenzhen Special Economic Zone (SEZ), one of the biggest and most successful in generating investment, manufacture and export, transformed Shenzhen from a village rice paddy in the late 1970s into a sprawling megacity with a population already estimated at 9 million by 2006.[23] Part of a cluster of zone-stimulated urban expansion, Shenzhen merges into the city of Zuhai – which has its own special zone – and Macao, now a gambling centre that rivals Las Vegas. Zuhai, Shenzhen, Macao, Hong Kong, Foshan and Dongguan constitute the seamless urban sprawl of the Pearl River Delta, the largest urban area in the world with a population of approximately 50 million in 5000 square miles, knocking Greater Tokyo[24] into second place.

When 12 per cent of arable land was lost to highways and industrial development around the zones, 20 million farmers lost their livelihoods between 1996 and 2005 alone. Zones were allowed to create their own land regulations and these gradually gave way to property markets. Urban land belongs to the state and rural land to the village commune.[25] Rural land needed for factories was easily transferred to the state, which reclassified it as urban, thus easing the sale of development rights. This generated a speculative market in land[26] and made those farming near the zones especially insecure.[27] Industrial development of farmland unleashed a further macro-social impact of the zones with far-reaching implications. We will witness the micro-social impact of land reallocation on individual lives later along the trail. In place of farming, villagers took jobs, rented out property, depended on family or lived on their compensation. Mass protests against land acquisition and compensation schemes have erupted all over China. In 2004 the Chinese government admitted to 74,000 riots in the countryside around loss of farmland, corruption, worsening pollution and arbitrary eviction.[28] These macro-social changes have created multiple asymmetries between rural and urban areas, generating a strong east–west divide that maps roughly onto a large gap in incomes, living standards and social benefits: all potential sources of social instability.[29]

At the beginning of 2008 China's zone experiment entered a new phase. In compliance with Word Trade Organization (WTO) regulations, tax holidays given to foreign companies were withdrawn, and differences between foreign and domestic investors levelled. Foreign companies now pay 25 per cent tax and this will increase their production costs. Will they continue to invest in the zones or will they shift their business to lower-cost offshore centres?[30] As China suffered the global economic downturn of 2008 and mass factory closures, its future as the world's factory looks precarious. Alongside these potential sources of uncertainty in the zones, China anticipates that future growth will be fuelled by consumption and property markets, already crucial in the big cities.[31]

Bridge to the City

The zones, and the dynamic between zones and the cities they co-constitute, reveal important information about how contemporary China works, and draws a macro-landscape to contextualise what follows. The Fuzhou Economic and Technical Development Zone successfully catalysed transfers of capital and technology from Taiwan, Japan and Korea. This fuelled a local version of the manufacturing and export boom launched China-wide in the 1990s. It was focused on larger scales of production, investment and profit: scales that produced Nike and Ikea, but not flip-flop, factories. While tons of Korean plastic granules run through the zone, these are the kinds of plastics that make high-end objects, not lower-value objects like flip-flops and plastic bags, which are made from polyethylene and EVA granules. The flip-flop trail, it transpires, does not run through the zones, as I suspected it might. In fact, it bypasses these drivers of new Chinese ambition.

Does the trail pass through the city itself then? Virtual evidence, in the form of websites claiming to manufacture and supply wholesale flip-flops, suggests that the flip-flop trail runs through Fuzhou. In pursuit, I follow the corridor created by the Min River north-westwards from the zone to 'Liberation Bridge', which crosses the Min River joining the north and south sides of the city. This bridge creates a junction in the city in two senses. First, it connects an older, crumbling, version of Fuzhou on the south side of the river, with the modern, commercial centre to the north. Second, 'liberation' belongs to a lexicon that connects the city with regimes and struggles past. The bridge, for these reasons, provides a viewing platform onto the city, connecting quite different urban topographies and, by this means, displaying some of the city's hidden layers. Cities are not simply described.

The first layer. The streets on the south side of Liberation Bridge are narrow and winding. Buildings are one and two storeys high, built in wood and brick, some are derelict and collapsing into ruins. This area awaits 'redevelopment' of its exposed brickwork, peeling plaster and paint, its leftover bits of posters. Its traces of lives once lived in houses which now have their fronts torn off, exposing their formerly private interiors to the street. Plants sprout from a jumble of ruined buildings, tilted at odd angles by decay. Tangles of overhead power cables just clear the rooftops. Commerce involves workshops and stalls, open to the street, revealing practices of making and mending. Tailors perform their craft in full view. Beds, splendidly dressed in shiny red satin covers, sit just off the pavement in open-fronted stores. Stacks of brightly coloured flip-flops peek from behind wooden counters. Three-wheeled bicycles, with large baskets at the back, shift goods around the city. This is a world away from the city on the north side of the bridge. This side consists of a functional world of family-run businesses, pre-dating the visual artifice of department stores and malls on the other side of the bridge. What Liberation Bridge bridges are distinctive architectures and street plans, distinctive styles of commerce and consumption.

The second layer. At the north end of the bridge are straight north–south and east–west avenues, lined with impressive architecture. Attractive commercial buildings are leased to banks, and to providers of insurance and shipping services. There are upscale shopping malls dominated by large department stores. Building and architecture are the most overwhelming activities in Chinese cities, and Fuzhou is no exception. It is full of the building sites which fabricate constant urban renewal. Women clear rubble, foundations are dug, cranes tower overhead, and grand scales of new building refashion old districts. The scale and speed of redevelopment are impressive. Architect Rem Koolhaas points out that Chinese architects design the largest volume of buildings in the shortest time for the lowest fees. Architectural design, stamped out from templates – like flip-flops – is ten times faster in China than the United States. Chinese architecture has become 'coincident with capital, speed and quantity'.[32] City centre property development is highly profitable.[33] Social costs in the absence of hospitals, factory dormitories and affordable housing in the city display the priorities of the financial (and social) forces shaping it. Central Fuzhou is solid, beautiful, new and urbane, in stark contrast to the older city at the other end of the bridge, which instead provides a fraying city boundary.

Among the mixture of monumental and more ordinary commercial buildings in the city centre, a shopping mall lies immediately at the north end of Liberation Bridge. This has a central atrium. Its tiered shops trade and display quite differently from the small, open, stalls on the south side of the bridge. There is glass, glitz and all is (on) display. Young women wearing the latest fashion in mini skirts, denim shorts, flat sparkly shoes and tee shirts, shop. Outside the mall is a branch of KFC where fashionably dressed affluent late teens and early 20s, with creatively expensive haircuts, hang out in small groups. Fast food chains – KFC, McDonald's and Pizza Hut – pepper the city centre, providing further venues for the young to meet.

The third layer. Next to the shopping mall is a small enclave of heritage buildings more than 100 years old, which have been carefully restored. This section of the city is modelled on the small historic quarters of Shanghai and Beijing, promoted as 'Old China' tourist attractions. This quarter of Fuzhou has red street lanterns, roofs that lift up at the corners and ridge at the top, iconic Chinese architecture, tiled in earthy pinks. These heritage buildings are three storeys high. They have windows with the traditional red and brown grilles. An upscale street market selling handcrafts and fast food establishes the commercial purpose of heritage.

The fourth layer regards the impact of time and politics on urban landscape, suggested in the name of the bridge itself. Liberation belongs to the lexicon of revolution. It registers Fuzhou's recent past and its ambiguous future. Liberation Bridge poses awkward questions about the coexistence of socialism and the private enterprise responsible for refashioning the city. Its name positions the bridge among the monuments to socialism's strategies, in the big and small brutalities of the Cultural Revolution. In raising awkward questions about the intersections between a centralised communist state and private enterprise, Liberation Bridge stands along with the giant statue of Mao Zedong in Wuyi Square, and the Wenlinshan Revolutionary Cemetery on the western side of the city. These monuments hold the past in the present, and challenge the authorities to account for the vanquished and the dead, and in this they tell a different story from the monuments to the market forces shaping the plastic city.

The Wenlinshan Cemetery lies on the west side of the city without explanation. It opens between 5 and 7 in the morning, and ashes are scattered by arrangement. The gatekeeper suggests the cemetery is for those who served in the 'revolutionary army' and 'as teachers and professors', especially those 'involved in nation-building'. It is not clear what these references mean today. The cemetery has no graves. It is a large garden with a low, angular, concrete, functional building in the centre. Inside the building is a bas relief of men, bare-chested, carrying long guns, moving in the same direction, in a manner that suggests struggle against adversity. This iconography of revolution is liberally scattered around this city, absorbed into the new topographies of private enterprise.

Trailing through the city there are only indirect traces of plastics: plastics turned into architecture, design and activity. Money generated by plastic – and other materials too of course – creates demand for services like banking, shipping and new forms of consumption in upscale shopping malls. Plastic profits create demand for new apartment blocks, to house those with the means to engage in these forms of consumption, and to profit those with an appetite for speculation. Plastics create demand for park, play and leisure spaces for the plastic middle classes. And plastics shape the city in ways that are subtler, and therefore more difficult, to discern, so that it becomes impossible to trace the flip-flop trail as its reverberations merge with other sources of accumulation. In this indirect sense of traces and undergirding, Fuzhou is indeed a plastic city, even as I fail to locate its actual sources of plastic production.

Fuzhou is a plastic city in another sense too. In the way in which the term is used by urban scholars, planners and architects to describe the spectacular growth of Chinese cities through ad hoc intelligence, improvisation and relentless building on an unprecedented scale: capitalising on 'the opportunistic exploitation of flukes, accidents and imperfections'.[34] Plastic urbanism is ever expanding, driven by the mechanisms of uncontainable markets and the human activities that turn them into everyday life. These are markets for manufactured goods generating new objects and opportunities, drawing still more rural migrants into the city's orbit. These are markets for migrant housing and the new social relationships they inaugurate with locals. These are markets for upscale housing and property speculation for those who accumulate fortunes in these, and other, markets. These are markets for manufactured goods, finance and services. Plastic urbanism is urbanism that exceeds central planning and municipal service provision for water, sewerage and electricity. Plastic urbanism is opportunistic. It is ad hoc. It is assembled by human ingenuity, around the requirements of people's lives. Plastic urbanism belongs to the people who mould it around their lives, as much as to urban planners and to architects. For urban scholars, plastic urbanism is urbanism without urbanity. It is utilitarian, lacking in refinement.

But Fuzhou is urbane as well as plastic. Rezoning its manufacture and attendant workforce into zones outside the city, key sources of struggle and improvisation around work, housing and food are removed from central areas of the city. Fuzhou aspires to urbanity, and the dynamic between urban centres and zones is crucial in shaping both. Fuzhou is not included in the descriptions aimed at the great cities of China by urban scholars. Although it lies at the centre of a matrix of manufacture and has a rapidly rising population, estimated at 8 million,[35] this medium-sized Chinese city has not attracted the same kind of attention as Beijing, Shanghai and Shenzhen.

If zoning laws have removed plastic manufacture from the city, and it is not in the zones, then where is it? I am scouring landscapes of different scales in the city of Fuzhou, its technical development zone, the larger landscapes of industrial and private enterprise China, but I can't find the trail. I can only find its reverberations and proximate territories. It is time to visit one of the city sites comprising the flip-flops web presence: Dai Wei's office/showroom.

Translation

Dai Wei's office is on the northern side of the city. Although it is only a five-minute walk from his modern apartment block, he drives rather than negotiate the traffic and the dirt that fills this short distance. His office comprises two 100 × 100 foot interconnected shiny rooms, with pristine white ceramic tiled floors. It is furnished to impress. Its three substantial desks – for him, one for his wife and one for a woman clerical worker – are matched with expensive office chairs. There are wood bookcases with glass fronts, modern grey metal filing cabinets, comfortable sofas and armchairs. On Dai Wei's desk stands a flat-screened computer. High ceilings betray the building's former use. This was once his family's flip-flop factory, before zoning laws, prohibiting noxious production in the city, closed it. This, combined with Dai Wei's rising fortunes, transformed the factory into the front office of a matrix of invisible flip-flop factories, supplying customers throughout the world. In this office Dai Wei connects flip-flop production with global markets.

Through the archway leading from Dai Wei's office is another room in which showroom-stands display furry slippers, plastic crocs – clogs with holes in the uppers – and 3000 *different styles of plastic flip-flops*. As a style falls out of fashion, Dai Wei assures its replacement with a more popular one, garnering trend information from his buyers. International buyers locate Dai Wei through his web presence. Photographs of gleaming offices and product lines like Dai Wei's, offer sanitised impressions of Chinese flip-flop factories, which turn out, on closer inspection, to be showrooms. Customers are emailed and orders processed in English and in American dollars. Middlemen like Dai Wei have English names – 'call me Bob' – and mobile numbers on which customers speak with them. Dai Wei knows that overseas buyers are unlikely to speak Chinese. This makes it impossible for them to navigate the flip-flop factories without a guide. He knows which factories specialise in which styles and qualities, and he commissions them on behalf of his customers. On his desk sits a small globe displaying his markets.

Dai Wei is a broker with 'partnerships', as he refers to his arrangements, with between 50 and 200 small to medium-sized factories. A small investment secures his position as a priority buyer, allowing him to check quality and production schedules and to monitor deadlines. Through his web presence, he gathers the orders from overseas buyers, which he places with his partner factories, carefully choosing the right factory-combinations to fill his orders. Through Dai Wei's orders and his export licence, small factories, which could not otherwise manage it, access international markets. Completed orders are trucked to his warehouse to wait for other orders. Or they are sent straight to the docks. Dai Wei has oversight of more processes than anyone else in the supply chain. In Dai Wei's office, I had hit a significant part of the flip-flop trail, if not the factories. Like his international customers, I can't find the flip-flop factories without him. And, unlike the other guardians of the flip-flop web presence, Dai Wei offered to help me. Others refused, suspecting I might be a journalist who would write condemnatory articles in the Western press about conditions in Chinese factories, and get them into trouble with the authorities. Dai Wei was curious about the project, unafraid of the authorities, trusted me not to expose him and took the time necessary to connect me with the world of flip-flops. Dai Wei is not, of course, his real name.

Dai Wei drives me southwards through the city in his sleek black 'Cherry', its small screen playing Chinese MTV-styled videos as he drives. He was born in 1976, auspiciously the year 'the Chairman', as he refers to Mao Zedong, died. He says that 'the poor and the old remember Mao, they were the soldiers of Mao', but 'the rich can forget' what he calls the 'crazy stupid years' of Chinese Communism. His vague, second-hand recollections of the Cultural Revolution bleed into a longer history of what he calls the 'dark ages', inaugurated by the 1949 revolution. For Dai Wei, the dark ages ended with the economic reforms of the 1980s, and his family's personal circumstances developed in tandem with the Chinese economy. He says: 'the world has opened up'. Party officials still 'speak like Mao' in support of their claim that the communist system endures. But Dai We knows that it does not. He knows that 'everything has changed', and that now, 'people have their eyes on money'. Last night he took a party of friends and family to a restaurant to celebrate his wife's birthday. His one-child family dine out frequently. They have a servant to do their domestic work and child-care, while his wife works with him in the office. In addition to a new Egyptian venture, Dai Wei tells me he is thinking of investing in a factory in Serbia. He speculates about the size of the Serbian population as though this information informed his calculations.

With what skills does Dai Wei navigate this (significant) part of the flip-flop trail, on which he commissions production and supervises overseas distribution? He understands both the human and technical sides of flip-flop production. He knows about different plastics, and the carefully guarded formulas he can't disclose. He understands sales, marketing and product design. He operates in Chinese, excellent English and the rudiments of other languages too. He has a practical grasp of lived-cultures, deftly gauging how to deal with foreign customers. He is adept at dealing with Muslims, steering them round the Chinese staple, pork. Pakistan is one of his biggest markets, closely followed by Egypt, Sudan and Ethiopia, though these markets are fragile and shift constantly. He thinks they like flip-flops in these places because they are poor, and it is a cheap shoe. It is hot in the desert and flip-flops allow air to circulate around the foot. It is easily slipped off in the mosque. He is adept at entertaining Europeans too, and suggests that he has exceptional facility, garnered through experience, with Germans. The world visits Dai Wei, but he does not visit the world. It is difficult to travel, he says, with a currency that buys so little. In these practical translations of material difference, he navigates the world, working on several levels of translation simultaneously. Between Chinese and English, between international markets and Chinese flip-flop design and production, and between everyday Chinese culture and the buying and social habits of foreigners.

The multiple translation skills with which Dai Wei navigates the flip-flop trail are the result of flip-flop profits invested by his father at the Fujian Vocational College of International Business. This is a new, grey, seven-storey building still in construction, with beautiful grounds and light airy stairwells. The college is an hour and half by road from Fuzhou. It lies on a coast famous for shipbuilding, seafaring and exporting people to Taiwan, the USA and other places favoured by the Chinese Diaspora. The 1500 freshmen arriving at the college each autumn are taught the key languages of international business – Japanese and English. The college approach is utilitarian: 'Every student should remember for what purposes you have come here. And what you should do when leaving' is written on the wall in Chinese and in English. 'The teacher is the ladder the students can climb'. 'Study more and use the knowledge you have'. Knowledge is for self-improvement. There are other instructions too:

Love your country.
Make friends with your classmates.
Respect your teachers and those with more experience.
Don't waste food and money.
Manage your study and rest.
Take care of the school's belongings.
Study hard for your dreams.

Fujian Vocational College provides some of the human fabric of the new China. It has produced tens of thousands of graduates since it opened. Its Vice President estimates that 10 per cent of its graduates are already millionaires, and 1 per cent are 'super-rich'. Students come from all over China in addition to Fujian Province to 'Study hard for your dreams'. The Vice President himself is an inspiring role model. His father is a 'simple illiterate peasant', he says, still living in his village. The Vice President rose by studying hard, a valued route to upward social mobility, underpinning the hard work that students anticipate will lead to business success.

After college, Dai Wei stayed in Fuzhou rather than return to Xiamen and his father's factory. He married a local woman and together they developed their business from the platform of the family flip-flop-turned-trainer business. With one little girl they are a thoroughly modern Chinese family. Visits to neighbours' houses service children's social needs in one-child families, and form fragile bridges between adjacent households. Dai Wei's parents live with his elder brother near their original family home, outside Xiamen, in the south of Fujian Province. More mobile than his brothers, Dai Wei's younger brother has moved to Guangzhou where he continues to explore the business opportunities it offers. His father still runs the factory in Xiamen. His grandfather is a peasant farmer. The family have risen from humble beginnings to bosses in one generation. Chinese social mobility is the product of the new business climate inaugurated by the zones, but spreading well beyond them.

Dai Wei's significance exceeds his own life. He and his father are the entrepreneur-fabric animating China's export-led growth. In future, growth will rely on consumption, and he is important in this regard too. Expanding consumption requires expanding middle classes and rising incomes, making it possible for wider sections of the population to consume. While 25 per cent of urban populations are currently counted as middle class,[36] this falls sharply in rural areas, where social structures are bottom-heavy with farmers. The Chinese middle class is proportionately smaller than the American, Japanese, Indian and Korean middle class, so there is room for expansion as a way of expanding GDP. Dai Wei remains important in China's future, just as he was significant in progressing things to the current position. On thick-soled, attractively coloured, flip-flops, he navigates the subdued polished and carpeted surfaces of his modern condominium. He wouldn't go outside in flip-flops, but inside his apartment they make his feet relax, he says. Changing into them, he avoids carrying outside-dirt into his pristine domestic space. They are particularly convenient, he thinks, around water, and in his family they are used in the bathroom, thus avoiding, in all circumstances, being barefoot. In Dai Wei's life flip-flops mark boundaries between outside and inside, between dirt and hygiene, between rich and poor.

Class[37] in part composes social structures[38] and, in contrast to the relative stabilities of North America and Western Europe, Chinese social structures are fluid. Dai Wei's trajectory shows this. Along with new social and economic opportunities, new, motile class positions are generated by people with the skills and resources to turn opportunities into personal, family and community advantage. Social structures are thus the local, regional and China-wide strata to which differences between circumstances and their outcomes accumulate. The sheer size and complexity of the Chinese middle class is only now, slowly, being unravelled by Chinese scholars.[39] Although still small as a percentage of population, numerically the Chinese middle class is vast, socially diverse and rapidly expanding.[40] Fortunately – for this is a vast topic – only a fragment of the middle classes, generated by plastic, is relevant to the flip-flop trail.

All lives are unique but share with others the social architecture positioning them. Class is a useful category in popular currency for gathering together those in similar circumstances. Even qualified by terms like 'plastic' or 'flip-flop', the middle class is a roughly drawn category, subsuming differences we might want to illuminate. Spatial biographies that embed mobility – journeys – on the other hand, expose important differences between the lives gathered together by the concept of class. Further along the trail, we will trace individual journeys that illuminate the social textures composing categories like 'factory worker'. At this junction, Dai Wei's journeys on plastic business expose some of the fine-grained textures of the plastic middle class. This approach both acknowledges commonalities drawn by class and disturbs them with the specifics of journeys, restoring biographical uniqueness to lives, which is denied by categorisation. The circumstances and the places connected by each worker and factory boss are articulated in personal journeys along the flip-flop trail. Journeys thus elaborate lives and landscapes, with detailed portraits of people and places, which the concept of class cannot provide, and often doesn't try to.

Factories, Bosses and Beginnings

The flip-flop factories are to the south of the city. Dei Wei connects them with the city through the routine journeys (in his Cherry) composing his life. These are local circulations between home, office, factories and the city's parks and restaurants. His routes through the plastic city, along with others, contribute to its fabrication. The area to the south of the city is a patchwork of industrial village settlements with hundreds of plastic factories specialising in flip-flops. Dai Wei guided me to these factories and around his network of factory owners. This seemed, in the circumstances, the right place to begin to understand the world of flip-flop manufacture: from the bosses at the top, and through them working down to the grassroots of the factory floor and the workers.

The most important thing about flip-flops the factory bosses taught me, is that the skill required to make them is quickly learned. Their technologies are simple, and only require low start-up capital. At their simplest, flip-flops can be cut by hand at home. In these simplicities their significance lies. Many factories began this way, with would-be entrepreneurs borrowing small amounts of money through kinship networks, informal moneylenders or shadow banks, to buy a used mixer, operated from home by two or three family members. In contrast, trainers are made through 20 separate processes requiring expensive machinery and substantial capital investment. Flip-flops, on the other hand, provide social advancement through factory production. This makes them a popular start-up for those with an inclination towards making things, as a way of making money and improving their social circumstances. Factory fortunes were made from humble flip-flop beginnings. Flip-flops provided junctions in the road where personal and financial resources can be audited, risks weighed and people navigate routes to becoming (or remaining) a factory worker, or taking a step up and becoming a boss. Flip-flops are about possibility and becoming. They capture the Chinese dream of improving circumstances, writ small.

Wang Fei was a farmer born on the eve of the Chinese Revolution. Against his small plot of land he borrowed money to set up as a peddler of household items in the late 1960s. The small amount of money he accumulated, he invested in a home factory in the 1980s, where his family cut flip-flops by hand from plastic sheets. Profits were gradually re-invested in more productive machinery, and later in buying a factory building. Wang Fei's factory was grown, like a crop, with increasing yields, year upon year. He was able to take a step up in technology to injection moulding in the 1990s through clever re-investment of profits. Injection moulding inaugurates a step-change in flip-flop fortunes. It brings a ten-fold increase in production and profits through diversification into plastic clogs (crocs) and boots. These higher-value items use the same technology but with different moulds. While flip-flops are limited in their sales value, clogs and boots better sustain the capital accumulation required to grow production.

A lively, busy man now in his 50s, Wang Fei lives in a big house in the grounds of his factory's 10,000 square metres of high-tech production, arranged over five floors. Architects' drawings in his office reveal plans for the new factory in glass and steel he will begin building next year. One of his sons is in the United States and another is in Canada. Both are studying international business, skills and connections that will be leveraged into further lucrative, diversified, international opportunities by the next generation.

Flip-flop fortunes, as Wang Fei's journey shows, lie in establishing platforms for more profitable plastic shoes. Flip-flops sell wholesale for between 40 cents and US$4, depending on quality and design. Profits are small, and margins tight. Small to medium-sized factories typically make 3 million pairs a year, with a sales value of 200,000 RMB. A typical 10 per cent profit margin brings in 20,000–30,000 RMB a year, making only small reinvestments possible without a shift to more profitable lines. Most factory owners don't make this transition. They stop at various scales of production and technologies that work with their capacities for risk, their industry, their effective decision-making and their luck. Thus flip-flops generate a differentiated boss class, ranging from small-scale home producers to large factories and fortunes like Wang Fei's. The flip-flop middle class is as diverse as their scales of production and the navigational skills with which they tackle the journeys expanding them.

Flip-flop start-ups are open to all except those unable to borrow small amounts of capital and those with no inclination to factory life and its risks. But this democratisation of factory start-up is also limiting as it generates fierce competition, especially in domestic markets served by small-scale production. Competition depresses retail prices and profits. Growing flip-flop factories, and rising up the plastic social structure, requires connections. Connections to lucrative overseas markets are particularly important. But export licences dispensed by the authorities guard these markets, and not all factories are big enough or well-connected enough to get them. Thus small and medium-sized factories rely on middlemen, like Dai Wei, for export licences and the skills to broker transnational connections.

But development of international markets is constrained by the same flip-flop mobility that expanded the domestic Chinese market. In the 1980s flip-flops were made in Taiwan. From Taiwan they migrated to China, as migrant, Taiwan-based, families sent machines back to Fuzhou. As Taiwanese factory conditions and wages improved, and the economy shifted from manufacture to services, so flip-flop production shifted to China. It is now en route to Vietnam, Sudan, Egypt and other parts of Africa. Dai Wei has invested in a factory in Egypt. He sent a Formula Man and eleven workers, four of whom remain many months later, as advisers. They transferred the machines, and their knowledge, wordlessly, to Egyptian workers who mimicked their work practices and scribbled their formulas in Arabic. In this way, new, translocal, co-productions are inaugurated. Wages and other production costs are lower in Egypt than China, and so Dai Wei thinks this is a profitable investment. The flip-flop business is open and mobile, making it a fragile basis on which to position livelihoods.

Developing flip-flop production involves taking advantage of different kinds of opportunities. These increased with the 1980s liberal economic reforms inaugurated by Deng Xiaoping. Dai Wei's father exploited a gap in government shoe supply in 1981 to develop his own factory. Until then, the Chinese government was the sole owner of shoe factories and supplies were centrally planned. Unable to meet demand, the government allowed private producers to fill gaps in the planned economy. Dai Wei's father's cousin, who had moved to Taiwan before the revolution, helped him buy a machine for mixing and rolling, and with this, Dai Wei's father set up production at home. With the right connections the home factories of 1981 became big factories in the late 1980s and the government, unable to compete with independent producers, closed its shoe factories, thereby generating further opportunities. Dai Wei's father's business still thrives. Shifting from flip-flops to trainers in the late 1980s, he invested in new technology and generated bigger profits.

Connections are important in building humbler scales of production too. He Jin and his wife He Zizhen, 30-year-old factory owners, expanded an opportunity opened by He Zizhen's father's connections. He started his factory in 1992, later in the liberalisation process, after working as an army truck driver. His army contact with party officials connected him with those who subcontract flip-flop production to smaller factories. Thus, through her father's connections, He Zizhen and He Jin gathered the capital and the orders to start their own factory in 2000. They live comfortably on the profits of their medium-sized factory, in a large apartment in the factory grounds. They are a middling example of the flip-flop middle class, and middle-scale flip-flop production. We will meet them again, further along the trail.

Jiang Qing, the mid-40s owner of a large, high-tech, factory has excellent connections. Her husband works in real estate for the army. Jiang Qing started her business, with her sister, making soles. She now lives in a spacious, expensively furnished apartment inside her factory grounds, with her husband, son and a servant. Her factory is big enough to provide dormitory accommodation for 100 workers. Factory size, it seems, correlates with the quality of connections. Dai Wei's father, He Zizhen's father and Jiang Qing, all have connections with what they call 'officials'. These provide crucial opportunities to grow factories as new opportunities open up. The Communist Party and the Chinese state crucially shaped everyday lives,[41] as state enterprises closed and private ones opened. With liberalisation and the transfer of assets from public to private, state to citizen, party officials had advantages and could create them for others. There are numerous examples of personal wealth accumulated by officials, whose influence provided benefit to their network. This is expected rather than resented. What matters is how someone who advances takes care of everyone else.[42] Opportunities and patronage secured new ways of living and new forms of social differentiation, making new, fluid social structures.

With what skills, apart from the skill of securing party connections, do factory bosses navigate their flip-flop journeys? They must manage workers in meeting production targets. Unreliability in meeting targets loses orders to other factories. Bosses must know which workers can achieve production targets at the required quality. Poor quality loses orders too. Bosses must secure enough workers to fill orders and then dismiss them when orders fall. They must decide when and how to invest in new machinery. Is it better to buy a big expensive mixer to serve two production lines, or two smaller ones? Finding strong and durable machines takes experience and good judgement. Injection-mould production is ten times more profitable than sheet production, but what is the best way to accumulate the capital to buy the machines this shift requires?

Class, Cities and Plastic

My search for the flip-flop trail led me through the special economic zone near the port, which is responsible for transforming China, and on through the plastic city of Fuzhou with its uneven topographies of past and present, socialism and capitalism, and on to the industrial villages to the south. En route I explored the human fabric making the new China and the plastic middle class. It seems that bosses and workers often share early life circumstances, but follow different routes, taking them to different places. Flip-flops make class, and they generate social mobility between classes in their unique capacity as a factory starter-kit. Rising opportunities, then, are not confined to the zones, but extend beyond them, making the city and industrial villages too. The social, political and economic forces creating the zones are the same as those creating smaller enterprise, for example the matrix of factories started by entrepreneurs with an appetite for risk and appropriate contacts. The zone and the industrial villages hosting the flip-flop factories, as we shall see further along the trail, pool workers and share distribution. They share adjacent peri-urban space, albeit segmented. They share the workers that move between them and pools of local skill. Most importantly, they share the idea of generating wealth through manufacture for plastic global markets. Home factories and industrial villages express the ingenuity and improvisation of humbler scales of ambition in commercial enterprise. They are part of a larger dynamic around the zones, a scaled continuum of enterprise. Whether the zones generated the dynamic for home-based factories or the other way around is unimportant. They are all part of the idea that things can be made and traded at different, accumulating, scales of return, making them part of the same human initiative and energy. They are part of the same idea of expansion in production, in profits and in the scale on which lives can be lived. The factories and the zones are both connected and disconnected, forming proximate manufacturing systems driven by the same ideas and lives.

5
Plastic Village

[S]pace is broad, teeming with possibilities, position, intersections, passages, detours, U turns, dead ends, one-way streets. Too many possibilities, indeed. (Susan Sontag, 'Introduction' to Water Benjamin, *One-Way Street*, 2006, p. xx)

Dai Wei drives through the dense patchwork of rural-turned-industrial villages south of Fuzhou, stopping at different factories, negotiating quantities, prices and delivery dates with bosses. We are finally in the production centre of the flip-flop trail. Before taking a magnifying lens to one of the factories, it is imperative to understand its immediate social context in one of the industrial villages. The village, not the city, at this point becomes a central character on the trail. This provides a way of piercing the surface of this landscape for its stories, revealing its built and social architectures. The Village, as it will be known, is a small area with, perhaps, 30 plastic factories, most of them producing flip-flops and plastic packaging. Like adjacent villages, it merges seamlessly into a cluster of what are units of local administration and decision-making, minimally distinguished from each other by marker stones at their boundaries, and criss-crossed by the journeys of those who live in them.

Four approaches to The Village present themselves as ways of gathering information about it. Sit on a stoop outside one of the small supermarkets and watch the village move past on foot, bicycle, motor scooter, car and truck. Or wander the main streets and the back streets; the factory yards and public spaces; the closely packed living spaces nestled against factories. A third way is to appoint a guide and follow them through the routines of everyday life, seeing the world from their shoes. A woman with a small child on the back of her bicycle picks up a metal bowl and beats it with a spoon to announce the arrival of 'the foreigners'[1] in The Village. As the foreigners become familiar there is a fourth way to explore the village, as guests, looking out through the windows of villagers' houses. All vantage-points provided their own version of The Village, and their combination, perhaps, provides a finer-grained portrait of it. But on this all vantage-points concur: the physical and social landscapes of The Village are made of plastics, by plastics and through plastics. This is the plastic village.[2]

Making the Plastic Village

This is the plastic village because plastic factories provide (social, material and built) fabric. The Village is dominated by dozens of factories making plastic shoes, straps and packaging: more of this in the next chapter. Factories are closely packed between small houses. Densely populated, The Village buzzes with incessant shift work and the intimate intersection of working and living space. This is the plastic village because bits of scrap plastic and blue carrier bags litter the ground. Waste plastic is incorporated into informal vernacular village architecture. Large sheets of EVA with flip-flop soles stamped out of them – leaving a latticework of coloured plastic – are made into a fence and placed around a house on the outskirts of The Village, vividly marking the property-line in hot pink and blue. Complete, uncut sheets of EVA fill the gap between the roof and the adjoining wall of a brick house, providing extra waterproofing.

The Village is plastic in the material, thermoplastic, sense too, of being a malleable substance, which can be moulded in many ways and is always being shaped into new emerging forms. Plastic, a shape-shifting material, landscapes The Village.[3] Factories stand on what was farmland until the mid 1990s. As The Village grows, it extends into what were, until recently, the rice fields from which The Village ate. The land-space between villages gradually disappears, and they merge into a single built environment, into one large, densely packed, industrial-residential landscape, vibrating with the human effort of incessant work. There are vacant lots awaiting factory development next to abandoned factories where production has ceased or migrated elsewhere. Everywhere is building, building and building. The sound of construction is layered with the soundscape of traffic and factory machinery, as flip-flops are stamped out of plastic sheets and rows of women pack them into plastic bags.

Plastics fabricate road construction and the circulations they support. A grid of paved roads connects factories, with containers waiting outside, to the main road and eastwards towards the port. The production and movement of plastics around a matrix of connections literally shapes these villages. Plastics fabricate traffic circulations, as well as the journeys of routine working lives, organised around production, encountered later along the trail. Plastics fabricate routine journeys of materials, objects and people, circulations – journeys – that feed flip-flop production and distribution. Workers arrive at factories on foot, on bicycles and on small, inexpensive motorcycles. They circulate the area wearing the flip-flops they, or others, have made in brightly coloured plastic. Trucks move the raw materials in and the finished goods out to China's inland trucking routes and to the port for export to overseas buyers. Tractors piled so high with boxes of flip-flops that the tractor itself is no longer visible, move slowly and noisily around The Village. Occasionally, in this mix of traffic, an expensive car goes by. A BMW 7 series for example, sleek and black, with tinted windows protecting its passengers from the villagers' gaze. There are less impressive cars too, but cars are a minority transport in The Village, driven by factory owners and middlemen like Dai Wei, checking on production. Buses, taxi-cars and taxi-motorcycles ply the main road, connecting villagers with the city to the north and places beyond.

Plastics shape the architectures of The Village, displaying the social distinctions they also generate. The Village road grid lapses into unpaved, narrow, winding back-alleys between factories where villagers and factory workers – distinctions unpacked later – live in densely packed housing, in simple two-roomed dwellings, with electricity but no running water or bathrooms. Grander two- and three-storey houses, sometimes gated, are set apart from these simple back-alley dwellings. These are architectural manifestations of plastic's rewards, which accumulate, building new (plastic) social structures. On the edge of The Village, slightly apart from the tangle of factories and smaller houses, smart new apartment blocks, five and seven storeys high, are nearing completion and offered for sale. Developers, as well as factory owners, have first call on ex-farmland, and for some housing has become a way of accumulating wealth. These apartments and the big houses in the village belong to those who make multiples of factory workers' wages from new entrepreneurial opportunities in plastic. They are monuments to aspiration, visual reminders of the rewards of success. Plastics make and circulate money, and they fabricate social distinctions.

Plastics fabricate population densities and the dynamics of settlement in The Village, as well as a further set of social distinctions, this time between migrants and locals rather than, as in the last chapter, plastic workers and entrepreneurs. Plastics have multiplied the population of the village to five or ten times its pre-plastics size, while simultaneously emptying other (rural) villages to the west of their working-age populations. Plastics have transformed village social relationships. 'Original' villagers live with 'strangers' whose familial relationships are transformed into new, long-distance, intimacies. Migrants outnumber original inhabitants of the village by five or ten times. It is difficult to get reliable figures, but informal estimates agree that there are approximately 1000 'original' villagers, or 200 families of five – a couple, their child and the husband's parents – in The Village. Rural migrants, on the other hand, are estimated to number between 5000 and 10,000, a figure that might be inflated as locals translate the experience of being overwhelmed into numbers. Migrant and local lives are closely intertwined, with local villagers renting rooms in their houses to migrants, whose rents have become a key source of income with the loss of farming.

Differences between migrants and locals are informal and lived, as well as formal administrative categories. Chinese citizenship is place-specific[4] and entwined with complicated versions of origins, as we will see. 'Yuanzhou', the Chinese word for 'original' villagers, and 'yumint', the Chinese word for migrant villagers, are registered on the ID card people carry and the police check. These official distinctions mark ways in which the Chinese state deals with its citizens, and locals may or may not attach importance to them, depending on the context. Factory bosses interviewed reported their preference for migrant workers for their flexibility and readiness to work hard. In the competition between workers for jobs, locals often reported feeling disadvantaged. But others reported no difference 'in face and work', between original villagers and 'waidren', which means literally, 'outside people'. Migrants are major contributors to the local factory workforce and the flip-flop factories could not operate without them. In this area the flip-flop factory labour force is estimated (by bosses) as 75–90 per cent migrant, and 10–25 per cent local. Local families cannot meet, and, sometimes do not want to meet when they have other options, the labour needs of the factories, which must then depend on migrant workers to fill orders.

Plastic is the dominant material in which the common objects of everyday life in this area are made. The Village's cups, buckets, baskets, bowls, television sets, radios, clothes, shoes and more are all made of plastic, and many are manufactured locally. This world is made *of* plastics as well as by plastics. A couple of well-stocked supermarkets, selling packaged food, drinks, cleaning products, toiletries and household goods like mops, buckets, enamel cooking pots, blankets and simple furnishings, overflow with plastics in all colours, shapes and sizes. Outside one of the supermarkets is a large plastic cat toddlers can ride on if they insert a coin. In the square, a cobbler mending shoes says he does not repair flip-flops because they are disposable. The elementary school comprises two blocks. Between them there is an unpaved play area, bounded by a wall and an elaborate gate. Above the school flies a red flag with one big star, and four small stars in yellow, on it. The village soundtrack rises several decibels with young voices as the children leave school for the day. Beyond the school are a couple of cafes. A woman is frying fritters in a large metal can outside the 'China Mobile' shop. Villagers and rural migrants alike have mobile phones. There is a library with a couple of shelves of books, an open-sided pool hall colonised by boys and young men. A young man positions a baby on the pool table while he takes a shot. Next to the pool table are a table football game and some old pinball machines, both fabricated in plastic. This is the plastic village.

Transitions

The plastic village is the outcome of an accumulation of multi-layered transformations over a long period. Some of these transformations are about the making of contemporary China and run through this village, as they run through the rest of China. Others are more specific to this area, and are about the arrival of plastics. Those best positioned to report on these transformations are those long-settled in The Village, who think of themselves as original villagers. These are people whose routine journeys required them to navigate a rapidly shifting landscape with the resources available to them. One way to access locals' stories on the subject of change is to join five women and two babies, 'women of leisure', as they describe themselves, sitting on a concrete stoop outside of a tiny kiosk-shop in the centre of The Village. The foreigners with their camera and recorder soon gather a crowd of elderly people, preschool infants, adults with erratic employment and those who are, for a variety of reasons, just passing by. This ad hoc village meeting on the subject of change seemed, in the circumstances, to be a viable research strategy.

Among villagers, elders are able to take the longest view. An 85-year-old man, Lin Lu, once a farmer, standing beside his wife recollects and reconnects the plastic village with its past:

I experienced the revolution, when Mao Zedong was in office. From Mao Zedong you have Deng Zhao Ping and now Hu Jintao, three prime ministers, so things have changed a lot especially in the 1980s when Deng opened up China, there was a lot of change. I remember when I was young, 7 or 8 years old, there were a lot of siblings at home and it was very hard to get food. The best time was during the time of Mao. I was a young man and so life was more carefree and we had farmland to plant groundnuts.... I wasn't educated and didn't want to go to school. I stopped at Primary two. Now you have to work. Then [in the past] you can't get your goods. It's not easy; there was only a provision shop. We used bills, not cash, coupons for clothes, coupons for food. If you were on a production line, each family would be allocated a few coupons. At the time of Mao Zedong my parents were farmers. They worked in the fields and they would be allocated points, and the points they would get, like 50 points, could be converted into coupons. In Mao's time if you wanted to be in business you couldn't.... Now we have the ability to do what we want to.

The government took my money: the entrepreneurs have taken my land. I am 85 and I am still working. No money. How can I retire? Our kids, three boys and four girls, don't have jobs; they live with us. The girls are married, but the sons still live with us. They are married too, but there are no jobs. If you don't work, there is no money. I use my fund I got from the government. I am living on the money that I got from the land sale. I have three granddaughters and one grandson. I was a farmer, now there is no more land.

Lin Lu's life spans a time of profound change. The defeat of the nationalist Kuomintang in 1949, inaugurating the establishment of communism, brought far-reaching changes in ordinary lives. Public and private land was merged, village fields were re-divided by the government, and redistributed as household plots in the 1950s land reforms. From 1954 to 1961 collectivisation initiated the commune–brigade–team system the old man describes, in which villages became units of government administration, divided into production teams and paid in work-points, redeemed against household necessities. The Cultural Revolution (1966–76) targeted 'reactionary' social practices like religious worship or festivals celebrating local gods, forcing them to become private activities.[5] And the economic reforms that began in 1978 led to the appropriation of farmland for industrial (plastics) production and land speculation, all in private hands, signalling state sponsorship of new forms of privatisation and individualism.

Lin Lu has had to navigate the far-reaching macro-level changes constituting modern Chinese history as they ran through The Village, reconfiguring the journeys composing his everyday life. Locals travel different kinds of journeys and experience different forms of dislocation from rural migrants in this regard, as will soon be apparent. Locals remain in place and their familiar world shifts around them, creating new lives in the same, but reconfigured, locations. Rural migrants, on the other hand, travel from old locations to new ones and, in these dislocations composed of distance rather than time, exchange their old lives for new ones. Travel is about time and transformation, as well as movement through space. The Village is not the same place, it is transformed by time – by new technical and social forces – but remains in the same location and retains (some of) the same people, who must live reconfigured versions of their old lives.

Life on Compensation

While locals navigate The Village wearing the same flip-flops as migrants, their sense of belonging is forged in calculations of long-standing connection, through land and ancestors. These calculations edit earlier migrations, in order to sustain claims to belong. They establish a false fixity that erases the mobility of locals, who were historically migrants from other areas. Stories about origins and mobility differentiate locals from rural migrants. Local villagers are different from migrants too, in the variety with which they secure the material substance of their lives. Although some locals live on factory employment and must compete with migrants for jobs, many have other options. As ex-farmers, they live on the proceeds from the sale of their land for factory development. While this may not always provide a living wage, there is often a cross-subsidy through the wages of household members with factory or related jobs. Locals can also rent out their property – the arrival of migrants increases demand for rented rooms – and live on the redistributed factory income of migrants. Like migrants, locals live on plastics too, if in a slightly different way. A 40-year-old man, Yu Jin, says:

> My son provides. I have two sons, one is working and one is still at school. My son works as a part-time porter carrying stuff in Fuzhou. Based on our income we do an annual budget, based on each season, setting out how much we will spend. It's not like if we have money we buy meat and stuff, we spread it out and budget over the year. I have no income. At my age it's hard to find a job, so we survive on the money I got from the land I sold. So it's about 20 RMB a month by twelve

months. But we still have to pay the hygiene and maintenance fees of the village. When I'm done I don't have much money left. The money we are paid for the land gets higher with age. So if you are 60 you get more, you get 30 RMB instead of 20. A Government official sold the land. They collect the money and then the person who sold the land will get a percentage of it. The remaining money will be distributed to the people of the village. The officials of the village council have the right to decide what they will sell. So we don't have much say when land is taken away. As villagers we are not aware of the policies of the government … so we just have to accept it.

We would like to work in the factories but we can't get a job. People from outside the province are more obedient to the boss. They are more submissive because of their conditions; so it is easier for the boss to work with them. That's why local people don't have land to plant any more; they don't have anything.

We are very good with them [the migrants]. There is no political collision. If you have money you can always go [too].… Rich people move on …

My relative rents rooms [to migrants]. Renting is part of the way we can get income, if you have the money to build a house. To build a house, depending on size would cost over 10,000 RMB.

As the ad hoc public meeting progresses, it gathers more people and opinions on the subject of change in the village. Things are better, things are worse, but all concur that life is different and change is part of life. Some stop to say they would like to move on to somewhere else with more opportunities and modern condominiums to live in, but stay because they lack the resources to move. The would-be movers have, perhaps, absorbed the *Zeitgeist* of transformation and the aspiration it enables, without the means to benefit from it. Richer villagers are more mobile, the new opportunities are unevenly distributed. Mou Sen, who wears a Calvin Klein tee shirt, says that his boss has made millions, but that he is only a truck driver. He thinks life is better now than before the factories. Others demur. They and their kin are being pushed into the towns by the pace of transformation and village life as they knew it is over. Those who have turned their land and housing into rental income, because they had access to the capital required for building, conversion or renovation, live as landlords and may also have jobs. Those who have sold their land but manage to find employment through new opportunities in the area for themselves or their children, rather than rely on a diminishing pot of compensation, manage to live comfortably. Those who rely solely on their land-compensation without other sources of income, like Lin Lu the 85-year-old farmer and his wife, struggle the most with the new circumstances. These personal stories are constantly interrupted by small noisy tractors carrying heavy plant, sometimes a cement mixer, or by bicycles, motors scooters and the occasional car. These passing vehicles squash the meeting into the walls of the shop and surrounding houses. The public meeting ends with an auction in which bids – of interesting stories to tell – to entice the foreigners home are placed. Mou Sen prevails, and provides a portrait of his life.

Mou Sen's house is large, detached from other buildings, and has a front courtyard which lies behind high locked iron gates. It is on the edge of The Village, and looks on to scrub land yet to become factories or condominiums. This substantial house is divided, and shared with Mou Sen's brother, his wife and their toddler. Mou Sen's side of the house has five rooms: two bedrooms upstairs, a bathroom with running water, a living room and communal space downstairs, next to a large dining room, which leads onto a kitchen. He shares this space with his wife and their 15-year-old son, a student at a college in Fuzhou. In its spacious dimensions, its arrangement of differentiated domestic space and in its material objects, Mou Sen's situation contrasts sharply with that of migrant workers, as we will see. He has large comfortable furniture, a polished dining table and chairs, a lounge suite with sofa and easy chairs, a large refrigerator, a fitted kitchen. It looks solid and permanent, if also a little shabby, because he can't afford the replacement and renovation costs.

Mou Sen was a beneficiary of the compensation from the 300 square metres of family farm, co-owned with his parents and brother, and relinquished in the industrialisation of farmland.

This was our farming land so we are compensated for that. Sometimes when the government wants the land, or entrepreneurs want it, through the government, we may not want to sell the land but we are forced to…. Our land is going to be turned into a factory and we get compensation. It's not enough for a child's education. I am not educated, so I want my son to be educated. Initially he was studying in a technical school, which is free because the standard is not good. I sent him to a better learning environment. It costs 30,000 RMB for three years. When we sold the land we got 150,000 RMB, but it comes down. You only get 20,000 because they take the tax away and for the proceedings. It's a historical practice [implying multiple formal and informal cuts to different interests].

Both Mou Sen and his wife, Mou Fang have jobs, releasing their compensation for projects, like their son's education, beyond daily survival. Mou Sen continues:

> She [Mou Fang] works in a factory. It's a very small factory set-up. It makes plastic bags and packaging. About ten people work there. The pay is very good though, depending on the amount she works. For each plastic bag she makes she earns one-third of a cent. It's not predictable or constant. She gets about 20 RMB a day. With 20 RMB a day, with our standard of living, what can you buy? A hundred grams of meat costs one and a half RMB, rice costs 2 RMB for 500 grams of good quality rice.
>
> I have been working in a factory for quite some time and the boss treats me well. I don't punch a card when I go to work and the boss is actually quite free with me. So I have freedom in my job as long as I fulfil my duties and accomplish what I am supposed to. I drive a truck transporting goods out from Fuzhou. I deliver textiles. The goods produced in the factory get exported to Europe: fabrics. Different kinds of fabrics, like the material you use to make ski-clothes. They don't make the ski-clothes, just the fabrics [containing plastics]. We have orders from overseas so we send them ...

Their lives, also organised by plastics and plasticised fabrics, are comfortable.

The route from Mou Sen's house to the centre of the village passes the pond. This tells its own story of the area's transformation. It is toxic, dirty, stagnant and full of plastic debris.

> This pond used to be pristine. We used to swim in it. Now, because of the factory ... it's just unsightly.... The living conditions here are very bad health-wise and [in terms of] the environment. The people who sold the land, they didn't actually use the money to improve the condition in the village. There is corruption going on in bureaucracy and government, going all the way up to Beijing. (Mou Sen)

The village environment and village life are consumed in industrial transformation. Rising prices of farmland, fuelled by factory construction and property development, transform it into further factories and high-priced condominiums. It is not that Mou Sen's family and the other villages can no longer farm, there is still vacant land that could be used for planting. But it just doesn't make sense. The land is too valuable now that it has more profitable uses. Once the irrigation plant was no longer viable because farming declined, and the detritus of industrialisation littered the landscape, the pollution and loss of irrigation water made it increasingly difficult to grow crops. Agriculture and industry became incompatible activities as this young grandmother, Ye Qun, says:

> The land was bought from us. They closed the irrigation plant. Because when they buy land they stopped the irrigation, so once the water couldn't come in we couldn't farm any more: and because of the pollution from the factory in the water. In the water! It's not good. It is polluted. This land that you see used to be farmland and now it's not.... About five or six years from now, when they want to develop this area, all this will be gone.

These villagers have lived through radical reconfigurations of their landscape and the lives they can lead and the journeys they can navigate through it. They anticipate future changes they cannot yet name.

Living Beyond Our Planting

On the other side of the village, from one of a cluster of densely occupied two-storey concrete buildings, a dim light bulb illuminates the hive of activity within. Tian Gang has just returned home from the flip-flop factory. Between six and seven o'clock, as day turns to night, streetlights light up and factories exchange one set of workers for another. The Village streets are alive with bodies on foot, on bicycles, on small motor scooters, as Tian Gang wheels his bicycle into the night streets and pedals the short journey home. He confirms the evening's arrangements from his mobile phone as he cycles. His wife, Tian Yi, serves his dinner of sticky rice and vegetables from a pot atop a single-ringed bottled-gas stove, immediately he gets in. She and their daughter have already eaten. The door from the street opens onto the main room in which the family cooks, eats, and entertains passing family and neighbours. A toilet is hidden behind a wooden partition. Above the main room, accessed from the back of the room via a wooden ladder, is their only bedroom. Tian Gang and Tian Yi share this with the 16-year-old-daughter who joined them, from the village in Jiangxi when she finished school, to work as a trimmer in the flip-flop factories. Make-do and recycling guide the improvised interior aesthetics of their home. A door becomes a table; plastic bags are used for storing food, and hung around the walls away from the reach of rats. Their public world of plastic production is also a private world of plastic consumption. Bowls and buckets, in bright colours, store water and provisions bought in the village supermarket. Aluminium is the second most ubiquitous fabric of domestic culture, made into cooking pots and pans.

Tian Yi, who serves tea to the gathering company in their main room, is a feisty woman in her mid 30s. She navigates her world in just two pairs of shoes, a pair of flip-flops and a pair of leather shoes in need of repair. Casually employed, she likes to work as a final trimmer in the flip-flop factories, but in order to stay in work does a variety of jobs, including sticking logos on flip-flops and making plastic bags. Part of a large, flexible, disposable labour force, when the factory work that relies on the Dai Wei orders dries up, she takes whatever work is available. Cheerfully she says she will do:

anything that brings in money. I'll pick up waste or dig sand on a construction site. Where there is money I will go. When it is not peak season [in the flip-flop factories] I will do that to supplement.... I have trimmed loose threads off clothes in a clothes factory in Fuzhou, I have cleaned up waste as a sewage worker, and I have worked in construction. No matter what it is, it is all about money.... I'll do anything legal to earn money.... When I have a job I am very happy.... We eat money. We are hungry for money.

Food and family form the fabric of connection Tian Gang and Tian Yi maintain with the rural life they have left in Jiangxi Province to the west. Two of their children, a boy of 5 and a girl of 6, are still living on the farm, cared for by Tian Yi's parents. Like other migrant workers, they see their younger children once a year. Their migration eastwards, and that of the entire working-age population of their village of 500 families, results, they say, from the Chinese government's ban on firecrackers in cities. This was the village industry in which they all worked.[6] But what one China scholar refers to as 'chains of unsettlement'[7] were established before the ban:

My cousin brought me over ... my father-in-law brought my cousin. No one knows who brought him. He's been here for 30 years. (Tian Gang)

People and objects of various kinds circulate along the routes rural migrants have fabricated in navigating between Jiangxi and The Village:

These are long beans, dried long beans. We brought them back from Jiangxi. We plant them ourselves on the farm. They are sun-dried so we can keep them for when we need them. We grow this pumpkin too. We slice it, sun-dry it and put on some salt. Then we put some glutinous flour on it and steam it. It is sun-dried, steamed and then sun-dried again ... we bring this because we plant it at home so we don't have to spend to get food. This is why we bring it back here, it's free at home.... We eat porridge for breakfast, with pickles, that's plain rice with vegetables in it. Lunch is rice with pickled vegetables and if we earn a bit more we will buy something else – fish, meat, a bit of duck, chicken, pork, ribs, pig's trotters. If we earn more we eat better. If not we don't eat so well. (Tian Yi)

Food travels from west to east and supplements the fragilities of a life on uncertain factory wages. Cash remittances travel from east to west to support family in Jiangxi. Remittances take many forms. They can be in the form of information, skills and ideas as well as money. Their impact on rural areas is uneven and depends on how they are used. Some rural areas are developing vibrant forms of commerce. Remittances channelled into petty commodity production and entrepreneurial activity that is income-generating has greater impact in stimulating local economies than remittances spent on building big houses and buying consumer goods in order to maintain, or enhance, local customs and social standing.[8] With cash remittances, Tian Gang and Tian Yi's rural families can 'live beyond their planting', as one rural migrant so eloquently put it to me. Such migrations are family projects. The implicit understanding is that the benefits of migration are distributed around the family.[9] Migration strategies are part of a broader dynamic, continuously transforming rural landscapes and creating new urban and industrial zones.

Tian Gang and Tian Yi's house fills up with family, friends and neighbours. These are, it seems, flexible categories of association that bleed into each other:

My siblings are all here in this village and big brother is throwing a party but we are not going. I have one elder brother, one younger brother and a sister. They work here. One attends the shop, selling electrical cables in a hardware shop, that's my brother. My younger sister works in the garment industry, but she doesn't work now because she has just had a baby. The husband of that sister is a motorcycle rider [taxi] ferrying people around. Most of their children are still in the village in Jiangxi because they are still young, except my eldest brother's kid who is old enough to come up. (Tian Gang)

These are our neighbours. We are all from the same village in Jiangxi. We are also related. We have a sense of kinship because we share the same family name. So I call him brother, but we are not blood related, but we don't distinguish that. We come from the same village. There are three households here [next door] from Jiangxi. Henan, Sichuan and Anhui are where our other neighbours come from, but we don't really interact. If we know them through working in the factories then we will talk to them and interact with them. But the kind of relationship we will have with them will not be like [those with] people from our village. You have to get to know them; so if you don't know them it becomes hard to interact. So that is the reason we don't interact. The person who lives behind the house comes from Fuzhou. We talk to each other. As long as they speak Mandarin we speak to each other. If the other person doesn't speak Chinese then it is hard for us to interact if we don't speak the same language. You need to have a common language to interact or you can't start that communication.[10] (Tian Yi)

The west to east journeys, from rural to industrial village, which Tian Yi, Tian Gang, their extended family and neighbours travel, are collective journeys. Since the 1980s more than 100 million Chinese farmers have left their villages for cities. A further 130 million rural people: 'lack sufficient land or employment to guarantee their livelihood.... They are the largest peacetime movement of people in history.'[11] Lives, and the journeys constituting them, provide a window onto bigger social processes. Migrants like these circulate between rural and industrial landscapes,[12] transforming them as they go. In the economic downturn in 2008, when factory production fell dramatically in China following a fall in world demand for Chinese goods, triggered by the banking and subprime mortgage crisis, migrants like Tian Gang and Tian Yi went back to their village farms where they rode out the recession, only returning when factory production recovered. Out of the 250 million rural migrant workers, 20 million lost their jobs in 2008.[13] They are part of a massive, flexible labour force making flip-flops and other goods, exported worldwide. They are the human fabric of the economic miracle of Chinese growth, and these journeys describe their lives.

The crowd passing through Tian Yi and Tian Gang's house all evening breaks up early as family and neighbours return to their own houses nearby. The factory workers have a 7am start, and those without work will make an early start too, hoping to secure a day of casual labour.

Cycling Through the Village

It is 6am as Tian Gang, Tian Yi and their daughter sit at the kitchen table with tea and rice. Filling his tea flask for the day, Tian Gang wheels his heavy black bicycle onto the street and starts on his journey through The Village to The Factory. A tangle of overhead power lines transmits electricity to factories and houses, democratising some of the benefits of industrialisation. In contrast to the low backstreet houses where Tian Gang lives, three- and four-storey apartment buildings line his route as he nears the Village Gathering Hall. The hall is a new building of monumental proportions, in the process of being finished inside with elaborate wood-carvings. It was financed by contributions from factory owners and villagers. Tian Gang's boss himself contributed 20,000 RMB. The Village Gathering Hall is part of the new economic order and the rising prosperity it has brought to the area. Its broader economic and ritual significance are detailed by China scholars.[14] Tian Gang suggests that the Gathering Hall marks his relationship to the village. He says it is:

> For prayer, to remember ancestors, ancestor worship, Taoism, people here have a belief in that ... ancestor worship is for people who live in this village. I don't belong to this village because I wasn't born here.

Tian Gang's ancestors lie a long way away to the west in a village in Jiangxi so the Gathering Hall is also a monument to his (dis)connection from the place where he now lives. Rural-to-urban migrants collaborate with 'locals' in establishing for themselves a distinctive status, which affirms the significance of family loyalties and 'native place'. As I suggested earlier, this is not as straightforward as it might seem. China scholars point out that chains of 'unsettlement', 'dislocation', 'movement' and 'resettlement' are prominent in the calculation of Chinese belonging.[15] In these calculations, Tian Gang's migration lacks the long time-span necessary to include him as a villager. He is a migrant in his own and others' calculations. But belonging is neither a settled matter nor a matter of settled place. It is about ancestors' journeys. In this framework navigation of particular routes, and sojourns along the way, become significant. Belonging is a matrix of travel; a matter of intersecting journeys, tangles of routes and roots.

Those who count themselves as local in this area have close connections with transnational migration and may themselves be returned migrants. The coastal cities of Fuzhou and Xiamen have deep histories of overseas trade and migration, establishing networks of family ties with Taiwan and beyond. As a mountainous province with better outward connection by sea than inland, Fujian has a distinguished history of seafaring and ship building, important activities supporting trade since the eighteenth century.[16] Prior to the 1980s economic reforms this was one of the least developed parts of China[17] and this period stimulated out-migration overseas at the same time as in-migration from other parts of China. In this churn of in- and out-migration, Fujian and Fuzhou migrants still supply the US and British Chinese diasporas with goods, information and people, shaping China Towns across Britain and North America.[18] Chinese Americans from Fuzhou are famously linked with semi-legitimate global migration businesses. These are semi-legitimate in the intersection of legal and illegal practices. Official migration channels transport students, business delegations, visiting relatives and temporarily exported labourers, like those whom Dai Wei sends to Egypt. Tens of thousands of workers rotate in and out of the overseas companies collaborating with Fuzhou. These migration journeys are organised through government-owned travel agencies, with legal-becoming-illegal migration when it contravenes the laws of receiving countries.[19] This is an area with a deep history of coming and going in migrant journeys of different scales and this challenges the designation of the 'local' as a counterpoint to the 'migrant'.

Along Tian Gang's route, abandoned crops and weeds are tangled in patches of wasteland between newly constructed buildings. This provides visual reminders that this was recently farmland, now a landscape in transition. A trickle of ground water, once a bigger stream, is clogged with bits of blue plastic bag. As he passes a small cluster of houses like his own, an old woman bends over a green plastic bowl set on an outside communal concrete sink with a cracked base, where she does her laundry. Women scurry about with buckets of water, collected from communal pipes, which they will use later for cooking and washing. The slap, slap of flip-flops hitting the ground generates a subtle soundtrack as Tian Gang nears The Factory and greets fellow workers arriving on foot.

As he approaches the factory gates, Tian Gang cycles past the recycling plant. Above the cement walls tower black and brightly coloured mountains of plastic scrap, waiting to be added to new flip-flops. Opposite the factory gates, wasteland suggests further factories yet to be built, factories planned on land that lies waiting. Condos might be built instead. It all depends on deals that are invisible to Tian Gang. As he wheels through the factory gate he passes the boss's house and the office at the entrance to the production floor. The night shift is pouring through the gate, heading home to all parts of The Village and the adjoining villages. Along with Tian Gang, we have arrived at the plastic factory where the flip-flops are made.

6
Making Flip-flops

I don't know [who these flip-flops are for] but they are very big so they must be for a foreigner. (Sun Chulin)

Tian Gang wheels his bicycle past the office where the boss, He Jin, and his wife, He Zizhen, are already in the office placing orders for chemicals and plastic granules, and turning new orders into production targets and work schedules. We met them earlier on the trail. They live with their baby in a large apartment over the factory they started in 2000, benefitting from He Zizhen's father's party connections. Tian Gang leaves his bicycle at the back of the trimming and packing section, next to the main production area. He picks up his single-blade knife and gets to work. As the day shift fill the places just evacuated by the night shift, production does not miss a beat. Flip-flops result from the continuous motion of people, machines, chemicals and hot plastics. The Factory[1] work environment is noisy, plastic-fume-filled and dirty. It is difficult to breathe. A layer of white and black dust settles over everything. Unpacking the production process reveals how flip-flops are actually made in the choreographies of machines and bodies. The production process also provides an opportunity to explore some of the lives of the flip-flop makers.

The Factory (1400 square metres) is arranged on two floors. The upper floor is airy and light, its floor tiled in white. It is filled with long rows of benches. Here, holes are punched into flip-flop soles, and PVC straps, bought from another factory in the area, attached. Downstairs is the main production floor, which is divided into two rooms. The outer room is used for trimming and packing, it is adjacent to the yard, where trucks pick up the packaged flip-flops. The inner room contains the main production area. It is closed on three sides, with one side open to the yard, where heaps of scrap plastic with sole-shaped holes lie waiting to be bundled for recycling. There are three production lines for flip-flop soles on the main floor, although not all of them are used at the same time. The Factory has no injection-moulding technology and this curtails the kinds of flip-flops that can be made and the profits. A medium-sized flip-flop factory for the area, its labour force of 200 expands and contracts with flip-flop orders. This flexibility is vital in protecting the fragile profit margins on which continued production depends. The Factory currently makes 2–3 million pairs of flip-flops a year, but has capacity to make upwards of 10 million.

The flip-flops, which supply cheaper and middle-markets, are made from PE and EVA. PE comes in different densities and molecular weights, and these produce soles of different qualities and durability. PE and EVA are combined with other ingredients like steric acid, calcium carbide and the blowing agents that make foam, as well as zinc oxide and the pigments that give the flip-flop soles their colour. The chemistries of The Factory, applied in secret 'formulas', produce a vast array of flip-flop soles. The higher-quality, more expensive flip-flops contain more new material and better ingredients, producing a sole with a denser and more durable finish. Cheaper flip-flops, on the other hand, contain more scrap material left over from previous productions, recombined with new material. This recycling is one of the advantages of thermoplastics like PE and EVA. EVA is regarded as a 'fresher', higher-quality material by some of the bosses.

Mixing and Rolling

Flip-flop production begins with mixing the plastic granules and other chemicals and then rolling the mixture into sheets of plastic. Sun Chulin, the 'Formula Man', works with the mixer. In it he combines plastic granules from Korea, chemicals he won't specify – formulas are secret – and scrap plastic, at 200° Celsius. The mixer Sun Chulin works is an integrated mixing and rolling machine. In some factories these processes are performed in separate machines. Mixing and rolling involve heat and friction. Sun Chulin feeds the granules and chemicals into the round barrels of the mixer, which is positioned to the side of the rolling machine. Scrap EVA is added later, when the hot sheets of plastic are put through the rollers. Sun Chulin and his wife, Sun Yi, work together, moving in intricately choreographed steps, around the mixer and each other. They work as a highly practised two-person production team, with a clear division of labour. In this hot, dangerous and skilled work Sun Chulin adds the formulas to the mixer. He then shifts his attention to the steering wheel at each side of the rolling machine, which adjusts the distance between the rollers. Through this adjustment he makes thicker or thinner sheets of either EVA or PE, depending on the order he works to. He wears thick gloves to stop his hands from burning, shorts, a t-shirt and flip-flops because it is a hot job. He pushes the heavy, hot, rubbery plastic sheets from the mixer between the rollers a number of times, until their consistency and thickness is just right. These are fine judgements. If thermoplastics overheat they spoil. He knows exactly when the plastic sheet is finished and ready to cool on the metal rack.

Sun Yi works as his assistant. Husband and wife teams are preferred by factory owners for their stability and practised interdependence. Obligations within family units are understood to extend to employers. Sun Yi works with broom and dustpan, gathering up bits of raw material that fall to the floor and feeding them back into the mixer. She works around the mixer-roller and her husband, often at the back of the machine pushing material in with him, while he works at the front. She wears trousers and a t-shirt, her long hair tied back into a ponytail. From the back of the machine she moves around to the front to clear up spilt chemical powders and plastic fragments to return to the mixing process.

The plastic sheets resulting from this integrated mixer-roller are usually in 2- or 5-metre oblong sheets of 2- or 3-millimetre thick plastic. They will later be combined, 3 to 15 sheets together, depending on the thickness of the flip-flop sole required by the order. After cooling the sheets are ready for the next process – vulcanising.

But first, here are the people behind the mixing and rolling. Sun Chulin and Sun Yi are in their mid 30s. They met in The Village while working in the same plastic strap factory and living in the same multi-occupied housing with other factory workers. Their biographies are unique to them: told in words and in the movements composing their routine journeys around The Village, around The Factory, around the mixer and around each other. Yet they also share the basic architecture of their lives with other factory workers, so that their story is not theirs alone. They share a matrix of journeys with different, as well as similar, geographies. They share former occupations in rural areas, and the decisions that brought them to this factory and to these jobs. They share the factory conditions and wages that secure production of competitively cheap plastic goods on global markets. And they share the interconnection between work and housing, as places of intersecting dwelling. The stories these circumstances generate are about how bodies and skills interface with hot plastic to produce a sack of flip-flops. Their journeys, and the skill with which they navigate them, are simultaneously unique and shared with others in comparable circumstances.

Sun Chulin and Sun Yi's lives are composed in journeys of varied distance and temporalities, in the traction between the soles of their flip-flops and other shoes and the surfaces through which they move. Footwear provides access to biographies and travel practices, and through these a rendering of mobile lives-in-action as well as the opportunity to imagine others in the same terms.

The boss gives the slippers we wear to us, but when we go outside of the factory we will wear the shoes that we buy. I have three pairs of shoes: one sandal, one slipper and one leather shoe. (Sun Yi)

I have two pairs, a pair of slippers and a pair of leather shoes. Because I work here all the time, I hardly go out, so I wear slippers. I don't know which country the slippers I make are going to, but I do know they are for export. Some go out locally to local people. I have never thought about who wears this shoe. I can't think about that person. We just hope if the business goes well we will earn more money. We don't think about who wears them. (Sun Chulin)

In slippers, their word in English for flip-flop, and in leather shoes too, Sun Yi and Sun Chulin navigate the routes through which their lives are produced, as they play their part in producing flip-flops. Most of their journeys concern routine survival – they are about working, sleeping, eating and servicing a matrix of family and friends.

Unless I am buying clothes I just shop in The Village. Previously it wasn't good; but now it is better. If we want to buy groceries, rice and stuff, we buy it in The Village stores. We eat rice vegetables, chicken, duck and meat; we buy that in the market in the next village. We don't each much seafood because we are not used to it. People in Fuzhou eat more seafood because that is what they are used to.... The cooker, the fan, the television, we bought it all in the local provisions shop in The Village.... We don't shop in the city [Fuzhou] except once a year we go to Taijung, which has a lot of garment manufacturers, and we go there to buy clothes. Clothes are expensive. They cost us 200 or 300 Yuan.... I visit friends in this village and in other villages.... Most of the people who live in The Village work in slipper factories. Or they work in strap factories, or other plastics factories here in The Village and villages around. (Sun Yi)

In slippers the couple navigate The Factory and the routine movements of plastic sheet production. Being a Formula Man is a skilled and responsible job, and Sun Chulin has been 'formulating' for six years. His knowledge of formulas, learned from the boss's cousin, lifted him out of the regular factory workforce. It took a year to learn the job, the only job in the factory that takes more than a few days to learn. He says: 'The man who taught me doesn't really run it any more so I am in charge.' Sun Chulin is on call 24 hours a day, sorting out problems and repairing machinery. His is one of only two continuous salaried jobs. The other is Production Manager. Sun Chulin is paid a salary of 3000 RMB a month. Other workers are paid piece rates, their earnings pegged to output, which depends on the volumes of orders and the speed at which they are able to work. Most of the other factory workers, who only have jobs when there are orders, earn between 1500 and 1800 RMB a month. When there are orders, but not otherwise, factory workers are protected by the 'government contract'. This stipulates a minimum wage of 800 RMB a month, which The Factory exceeds in order to compete with other factories in the area. The contract also controls the age of the labour force – there is no evidence of child labour in flip-flop factories – as well as working hours, which must not exceed 50 a week, except on a voluntary basis. Sun Chulin says: 'I like this job. The boss pays us on time and treats us well.... I don't think anything is bad. I am a worker so there isn't anything I would ask for more.'

Working and the rest of life, factory and home, are intimately connected: 'every time we change jobs we change houses' (Sun Chulin). Sun Chulin has had four jobs since moving to this area, only latterly working with his wife, and consequently they have lived in four different houses for approximately two years each. The connection between work and housing is about the proximities that service long work shifts, and maximise disposable income through lower rents or employer-provided housing. Unlike bigger factories, The Factory has no dormitory accommodation, but Sun Chulin and Sun Yi live in one of two makeshift dwellings constructed inside the factory itself 'for convenience. I can attend to the machines' (Sun Chulin). This is not an unusual arrangement. Domestic and workspace are intricately interconnected.

Bigger factories often have purpose-built accommodation, and this is popular with migrant workers who cannot always rely on local kin support and don't have housing-land at their disposal. Purpose-built accommodation is often arranged as double rooms for husband and wife teams, sometimes with space for children. Other kinds comprise single rooms and dormitory accommodation with bunk beds. Kitchens and bathrooms are usually communal. Wage levels account for accommodation, with those factories not providing accommodation paying higher wages to allow for rent. Accommodation outside of the factory rents for around 100 RMB a month for a simple, two-roomed, dwelling. The Factory pays live-out rates to its workforce, providing makeshift accommodation for only two families, who have over time come to form part of the skeleton workforce, retained throughout the cool season when orders are low.

Sun Chulin and Sun Yi's in-factory home is a single-roomed dwelling, built from concrete blocks. It is finished inside with a rough grey concrete skim on the walls, and has a concrete floor. It is located at the back of the production area inside the factory building itself, next to the open side of the factory adjoining the scrap yard. The walls of the house provide a barrier against the factory, as well as storage and hanging space. Sun Chulin's suit hangs on the wall along with woven plastic sacks containing food and other items for everyday use, posters and the adhesive-ghosts of posters-past. Suitcases and boxes provide storage for clothes. A clutter of shoes spill-out from beneath a table made from layered bricks and wood planks. This holds a television, with a radio and tape player on top. The television is positioned to be watched from the bed, which doubles as sofa and as a play area for their 5-year-old son.

Their furniture and fittings are assembled from found objects. Household objects are multi-purpose and cleverly recycled. A dead fluorescent light tube becomes a towel rail. Brightly coloured plastic stools stacked in the corner provide seating for guests. The kitchen area is on the opposite side of the room to the bed. Here, another layer of bricks and wood planks provides shelving for cooking pots in enamel, and buckets and bowls in plastic. A large rusty gas bottle provides the fuel for cooking next to a stand with a gas ring on top. There is no running water. This comes from the bathroom that serves the factory workers, and which Sun Chulin, Sun Yi and the boy must also use for personal hygiene. There is a second small kitchen where they store some of their things, outside the door to their house under a plywood box type building on stilts. This houses their neighbours, the only other family to live inside the factory.

The journeys Sun Chulin and Sun Yi make around their world in flip-flop slippers and leather shoes are small routine journeys. These are movements around the factory, the few yards between the mixer and their living space, the streets around the village for shopping and, once a year, into the nearby city of Fuzhou to buy clothing. Their flip-flops also take them on longer journeys, back to the villages in which each of them was born in Sichuan Province to the west. Villages they each left independently in 1992 to be in Fuzhou near the factories.

It takes 36 hours to get to my village. Thirty-six hours only on a train, then I have to take land transport, a truck or a car, another four hours to the village. I go back for school holidays. There are two school holidays but I only go back for one, for two months. I have a daughter who is 13 and studying in secondary school. My parents are taking care of her. I am not sure if my son will stay here or go back to my village in Sichuan. Depending on the conditions [in which they live and work] we will see where we will send him to school.... I miss Sichuan a lot; that is why I go back every year. My parents and my daughter are there. I don't want to be outside, I want to be in the village. Every time I go back there I don't want to come back here. I will go back for good one day. I don't know when I can do that because when the family run out of money they ask me, and I feel bad. So I don't know when I will go back there.... People from Sichuan work all over China because there are no jobs ... it's not developed; because there is no money there and we have parents to take care of. It's obvious ... this is what we have to do.

Farming doesn't bring us any money, and we have parents, who needed to be fed, and we have living expenses and that's why we came here to work. Sichuan is not one of the developed zones in China so there is not any prospect there. People who farm there plant enough to sustain themselves, but that excludes living expenses such as education and other stocks such as meat, poultry, fish; things that are beyond our planting. The price increases make it hard for us, and then ageing parents, medication and the cost of living. So with our farming self-sustaining method, it doesn't sustain any more, so we have to go out and work to feed us....

My first train ticket [to Fuzhou] was from my parents, through the money they earned from farming. But a friend from my village gave me a place to stay here and when I earned money I gave it back. She helped me get out of Sichuan in the 1990s when Fujian was opening up ... and I found work in a strap factory. (Sun Yi)

Sun Yi's conception of the 'obvious' difference between the rural and the urban-industrial as differential levels of social and economic development generating migration magnets, articulates what China scholars call 'cultures of migration'. By this they mean that migration is widely anticipated as a means of attaining economic and other life goals, as well as a rite of passage for rural youth.[2] Scholars also point out that the capacity for innovation and development in rural areas is not necessarily less than in urban areas. It is, however, circumscribed by cultures of migration, which see out-migration, not local innovation, as a solution to the problem of household incomes out of step with expenditure, as Sun Yi describes. In the centuries preceding the Communist Revolution, rural areas were thriving centres of commodity production and in- as well as out-migration.[3] However, urban residents' incomes today are four times higher than those who live in the countryside, and this differential prompts rural–urban migration. Urban residents also have better health care, education and social welfare benefits. Yet 800 million of China's 1.3 billion people still live in the countryside,[4] sustained by US$30 billion dollars of remittances from urban relatives,[5] Sun Chulin and Sun Yi among them, making their story part of a bigger story.

Rural migrants have also reconfigured the villages surrounding Fuzhou, transforming a once rural village into an industrial village. Early 1990s migrants had the biggest impact of all as they built the factories they would later work in, the roads connecting them and the housing needed to accommodate an expanding industrial workforce. This was Sun Chulin's experience.

I was a construction worker when I first came. Then I worked in a shoe factory; a strap factory was the first one. I worked in a strap factory and I also still did some construction to supplement my income. The construction wasn't paying well so I stopped: I was introduced to this factory by a friend. When I was in the strap factory I was doing the mixing, then the supervisor there came over to this side [factory] and that's why I came too. (Sun Chulin)

Pioneers like Sun Chulin had a hard time too:

Initially when we came here it was bad because people discriminated against people from outside of the province. Now things have improved. We came here as labourers and helped to earn money off this free zone, this free industrial zone that's happening in Fujian, that starts to build the economy. The government, the Ministry of Labour, came in and stood up for us, and it made things better for us, and it's good, because in the past they didn't pay us. They say they cannot pay the [migrant] workers, so we complained to the Ministry of Labour and they came in and stood up for us. [They pointed out that] All these people come from outside of the province to work, they are feeding households back in the village, so they have parents and people to take care of, so they have to be paid.... When we first came [and soon after they were married] we had living expenses so we borrowed money from the boss, just like about 50 RMB, and after we worked the boss didn't pay our wages, the boss wanted to get the money back. Sometimes there was even abuse, like they would hit us. We went to complain to the Labour Ministry. (Sun Yi)

Early migrants improved conditions for later migrants, and they provided the connections which eased others' journeys.

Vulcanising

The production process rolls on. An Qi takes it up after the thin plastic sheets come out of the roller and have been left to cool. She works on a table with an oblong piece of wood, the size of a plastic sheet, and has a wooden handle that looks like a wide paddle. On top of the paddle she carefully places thin sheets of EVA or PE on top of each other. An Qi shows a practised dexterity in assembling the sheets, checking that she has the right number of layers, by weighing them on a handheld scale with metal weights. Flip-flop soles are made in different thicknesses (qualities) and colours according to customer orders, and it is An Qi who assembles plastic sheets so as to meet these requirements. Today An Qi is assembling soles in dark blue, electric pink and green. She works alone, although she may have an assistant during the 'hot' (busy) season (December to May) when the volume of orders is high. Men do this job too, and gender is less important than speed and accuracy.

Carefully assembled plastic sheets are placed ready for vulcanising. In this cool season An Qi alone does this. The vulcaniser is a machine that melds the thin plastic sheets that An Qi has piled into the required colours and thickness, into a single sheet of plastic, from which 22 or 24 soles, depending on their width, will later be cut. The melding in the vulcaniser uses electricity and steam to make chemical changes through pressure. The vulcaniser is a square machine with metal shelf-like trays approximately at eye level. It combines the piles of thin sheets into one thick sheet at a press of the lever. A temperature gauge on the top must be carefully monitored, as over- and under-heating spoils the plastic. A red curtain is pulled across the vulcanising machine while it is working, to stop the hot sheets of plastic from popping out of the metal trays. An Qi wears thick gloves against the heat. A small electrical fan next to the vulcaniser cools the air, making the work-temperature bearable. Her movements are continuous. She divides her time between layering and vulcanising, each with its own rhythms and movements.

The need to live 'beyond our planting' (Sun Yi) drove An Qi, An Sen and the other rural migrants, to the factories from their home in Jiangxi Province. As a vulcaniser and finishing trimmer as well as fitting in wherever she is needed, An Qi manages to stay in continuous work at The Factory. She makes 1800 RMB a month when vulcanising, and a similar amount, at 5 cents a pair, if she trims fast. An Sen bundles and weighs the scrap EVA and takes it to the recycle plant. He was once a construction worker, but he caught tetanus and now has to do lighter work. An Sen's tetanus prompted An Qi's journey to The Village to nurse him. She arrived to find him too ill to walk and tried to persuade him to return to the village. When he pointed out that if he did their children would have 'nothing to eat', she stayed to take care of him. She now earns the money that funds their children's education. Although China scholars point out that the extra two years' schooling average remittances provide in rural areas have little impact on future earnings, as children anyway follow their parents to the cities, education is still regarded as an investment in the future. Workers' knowledge of the real relationship between education and employment opportunities coexists with the conviction that education transforms the fortunes and opportunities of the young.[6]

An Sen and An Qi's house is a single-roomed box, constructed from plywood. It sits high on stilts inside the factory building, at the far end of the production area, and must be accessed by a ladder. The window is cut out of the plywood wall. It opens onto the main factory production area, the sole source of light and air. Their electricity hook-up and their water come from the factory's supply. They, too, use the communal bathroom, and, preferring not to cook inside, they use the kitchen-nook beneath. Their room is a bed-sitting room. Their mattress is rolled out at night. Their corner sofa is in brown leather and mended with sticky tape. They have the same kind of makeshift furniture as Sun Chulin and Sun Yi, except that they have a wardrobe made from fabric. They also have a small fan and a TV as well as a mobile phone.

At 8pm, with her working day over, An Qi sits on the floor of their bedsit in her pyjamas. Her husband arrives with his brother and sister-in-law, and they strike up a game of cards while they smoke. The noise of factory machinery, now operated by the nightshift, is deafening. They have learned to sleep through it.

The boss built this space here, so as long as we don't have to pay rent it doesn't matter to me where we live: as long as we don't pay rent. The boss said 'Why don't you get your kids here so we can build another room for them?' And I said 'no'. If my family are going to move here they are all going to sleep in this room. I don't want to bother the boss....

The noise of the factory runs 24 hours, all night. When my son visited here, he was here for a month during school holidays, he can't put up with the noise. This allowed him to understand the hardship his mother is going through. He promised me to study hard. Then I said you don't have to come here to stay any more. In the holidays there isn't anybody on the [university] campus and I am not comfortable with the students who are there, because nowadays kids are a bit crazy, a bit badly behaved, so I asked him to come here in the holidays. (An Qi)

With An Sen's brothers, their wives and grown (working) children settled around The Village, An Qi and An Sen have created a version of the family at a distance from Jiangxi, although they return for a week each year to celebrate New Year.

Stamping-out and Moulding

Moving on to the next production process, cooled sheets of thick vulcanised plastic move through the main production area along one of two different routes. The first is at the hands of Fan Yuan, who works in shorts, a t-shirt and flip-flops, with the help of his brother-assistant. Fan Yuan stamps plastic sheets with a sharp, sole-shaped, cutter mounted on a table that makes soles one pair at a time. Sheets of uncut plastic lie in a pile and each is, in turn, placed under the descending sole-shaped cutter. Using a wheel to position and lower the cutter onto the plastic, Fan Yuan operates a foot-pedal that forces the cutter through the sheet, using his hands to manipulate the plastic into exactly the right place. Moving the sheet along, he brings the cutter down on the next pair. When 22 or 24 soles have been cut, the latticed plastic sheet is discarded for recycling. Fan Yuan's assistant ties the soles into bundles ready for shipping or strap attachment, depending on the degree of finishing required. Foot and hand coordination are the skills required in this part of the production. Cutting with minimal waste of plastic and getting the right number of pairs from a sheet, demand spatial skills and split-second timing, as well as the speed required to keep production volumes on target. Cutters come in all sizes and shapes. When fashion dictates a new shape, or a shift into children's sizes, a new cutter is made by a mould-caster if the factory does not have the appropriate mould in the store.

The second process involves sheet moulding. Plastic sheets are placed on the shelves of a machine and a row of moulds descends simultaneously onto the sheet of plastic, deeply indenting it in the shape of eleven or twelve pairs of flip-flop soles. Zhang Li operates this machine wearing thick gloves against the heat. Soles can have any pattern pressed into their top and bottom from the metal moulds, just as they can be any colour by adding pigments to the mixer. More high-tech than cutting, sheet moulding produces eleven or twelve pairs of flip-flops simultaneously. They are then cut from the indented sheet with a blade. Zhang Li is adept at timing and handling hot metal and plastic, which must be listed among the skills with which she navigates the journeys composing her life.

Cutting, Making Straps and Packing

The production process moves on once more bringing Tian Gang back into the frame. He does the cutting following sheet moulding, his wrist moving swiftly in a figure of eight, as his knife blade separates one flip-flop sole from the next. The remaining sheet, with sole-shapes cut out of it, falls to the floor beneath the cutting table from where it, too, is bundled for recycling. Tian Gang says: 'I cannot take up a pen: I can only hold a knife.' After cutting, the fine finishing-trim involves two or three women, who sit in the outer part of the factory used for packing and shipping, working with small hooked knives and wax for sealing any splits in the edges of the sole. They chat while they work. This is the only place in the factory where conversation is possible above the noise. Their work, like Tian Gang's, takes fine motor-skills, dexterity and good eyesight.

Bundles of flip-flops from both stamping-out and moulding are sent to the upstairs area for strap attachment, unless they are being shipped partially finished for customer completion. Women attach straps using foot-pedal operated machines, to punch holes in the sole through which the strap is fixed. Most factories buy their straps from specialist factories, although some of the bigger factories have their own strap production facilities. This involves a more advanced technology called injection moulding, in which hot plastics are forced under pressure into multiple

V-shaped moulds. Straps add further variation in design, as they come in different shapes, colours and materials, with PVC, fabric and beading adding distinctive finishes. The flip-flops are then packed in the large white woven plastic sacks in which they enter the haulage system. Sometimes they are first packed into individual plastic bags. An adjacent world of plastic packaging operates from neighbouring factories.

A third method of making flip-flops involves the injection-moulding technologies that make straps, in which plastic granules, EVA and PVC, and other chemicals are fed into a machine at high heat and pressure, as liquids. When the plastic cools it takes the shape of the mould, and a complete pair of flip-flop soles emerges ready for trimming. This makes more expensive flip-flops and has the flexibility to swing production into boots and clogs, using different moulds. This method uses fewer workers and more machinery. Injection moulding is the technology of higher profit margins and factory growth. The Factory doesn't have it and this limits its future.

How Many People Does it Take to Make a Pair of Flip-flops?

The world's simplest and cheapest shoe is made through ten different production processes. These are weighing and mixing, rolling, weighing and assembling the plastic sheets to the correct thickness, vulcanising, stamping or mould pressing, trimming, strap attachment, bundling and packaging into sacks, shifting the sacks to the yard for trucking, and clearing up scrap. It takes a minimum of 12, or more usually, 16 to 20 people to produce a single pair of flip-flops. These include the 'Formula Man' and the 'Production Manager', who manages production targets and calculates the output of each production unit. Workers' output and reward involve units of collaboration, like Sun Chulin and Sun Yi who work the mixer, and Fan Yuan and his brother who work the cutter. The reward structure pays by the piece, rewarding production speed at the required quality, except for the Production Manager and the Formula Man, who are salaried. This calculation of personnel and production processes excludes the work of the factory owner (and wife) in taking orders, securing raw materials and negotiating delivery and distribution. It excludes the ancillary trades in machine and mould making. Adding these it takes more than 20 people to make a pair of flip-flops.

Some parts of the production process are gendered, others are less so, and flexible attitudes prevail. If someone shows that they can do the job it is theirs. Alongside this flexibility are more entrenched images of male and female labour. Men generally do 'dangerous' work, involving high temperatures and sharp instruments, with wives enlisted as assistants, as we saw. When women tackle dangerous work, men often help them. Women generally do the 'easier' work demanding dexterity. Flexible gendering is combined with ideas about family and work with couples, and sometimes their grown children, working as production teams, a concept bequeathed by earlier regimes of collective working. Workers are ideally young (20 to 40), but not too young. Families are preferred to single young men by factory owners because their obligations make them more reliable. A worker is as 'good' as his or her output, calculated by production managers and factory bosses in time and quality. Family and friendship networks frequently source new workers, hired on a trial basis, while the quality and quantity of their output in comparison to the rest of the factory workforce is assessed. Packing and cleaning are largely women's jobs, but men do them too. Men do most of the cutting. Men own most of the factories and wives work in the office in support roles. But there are flip-flop factories, and large ones too, owned and run by women, usually women whose husbands who have connections with officials, as we saw earlier along the trail.

Flexibility lies at the core of flip-flop production. This involves flexibility between different parts of the production process, with workers mastering a number of different processes. Other kinds of flexibility are important too. Few workers in this industry have stable jobs, apart from the skilled and trusted. Instead, workers arrive to fill orders. Large orders draw in workers and generate continuous shift production. Factories operate continuous 24-hour production with a swollen workforce when demand is high and minimal production with a skeleton workforce when it is low. No orders, no work. Workers migrate between the factories clustered in the area, in order to secure more continuous, if still precarious, employment. As one factory owner put it: 'They are living in houses nearby, if you need more workers you can call them to come and the pay is according to the pieces.... Workers keep moving.' Their mobility, in small circular journeys around the area, keeps them fed. Thus flip-flop production relies on a locally available labour force with a range of navigational skills, including the skill of surviving on discontinuous work and fluctuating wages. Managing everyday life on these terms involves skills beyond those demonstrated in factory production, in living with insecurity and getting by in precarious circumstances, with the farm back in the village filling in during lean times.

Flip-flop production is as mobile as its labour force. The dynamics that brought production to China from Taiwan and elsewhere will soon shift it onwards to cheaper production centres in other countries.

At 7pm the day shift replaces the night shift and production passes to different hands, mobilised by different feet, providing a fragile social architecture for another group of lives. Tian Gang picks up his enamel tea flask and collects his bicycle from the packing and trimming area. He wheels it into the front-yard, past the office where the boss and his wife are still working, and out through the high metal factory gate onto the road and back through the village, reversing his morning journey. As night falls and the moon rises, the yellow streetlights cast a ghostly light over The Factory. The streets vibrate with all forms of movement signalling the end, and the beginning, of the cycles of continuous flip-flop production; workers move in and out of the factories as thousands of journeys cross-cut The Village.

Dai Wei's contacts with bosses brokered my access to The Factory. I was allowed to spend several days there, with Singapore artist and photographer Michael Tan, who roamed the factory with his lens. For my part, I interviewed workers and made notes and drawings. Interviews with workers had to be fitted into the rhythms of flip-flop making. Consequently they were fragmented. Michael translated my questions into Chinese and their answers into English. After several days, during which the boss was mostly absent, he returned and asked us to leave the factory immediately. He said that we were interrupting production. He expressed concern that our detailed drawings, photographs and notes, could be used to set up a flip-flop factory of our own. Workers had begun to question what we would do with the information they had provided. They expressed anxieties about losing their jobs, and the potential for trouble with officials. We left immediately, upset that we had caused this kind of consternation. Sitting outside of the factory, possibly looking somewhat forlorn as the day shift left, we were invited into the homes of some of the workers, who seemed happy to continue to speak to us privately. Leaving me un-chaperoned in the village also caused Dai Wei some anxiety, only partly assuaged by Michael's arrival. He felt responsible for me because he was (he felt) sponsoring my stay in collaborating with the research. He cross-examined me on Michael's Chinese credentials. Michael's family migrated to Singapore from Fujian, and he had often, as a child, visited his grandmother here. Only partly reassured, Dai Wei would check on me every evening as I returned to the hotel. Of course, he risked trouble with officials himself in helping with the research and, although he and his family were kind and generous in spending time with me, he was relieved when I returned to London. We stay in touch. His business is thriving and he now travels all over the world.

7
Logistics, Borderlands and Uncertain Landings

The flip-flops made in the The Factory are bundled in white woven plastic sacks,[1] and packed into large metal containers. These have the names of shipping companies on them and they stand outside of the factories while they are filled with flip-flops. From here – a major junction on the trail – flip-flops move in all directions. They move east to Australasia, south to Singapore and Japan, westward to many landing points on the African continent, and still further west to the US, Canada and South America, as well as north to Europe and Scandinavia. Flip-flops quietly connect Fuzhou with the world. These trails write their own stories. They narrate journeys in containers, on ships and on feet; journeys unfolding lives and landscapes, proffering glimpses of life in Marbella, Dhaka, Medicine Hat, Moscow, Sydney and Singapore.

Staying true to my own rules of the road, intended to bring consistency to an ever expanding matrix of possible routes, meant following the largest volumes of flip-flops. The same logics had led me to Korean petrochemicals and Middle Eastern oil earlier on the trail. The trail forged by the largest volumes of flip-flops passes through the port of Singapore; it then goes west, navigates the Red Sea, and on to the port of Djibouti. Here they are shipped overland to meet a rising demand for cheap shoes in the east African state of Ethiopia.

Ethiopia is a large emerging market for cheap Chinese goods. Conditions here particularly support demand for Chinese flip-flops. Ethiopia has a low GDP and a large population (approximately 84 million). In the absence of other options, large numbers of Ethiopians buy cheap shoes. They are a step up from being barefoot. In Ethiopia flip-flops capture a greater slice of everyday life in being worn on more journeys by more people than in other places where their use, perhaps as a beach accessory, is less frequent and more specific. The social and technical mechanisms, the lives and journeys propelling flip-flops along this route are, of course, specific to it. Other routes would expose different landscapes and lives lived in different circumstances.

Logistics

Flip-flop journeys are organised by the matrices of travel practices covered by the term 'logistics'. As with travel by people, we benefit empirically and analytically from taking object journeys seriously, from unfolding their social and technical substance. Inevitably this is circumscribed by practicality. Flip-flops on the move in trucks and ships pass through the interstitial spaces connecting territories across international borders, like docks, distriparks and bonded warehouses. They briefly become part of the lives of handlers, loaders, port operatives, gantry crane drivers, truck drivers, sailing crews and caterers. The investigation of transit is a large project in its own right and involves particularly inaccessible spaces, placing it beyond the scope of this book. Taking journeys seriously for their specific forms of traction and social textures means acknowledging this, even if investigating these traction-points is ruled out on account of its impracticality.[2]

Logistics articulates the human-technical, material activities of translocal connection. Logistics generates the systems, routes and travel practices transporting objects from place to place. Logistics constitutes globalisation's connective substance: its machines, its transport networks, its timetables and its software. To this list I want to add its feet, its hands and its human energy. Logistics constitutes the technical-human substance glossed as flow in accounts of global mobility.[3] Looking more closely at logistics, it becomes apparent that rather than flowing, objects lurch along, stopping and moving, propelled by systems that roughly coordinate people and machines, moving things along a shifting, untidy, inchoate network of routes and trails. Logistics calculates the human-technical input and the routes by which objects are shifted from production centres to distant markets and lives. Logistics moves objects connecting places. It maps the possible configurations of journeys. In this it composes the social and technical organisation of global movement itself. Logistics has its own geographies, composed in maritime, trucking and other cartographies, fabricated in IT software algorithms and in the technicalities of locomotion. To this conception of logistics I would like to add the lives and journeys of the locomotion-operatives. For me, logistics is as much about the hands and mobile lives objects pass through, as it is about technicalities of motion.

Ports

Ports feature prominently in the calculations of logistics. Ships deliver large quantities of goods at competitive rates. Calculation of port costs as a percentage of the delivered price of goods, important in transporting low-value and low-margin objects in particular, establishes a matrix of routes. Fast, highly mechanised unloading reduces port and journey times and is crucial in shaping ports. This makes some ports, the routes running through them and the shipping companies who operate them more attractive than others. Calculations such as these constantly reconfigure a shifting matrix of distribution geographies.

Ports appear in different sizes and handling capacities. While ports are all connected to each other, they have quite specific relationships with the national economies in which they are situated. Rotterdam, for example, is a highly significant contributor to the Dutch economy, which in turn supports the port's development with investment. This, in turn, impacts the scale on which the port can operate, and the global networks it can sustain.[4] Ports are increasingly privatised, so deals struck between government structures and hence public investment on the one hand, and commercial interests on the other, are also important in making ports and their scales of operation. Ports are shaped by the influence of their more powerful tenants. Companies like Reebok and Toyota, for example, have bargaining power over charges and other conditions in some ports.

Ports are shaped by their hinterlands in other ways too. Local and national politics, local labour practices, levels and types of social organisation, transport infrastructures, the distance from ports to markets, and the circumstances which prevail on international borders, all impact ports. Ethiopia's import–export logistics are complicated by its landlocked location. Cheaper water transport ends at a distance from key markets. Equally problematic are Ethiopia's relationships with neighbouring states, which have jurisdiction over its closest ports. These are in Eritrea, which was once part of Ethiopia, a circumstance which subsequently engulfed the area in a war of accession between the two states; in Somalia, with which Ethiopia has an equally difficult relationship; and Djibouti. An independent territory surrounded by Somalia, Djibouti operates under the security provided by Ethiopian and African Union troops. Fragile circumstances in Somalia inflect this region. Widely regarded as a failed state run by warlords on land and pirates at sea, Somalia's technical and social infrastructures are poor. These factors inevitably inhere in logistics.

Containerisation

Containers, the large metal boxes in which objects travel, configure port geographies. Containers appeared on the shipping scene more than 50 years ago and have since generated new logistical practices collectively referred to as 'containerisation'. Containerisation has transformed the transportation and handling of cargo. It has increased the scale on which goods can travel. Large, 40-foot containers transport thousands of flip-flops at one (mechanised) handling. Containers make loading and unloading faster, reducing port handling and journey times, and this, in turn, continually recreates port geographies. Just as transport costs are reduced in cramming more flip-flops into a container, so increasing the number of containers on a ship reduces cost too. This reverberates in the size of ships.

The ships that plied the translocal seaways of the eighteenth and nineteenth centuries were small. The new, 'post-panamax' container ships, so-named because their size makes it impossible for them to navigate the Panama Canal, have capacities greater than 4000 TEU (twenty-foot equivalent units of cargo capacity) with some ports planning for 10,000 to 12,000 TEU container ships.[5] Giant container ships require special loading facilities; they need large spaces and giant cranes. Giant cranes speed up unloading and use fewer, more skilled, workers, reducing docking and journey times, and costs.

A minority of ports have the space, the capacity to attract capital investment, and the political support required to upgrade their facilities and enable them to handle giant container ships. This results in ongoing reconfiguration of port geographies. A hub and spokes system of ports both concentrates facilities into mega-hub ports and spreads shipping routes to an extensive network of spokes ports, serving smaller ships. Fuzhou, like other ports on the eastern seaboard of China, is a feeder, or spokes, port. Flip-flops loaded into 20- and 40-foot containers in Fuzhou must first travel on smaller ships and connect with a mother ship in the closest hub. Shanghai and Singapore, the closest hub ports to Fuzhou, are strategic locations on global shipping routes. So the geographies of international shipping are arranged around the logistics of containerisation.

PIL

Dai Wei's logistics service selects the most cost-effective shipping line for the flip-flops he exports. PIL – Pacific International Lines – which sails through Singapore because it is a Singapore-based company, often carries flip-flops from China to global markets. This is no coincidence. The story of PIL is part of the flip-flop story too. In fact PIL has two stories. One is the story of international shipping and the emergence of the current geographies of port concentration and capitalisation. The other is closely tied to developments in China and also provides the substance of the flip-flop story. This is the story of flourishing industrial development and private enterprise in a niche expediently opened by late communism.

PIL was set up in the late 1940s to challenge the British and Dutch colonial monopoly over the China seas. The company and its founder, Y.C. Chang, was part of the historic straits migration circuit between Fujian Province and Singapore. Chang left Xiamen for Singapore in 1937 to find work and escape the war in China.[6] Small trading at that time was complicated by a shortage of ships for transporting goods, and by the colonial monopoly of what shipping there was. Starting with one ship, Chang built his fledgling business by shipping Chinese goods from the big state enterprises to the rest of the world throughout the 1950s and 1960s. He roped in investors and relatives and traded on his personal networks in China.

By the 1970s PIL had stable routes between China and the Persian Gulf, the Red Sea and East Africa. It made these places part of the same world. It established a network of social relationships along its routes. Selecting skilled and experienced ships masters, engineers and crew, it further developed working experience and skills. 'Old hands at shipping know the kind of knowledge I am talking about cannot be learned in one day.'[7] PIL became a global shipping matrix that held its shape as it moved.[8] Deepening its specialisation in China trade, PIL plied African and, in particular, East African routes through the 1970s and 1980s. These remain important today:

> But there is a lot of cargo that we can bring from China to Africa. Africa is a niche area of ours – we cover routes that may not be as profitable but are still in demand.[9]

Djibouti was on an important destination for Chinese goods by the 1970s and 1980s. In no small part because of its position as the Chinese government's shipper of choice, PIL was able to leverage-up to containerisation in the 1980s. Shipping lines unable to do this stayed small and became less profitable.

In the 1990s PIL fully containerised its growing fleet and so established a more extensive transnational network. This was coincident with the end of state-run monopolies and the development of private enterprise, driving Chinese exports all over the world. The same human energy, commercial savvy and *Zeitgeist* that created the flip-flop factories generated the means to distribute their products. The social and political processes producing the zones, the industrial villages and the factories were the same as those driving the expansion and mechanisation of shipping routes and ports. New scales of operation required new kinds of transport and logistics. Globalisation's trade networks grew along with the volumes of goods that must be moved from place to place. They are part of the same logics.

By the 1990s PIL had its own offices in Djibouti. It has now grown into a global network of container ports, feeder ports and inland distriparks. Its distriparks are spread throughout China and provide warehousing, trucking and container depots. PIL Logistics offers consulting, forward-hubbing, warehousing, transport management, vendor hub consolidation and domestic distribution services. It controls the entire logistics chain. PIL's story reveals an interconnected world of Chinese consolidation overseas and factories, however fragile this might in the future prove to be, as newer and bigger operators enter the global moving industry.

Flip-flops leaving The Factory are propelled along these distribution networks. Loaders lift them into containers and truck drivers take them to the port in Fuzhou. Here crane operators load them onto feeder ships, which meet up with mother ships at the Singapore hub. Here, crane operators reload them. At the hub port nearest to their destination, they leave the mother ship, and are reloaded once more onto a feeder ship for the trip to Djibouti. Truck drivers, sailors and dockworkers, whose lives we know little about, propel them on their way. Investigating these lives, composed on the edges and in the connection-points between nation-states, is another project.

A few comments on seafaring must suffice. China has the fourth largest shipping fleet in the world. But it is the second largest supplier of seafarers, who operate the vessels weaving translocal connections. Eighty-five per cent of the world's seafarers are from the global South, with the Philippines as the number one supplier. In an industry which must reduce transportation costs in order to remain competitive, Chinese and Philippine seafarers form a low-cost labour force. Like flip-flop factory workers, seafarers are employed flexibly, on a voyage-by-voyage basis.[10] Investigation of their conditions of employment reveals tensions between crew space and cargo space, concerns over cabin accommodation and on-board facilities, as well as discontent over pay, over sea-lifestyles, over risk and accidents.[11] And so it is with the shifting, itinerant and poorly paid labour force of the high seas that the flip-flops from Fuzhou (made by another itinerant and poorly paid work force) make their way towards Ethiopia.

On the way they encounter new uncertainties. These uncertainties travel beyond the places generating them and have far-reaching implications. Uncertainties so far encountered on the flip-flop trail appear more geographically confined to the locales of their evident production. This is, perhaps, misleading. It might be more accurate to say that, uncertainties encountered so far are magnified locally, while their global resonance is opaque. But translocal journeys sometimes amplify the uncertain and fragile textures of globalisation at a macro-social scale, making them hypervisible. This is the case on the next leg of the flip-flop trail.

Seizure

The Gulf of Aden, which connects the Indian Ocean to the south and the Suez Canal to the north, is one of the world's busiest trade routes. Cargo from China and Southeast Asia, oil from the Middle East and the Fuzhou flip-flops must navigate the Gulf and the forms of seizure which now operate within it. In this zone, the circumstances shaping life on land seek redress on the high seas. Sudden attacks and seizure are commonplace. In the fluid sea territories worked by Somali pirates,[12] ships are captured and cargos and crew are held to ransom. Although piracy has been present off the Somali coast since the late 1990s, it reached a crescendo in 2008, netting an estimated US$30 million in ransom payments,[13] and publicly showing piracy to be a viable and lucrative strategy. Here in the Gulf of Aden, the actuarial calculations of shipping insurance take a new turn, and new rules of global seafaring must be applied. These involve military escorts and private rescue and security services. Seizures reroute cargos, forcing them around the South African Cape and raising shipping costs. The Gulf of Aden has become a zone of intense geopolitical significance impacting the global geographies of transit.

The pirate base in Puntland is considered the perfect environment for this lucrative business.[14] The average ransom in 2008 was estimated in the region of US$2 million. Pirate wealth is conspicuously consumed on land in big cars, houses and multiple wives. It is highly organised, skilled and tightly structured. Pirates are ex-fishermen with expertise in seafaring;

they are ex-militia who served clan warlords; and they are technical experts who run satellite phones, GPS and other technologies of seizure.[15] If the Somali government and the ruling clans are not directly involved, they benefit financially. Reworking the organisation and practices of global shipping routes, pirates use mother ships to increase their range. They seize fishing trawlers to use as staging posts for attacks.[16] Piracy is locally regarded as legitimate. Pirates see themselves as defending Somalia's natural resources, something its government is too weak to do, and ransom payments are regarded as legitimate forms of taxation and reward.[17]

Piracy in this area is now declining following public (state) and private military intervention. Private security, a burgeoning global industry, is having an impact. A company called Protection Vessels International (PVI) Ltd, based in the UK rural idyll of the Cotswolds, non-coincidentally set up in 2008, claims to be 'the world leader in armed maritime security'. Fielding ex-marines in current trouble spots[18] it has succeeded in reducing piracy in this region through private military intervention. New clusters of piracy now trouble other shorelines where life inland is equally precarious. The Niger Delta area, especially around the south-eastern Nigerian city of Port Harcourt, where oil companies and local land rights activists argue about oil and pipe sabotage, has become the leading pirate hotspot. Clusters around Cotonou, Lome and parts of Sierra Leone, as well as around Indonesia and Colombia, have appeared.[19]

Like the systems they raid, pirates are part of a global, shifting, socially and politically generated flexible matrix of *redress*. They are redressing their circumstances as well as the neglect and profiteering of their government and the authorities administering their lives.

The social relationships and the calculations of seizure are not confined to the seas, but extend to the land from which attacks are launched and the spoils consumed. I made two attempts to visit Somaliland (2009 and 2013) and one attempt to visit Djibouti (2013) in order to research this part of the trail. Both failed. The closest I could get involved flying from London to Addis Ababa and renting a car in which to drive to the border town of Dire Dawa on the Ethiopia–Somali border, where I expected to witness the arrival of the flip-flops. On the border, once more travelling with Michael Tan who was taking photographs, we learned that the trail splits. Some of the flip-flops land at the port of Djibouti. They pass through customs and are trucked along the main road to Dire Dawa. But other flip-flops land on the Somaliland coast around Berbera. These cross the Ethiopia border illegally, avoiding customs duties. Both trails end up in the same place, on Ethiopian markets in the border region and in the capital city. This fork in the Somali trail tantalised and eluded me.

By 2013 the situation was worse than in 2009. Djibouti, a tiny territory with a GDP per capita under US$3000, a serious water shortage and little potential for agriculture,[20] erupted into riots following the 2013 elections, coinciding with my planned visit. Guelleh's Union for the Presidential Majority has ruled this one-party state since 1999. But government detention of moderate Islamists from the opposition provoked battles between police and protesters. The opposition claimed that the elections were rigged and in response the government placed the mayor under house arrest.[21] Thousands of US troops are stationed here in the US's only military base in Africa. Djibouti and Ethiopia have been enlisted as allies in the 'war on terror' because they share the region with what some commentators regard as the Somali terrorism incubator. On account of their political sensitivity, these riots were not much reported by the world media, and the UK Foreign and Commonwealth Office (FCO) did not issue a travel warning. My soundings on the ground, however, suggested that this was not a good time to visit Djibouti.

The UK FCO has long advised against all travel to Somalia, counselling UK nationals to leave immediately as 'kidnapping for financial or political gain, motivated by criminality or terrorism, remains a threat throughout Somalia'. Cameron, the UK Prime Minister, described the region as a 'magnet for jihadists'.[22] This warning failed to distinguish the relatively peaceful circumstances of Somaliland, which seceded from Somalia in 1991 and through which the flip-flop trail passes, from those of the rest of the country. A hypersensitivity to terrorism in this region persists. It follows from the attack on an Algerian gas plant (January 2013) and the launch of France's military intervention in its former colony, Mali. This intended to dislodge the breakaway forces in the north, backed by al-Qaeda, who seized control of northern Mali in a military coup in March 2012. Dislodged from Mali, this inchoate mobile network supports local movements and challenges state governments over minority rights, governance and the distribution of resources to broader publics struggling with multiple insecurities in basic living. It has spread over northern and western Africa, armed with weapons used in recent military interventions in Libya and elsewhere.

The borderlands between African states, where governments' authority falters, host these loose, itinerant military forces. Elsewhere in west and east Africa, Islamist groups, which may or may not have al-Qaeda connections, are openly in control. Boko Haram run parts of northern Nigeria from their stronghold in Maiduguri, and Al Shabab openly organise in parts of Somalia.

In respect of these gathering uncertainties and their implied threats to personal security, I modified my travel arrangements. I arranged through contacts with their diplomatic representatives in London, who agreed to issue me with a visa, to follow the flip-flop trail through Somaliland. I would shorten the trip to a few days, thereby reducing the risks. I arranged to fly through Addis straight to the port of Berbera. Here I was to pick up the trail with a driver, police escort and personal security guard, and be driven to the Ethiopia border. But first I had to fill out risk assessment forms at the university. The FCO warning invalidated my travel insurance. At this point my trip was brought to the attention of the vice chancellor, or warden, as he is called at this particular London college. In the lively exchange of views that ensued, he absolutely insisted I cancel the trip. Thus my narrative of the trail through Somaliland relies on secondary sources alone, the only part of the trail, apart from the high seas, which I could not explore directly.

An intrepid foreign correspondent[23] in Somaliland describes camels, sheep, goats and cattle, traded in the inland market town of Hargeisa, being herded by pastoralists, along the road to the port of Berbera. Their fragile circumstances made still more precarious by armed conflict and drought. He goes on to describe the Somaliland port of Berbera as 'stretches of wasteland covered with rubbish and dotted with rubble and ruined buildings, its scruffy vendors, shacks and broiling heat'.[24] The livestock outnumbers Somaliland's 3.8 million people. Once supplying meat to British and Indian troops in the outpost of Aden (now Yemen) when it was a British Protectorate, Somaliland is now the Middle East's butcher, supplying Saudi, Yemen, Egypt and Oman. Meat and remittances sustain the Somaliland economy, along with the UN-funded pirate prison in Hargeisa (built in 2010), which no other jurisdiction wanted.[25]

Somaliland isn't internationally recognised as a state. But Somalia is number one on the failed state index, a multi-dimensional measure of state dysfunction.[26] It is described as a 'collapsed state', and has three sub-zones. These are Somaliland to the north, a coastal territory next to Djibouti stretching along the Gulf of Aden. Puntland in the north-east also runs along the Gulf of Aden and then stretches south, along the Indian Ocean, where it meets the third sub-zone. Although Puntland and Somaliland are technically part of a federation headed by a single transitional government, they operate as semi-autonomous states. The president heading the governing coalition maintains only limited control over his putative territory with the support of African Union and Ethiopian troops. In the third zone, to the south around Mogadishu, Islamic courts, warring clans and warlords hold sway: 'Security institutions remain chronically weak, corrupt and factionalised, practically indistinguishable from clan militias.'[27] The situation here improved throughout 2013. But after 20 years of civil war generating legions of armed, unemployed, young men, Somalis live in conditions of grinding poverty and violence.[28] As one commentator put it, 'Somalia is one of the poorest, most violent, least stable countries anywhere on earth.'[29] Since 9/11 the 'Islamist vision of a political order'[30] that holds sway in the south, combined with its failed state status, has placed Somalia in the forefront of anxieties about terrorism. Through the inaccessibility of Somalia, the flip-flop reveals this epicentre of current global insecurities.

Half of the Somali population currently relies on food aid,[31] the delivery of which is compromised by the land and sea security situation. And yet, as one expert in this region put it, the Somali people somehow manage:

In the face of overwhelming adversity they have created thriving businesses, operating entirely in the informal sector, and hospitals built and maintained with money sent home by the Diaspora.[32]

Piracy and other terrestrial forms of seizure are how Somalis manage in the absence of other opportunities. Ethiopia is deeply embroiled in Somali politics and has an obvious interest in stability on its borders. Eritrea fights a proxy war against Ethiopia in Somalia: a continuation of a 30-year war of liberation. This re-erupted between 1998 and 2000 and may not be over yet. This is a zone of conflict and poverty where postcolonial borders are renegotiated through armed struggle. Yet ordinary life and trade in footwear continue, despite these difficulties.

Fork in the Trail

Across Somali landscapes flip-flops travel to Ethiopia through one of two intertwined transportation and logistics systems. These have far-reaching implications for those transporting, trading and handling them. These are, loosely, 'official' and 'unofficial' systems. Official systems involve unofficial elements just as unofficial systems involve official aspects. Official and unofficial routes, then, are not entirely separate systems of travel and arrival. While the designation 'official' is composed through multiple practices and social relationships, formality and legality define it. Official and unofficial systems are composed of different transport logistics, different geographies, different social and labour practices. They articulate different lives and they carry different scales of risk and reward. Official and unofficial systems become entangled at the beginning and end of the transportation chain, blurring the boundaries between them. It is nevertheless important to untangle key elements in these routes for they compose different social fabrics, lives and opportunities along the trail.

Flip-flops shipped officially by companies like PIL are unloaded in Djibouti. Ethiopian traders, with government-issued import licences, place orders through middlemen like Dai Wei. When flip-flops arrive in Djibouti, import and landing charges, paid through port authorities, apply. The borders of Djibouti connect with Ethiopia, avoiding Somalia. Passing through the inland port of Dire Dawa, where Ethiopian duties are levied, they are driven along the main road to Addis Ababa.

The road from Dire Dawa to Addis Ababa is tarred, with a single track running in each direction and a white line in the centre. Open trucks with people standing in the back, donkeys and mule carts are the main forms of transport. Scooters and rickshaws increase near the towns. So too do the number of people waiting for blue and white buses, taxis and minibuses with slogans like, 'Jesus is the only way to heaven' painted on them. Isuzu and Nissan container trucks pass along the road at high speeds. In towns, like Mieso, Abse Teferi or Adama, container trucks are parked on the roadside while truckers take a break. Roadside mechanics work beside piles of truck tyres. Kiosks selling bananas and provisions line the road as it passes through towns. At Metahara there is a sugar plantation, in other places along the route, different kinds of agriculture come into view. Circular thatched huts with mud walls are interspersed with single-storey concrete block buildings. Routes are full of life and full of commerce. They are not just corridors for transit.

Many people walk along the main road. Sometimes they are barefoot. Some wear moulded plastic or leather sandals with a single strap across the toe. Some wear plastic sandals with latticework tops. Many people wear flip-flops. Journeys on foot magnify the significance of footwear. Cowherds walk with sticks draped across their shoulders, their hands dangling over the stick. Some carry automatic weapons instead of sticks.

Walking is the way most people travel here and the road vibrates with the traffic of multiple activities and journeys. On the outskirts of Addis Ababa, the number of people walking, and waiting at bus stops, increases. The road crosses the railway tracks once more, revealing large groups of people using the line as a pathway. At a road construction site, sunburned Chinese labourers in classic straw pointed hats are busily improving the transport infrastructures of urban Ethiopians.

Unofficial transport systems have their own geographies and logistics. These prioritise secrecy and flexibility, but connect with official systems at various points along the route. Following these trails involves us backtracking along the official trail. Contraband flip-flops (electrical and other goods) that have crossed the Ethiopian border without the payment of import duty, pass through Somalia's less regulated border-points with Ethiopia. These border zones are beyond official regulation, and the boundaries between what is possible and what is impossible shift constantly.

Contraband flip-flops are often moved with the complicity of villagers living in border regions, whose lives are shaped by the possibilities these forms of transit bring. Transit is organised by 'contrabandists', as they refer to themselves, and forms a part of a spectrum of seizure and evasion, sharing the same underlying logics and circumstances as piracy. Unofficial activities are invisible. Contraband is mobilised by mobile phone, it is hidden in the back of cars and under loads carried by donkeys. Researching invisible activities is challenging. Working with what I could see, I slowly learned that seeing is also a matter of knowing. And knowing depends on investigation, which in turn relies on visibility.

Borders and their checkpoints, where contraband is audited, are important in sustaining local lives and livelihoods. Armukala, a small Ethiopian border settlement just outside of Dire Dawa, straddles the border between Ethiopia and Somalia and between officially imported goods and contraband. Although Armukala lies on the main road connecting Djibouti, Dire Dawa and Addis, it is a smuggling, as well as an official, route. It is faster than the back routes crossing the border, which contrabandists sometimes use. Around 20 trucks a day pass through the Armukala checkpoint carrying legally imported goods. Around eight of them are carrying flip-flops. Cars with false plates carrying contraband also pass through the checkpoint at high speeds. A camp has grown up around the checkpoint and people live there in makeshift housing, because it provides opportunities of various kinds.

Abel, the policeman who works this checkpoint, suggests that the authorities sanction the passage of contraband, that there are 'agreements' between the government and the police about what gets through, further complicating the boundaries between what is and is not official. The checkpoint supports parallel systems of regulation too. Abel refers to 'freelance police', which, like the freelance border patrols shadowing official patrols, operate throughout this region. Abel suggests that contraband flip-flops, oil and sugar move freely through this checkpoint, but that their passage depends on the 'political situation' and the relative strength of 'security' at any given time. Navigating checkpoints auditing borders between systems, and between nation-states and their complex, layered authority, demands considerable skill, as we will see.

Because it was impossible for me to trace the contraband flip-flops back along the trail to their Somaliland landing place, I don't know at which point on the trail they cross over and become contraband.[33] They are official when they leave Chinese factories, because the opportunity for tax evasion has not yet arisen. Abash, a contrabandist, whose armed security sits nearby while he tells his story, says: 'We are using the Somaliland ports', implying that contraband operations extend to their shipment from China. Abash implies that some Chinese shippers are prepared to land their shipments on the unregulated coast of Somaliland. He has not met these Chinese traders because his job does not extend that far back along the logistics chain. But he knows Somalis who deal with them. Rahel, an official importer-driver who trades legally through Djibouti says: 'There are Chinese illegal traders who collaborate with the Somalis.' The unofficial logistics chain might stretch back to China, with Somalis operating as middlemen between Chinese shippers and Ethiopian traders.

It is also possible that flip-flops become contraband when they land in Somaliland. This depends on whether Somaliland attempts to control imports or charge duties. If it does and these are evaded, then here begins the zone of unofficial business. If Somaliland makes no attempt to collect import duty, goods landed along its long coastline freely make their way onto the markets of Ethiopia, becoming contraband only when they cross the border.

Either way, contraband flip-flops travel through the big markets in Somaliland around Hargeisa, making them important distribution centres for smuggled Chinese goods of all kinds. From here, contraband flip-flops are shifted to Addis Ababa. Abash is understandably cagey about how they are moved:

There is a market place around the Somaliland border so we buy very cheap. I cannot know (or tell) exactly where it crosses the Ethiopia border. But I know there are Somalis and Ethiopians on this market. So many goods we buy from Somaliland. It's legal. It's a free market. Now there is a security system on the border. Because before we can say there was no security system. The Somalis are free. Nowadays since the war between Ethiopia and Somalia there are soldiers and politicians.

Running the Road

Abash is a clever 30-year-old Ethiopian, smartly dressed in jeans and t-shirt. He has worked in contraband for ten years, learning the trade and progressing within its networks of skill and trust. A male relative – women don't work directly in contraband as it is considered too dangerous – trained him when his father, with whom Abash worked in a small carpentry business, passed away. When his mother died too, he became financially responsible for his family, with only a high school education and no prospects of formal employment. Like carpentry, contraband was a family business, and a logical way for Abash to meet his family obligations. He now funds his sister's economics degree, a pathway he would have liked to follow too. He plans to study economics and become a legal trader when he has earned enough money from contraband to finance it. But legal trade takes 'strong capital', which Abash doesn't have. In place of capital, contrabandists take risks. The penalties are long prison sentences. Abash doesn't specialise in any particular product. He smuggles clothes, electrical goods and different kinds of shoes, including flip-flops. What he smuggles depends on the season and availability. There is high demand for electrical goods at Christmas, and for clothes at Easter and at New Year, which in Ethiopia falls in September.

Abash is in charge of 'security' from the Somali side of the border to Addis. He grew into this important position over many years. He is understandably evasive about the shifting matrix of routes he works. There are 30 cross-border routes around the Ethiopian border town of Jijiga alone, and a similar number around Dire Dawa. The border is made especially porous by the political situation in Somalia. Abash's skill is in reading the strength of security at border and road checkpoints. He does this by gathering intelligence from those in lowly positions at checkpoints and border crossings, people working as janitors and gardeners. These are people who know when the authorities are paying attention and when no one is watching. Timing is crucial in moving contraband. Abash is especially skilled in calculating when to move, and in maintaining an effective network of informants.

> We know the security situation. We know when to bring our goods to Dire Dawa. We check security at the police station and at the checkpoints. Villagers bring them [the contraband]. We arrange for someone to pick the goods up from them at a certain point. Sometimes it is very risky to give the villagers the contraband because some of them are not up to it. When we select them we see their confidence and understanding. It can be very difficult. Sometimes we use a car that cannot be identified instead. It depends on the quantity of goods. If it is small we use a donkey and sometimes we use a camel. Sometimes we use a car and change the number plate of the car so the police can't track it. There are so many ways and routes and they change. Now it is very difficult, very risky. They [contrabandists] are changing routes, shifting between them. They only stay for a while, make a deal and move on. (Abash)

Abash is only responsible for part of the route. Others bring the flip-flops from Somaliland ports to the markets in Hargeisa. Thus contraband logistics are fragmented as well as constantly shifting, factors which increase the security of the trail. Only the 'big boss' in Addis has oversight over the entire contraband logistics chain.

Contraband is important. It forms part of a broader strategy for survival among local people, who counter government interference in their lives by these and other means. An ex-smuggler university student, who quit smuggling when his brother got a job in Chicago and funded his university education instead, reports:

> The tax system and the economic system are not good for the traders so they are blaming the government system. That's why they are strengthening it even. Nowadays some political types are trying to rearrange the economical system so the traders can work. And we can. The supply in the market and the recent elections ... the government said it would improve things. But nothing happened. So now these traders are lying to the government about their income. They like their

income. They hide their revenue. It's the same everywhere.... The system doesn't allow them to live within the system.

[And for the smuggler] It's an easy way to make money. It pays well. So why do I want to waste my time working hard, studying? Unless you have strong capital it is very hard. They inherit from their family, or you have to win the lottery. Strict divisions: the rich, the middle and the bottom. It's very hard to move up. You can move down. There are some people who make money from nothing – the Gurage. They work. They do everything, starting from polishing shoes. They work hard. They are hard people – working very hard.

I was fortunate to meet this former smuggler-turned-student, now studying at the University of Addis Ababa, through my connections there. He agreed to work as a research assistant on this leg of the trail for me. He introduced me to the contrabandists and reassured them about speaking with me. Despite his assurances these meetings in Addis were always tense, often moved at short notice from one place to the next, sometimes abruptly terminated and always supervised by armed security. In some small measure I experienced, if vicariously, the ways in which smugglers operate.

The normative frameworks that legitimate contraband acknowledge a lack of opportunities and the difficulty of securing a living in the face of residual government hostility to private enterprise. The Marxist Derg ran Ethiopia until 1991. Contraband's legitimacy is also rooted in a sense that those in positions of authority attend to their personal requirements at public expense. In this context, the power and regulatory authority of the state, exercised through import duties and other taxes, are widely regarded as legitimate targets for evasion and seizure. Tax evasion is seen as a legitimate protest at the treatment of Ethiopians by their government, although as these things go, levels of corruption in Ethiopia are lower than in other parts of the continent.

Bush, Borders and Getting By

Borders, and the bush land surrounding them, across which flip-flops travel to markets, appear to be marginal, outlying, territory. But they are more than just the terrain crossed by the trail. Bush and borderland have a significant social texture. We already know that border checkpoints shape the lives lived around them. Bush and borderland are not only connected to regional and international markets through the circulations of legal and illicit goods like drugs and arms, as Abash suggests. They are 'the only conceivable frontier of wealth creation in an area that has no viable industrial base … [or] prospects for gainful employment'.[34] Borders generate and route crucial financial and commercial relationships, linking them with cities and making them important to distant urban economies.

Abash delivers cheaper shoes to a population struggling with the costs of living. Legal flip-flops cost 15 birr, while illegal ones are only 10 birr. 'There are different kinds of customers', as one middleman trader puts it, with varying amounts of income available for shoes. The cheapest flip-flops are contraband. They are also the poorest quality. These two factors put them within the reach of more Ethiopians. Eighty per cent of Ethiopians live on less than US$2 a day,[35] and there is an understanding that prices must account for a person's situation.[36] The price of shoes contributes to social differences and, ultimately, to hierarchies. For a large proportion of the Ethiopian population, whether they walk shod or barefoot depends on the passage of contraband through borders. Difficulties in unofficial circulation produce shortages, which raise prices and cancel out the advantages of smuggling for poorer customers. Being shod is a delicate thing. It depends not just on illegal circulations of shoes, but on the deals and bargains that governments of nation-states strike with their citizens. Shoes expose the dealings of states and the operation of cross-border trade. These are not just shoes, or just routes. Both compose and reveal social fabrics in Addis and the borderlands to which the city is connected.

8
Markets

In post-socialist Ethiopia, where strong centralising tendencies prevail, all roads lead to Addis Ababa. And in this capital city, where the ancient and the modern collide, all roads converge on the Mercato. Roads are acknowledgements of journeys; formalised pathways, etched by feet and by wheels. They are both a materialisation of travel, and a testament to its salience. Their very presence announces the significance of the places they connect.

The Mercato is Africa's biggest open market and a place of significance. The arrival of flip-flops initiates a burst of frenetic activity as trucks, piled high, drive slowly through the market, edging a passage through a dense sea of people, who are milling around and passing through. As the trucks shudder to a halt in front of a row of wooden kiosk-shops, they lower their cab-heads forward, as if to take a bow. Un-loaders and shop assistants spring into action. The space between the delivery trucks and the shop fronts is the most kinetic and noisy part of the vortex that is the Mercato. Amidst the heaving and shouting, the walkway is piled high with white plastic sacks. These are quickly bundled into the row of flip-flop shops and stowed behind counters, so that the tiny kiosks, a high wooden counter at the front providing the platform for commercial transaction, are bursting with flip-flops in every colour. Just as they led us through Somaliland and the uncertainties of the Ethiopian-Somali border, so flip-flops lead us on a trail through this city, making it legible as a matrix of commercial-trading activities.

Measuring several square miles, the Mercato is organised into sections by types of goods, and scales and styles of trading. Estimates suggest that the Mercato's central business core supports 13,000 employees, working for over 7000 business entities, including 2500 retail shops, many of which are open stalls and kiosks. It sustains 1500 service businesses and 80 wholesale operations,[1] making it a diverse and important commercial hub. Some of this diversity is registered in its architecture. One- and two-storey buildings, constructed in cement, provide back-office and wholesale space, while wooden-hut-like shops – kiosks – support retail and wholesale operations. A new mall retails specialist Chinese goods. These layers of wood and cement only come into view on Sundays, when the Mercato is less busy. A heaving mass of human fabric in motion dominates at all other times. Less formal and more mobile architectures, consisting of wooden tables and cloth placed on the ground, focus the transactions between customers and traders of lower-value items like fruit, vegetables and flip-flops. Ambulatory forms of commerce prevail too, as traders, sometimes children, circulate the market selling small portable items, like chewing gum and cigarettes, from boxes worn around their necks. Newspapers can be rented for a few cents from a man standing on a corner. The commercial activity of the Mercato is multi-scaled and multi-purpose, registered in fixed and in mobile structures and in bodies.

The exact size of the Mercato is difficult to determine. Its porous, shifting boundary tapers into the city around it, creating a peripheral market zone. This is a zone of small dwellings in cement and wood, supporting low-value commercial activities such as hairdressing, food preparation and tailoring, dominated by women traders. These home-based commercial activities have low start-up costs, they are skill-intensive, and they are embedded in the everyday lives of those who live and work in the same space. The peripheral zone declares a politics of space in which commerce is integrated into domestic life. This involves doing others' laundry, making food for sale, collecting plastic waste and selling small piles of vegetables from the doorstep. Estimates of Mercato commerce exclude these domestically embedded activities. The Mercato simultaneously registers and underestimates Addis's commercial activity. It stands in stark contrast to other, more modern, commercial centres, for example in the Bole area close to the airport. This area supports translocal logistics companies, in addition to contemporary-styled cafés, restaurants, shops and malls.

Flip-flops navigate different scales of trading and grind a lens through which to view the Mercato-matrix. The concepts 'wholesale' and 'retail' differentiate scales of trading, but in practice intersect. Traders discount bundles of flip-flops bought for resale in village kiosks at the same time as they retail them one pair at a time. The Mercato operates as a wholesale distribution centre for the rest of the city and the surrounding villages, as flip-flops move along small back roads, in ever-smaller bundles, into still more remote areas. In this way the Chinese footprint extends deep into the Ethiopian countryside, and into the lives of those who purchase only a single pair of flip-flops once a year.

Goods are both concealed (in the back of kiosk-shops) and displayed in large piles. The market is segmented. Entire streets are dedicated to bright coloured plastic buckets and water carriers – all from China. The same holds for shoes. Different styles have their own areas of the market: leather shoes, ladies fashion shoes, men's shoes, children's shoes and flip-flops constitute the geographies of the market. Fresh produce, hardware and so on are separated and clustered too. Certain streets display electrical goods, others textiles or clothes. The Mercato provides everything from washing machines to groundnuts, making it the shopping centre of choice for the masses. In addition to being divided by types of goods, it is also divided by styles of trading. In some sections prices are fixed by the trader, in others consumers can 'make an offer', as one informant referred to barter. Estimates suggest that as much as 70 per cent of the goods traded in the Mercato are made in China, and a high proportion of these are smuggled. Of course, unofficial activities are not documented in official figures. But the Chinese footprint, in plastics and fabrics, is visibly extensive. Flip-flops sample and reveal activities beyond their strict significance. Everyday life in Addis, and in the rest of Ethiopia too, is fabricated in plastics, which have travelled the forked road from China.

The City in Shoes

The Mercato reveals Addis Ababa in shoes. Shoes in leather and in plastic, in all colours and styles, some following global fashion trends, and others that are more local in their styling; are displayed in heaps, on stalls and in kiosks. Shoes are gendered, with (some) styles, aimed at women, sporting high heels and elaborate decoration. Flat, plastic shoes, like ballet slippers, also worn by women, and described by them as uncomfortably hot, are plenteous. Leather sandals are popular too, judging by their ubiquity. Plastic sandals, with a buckle and a heel strap, which cover the whole foot in a lattice pattern, are also popular. I witnessed these on men and children's feet, navigating the road from Dire Dawa to Addis. Flip-flops, the simplest and cheapest option of all, are there in abundance. Other places will have other shoes, in other styles, in other fabrics and at different prices.

Shoes reveal places and anticipate lives. A pile of shoes is potentially a pile of lives, shoes waiting to be animated in daily activity. What lives are lived from a pair of pink plastic high heels; a pair of flat black plastic ballet slippers; a pair thick-soled leather sandals; a pair of trainers or a pair of flip-flops? What forms of locomotion along the roads of life do these shoes anticipate? Shoes are translocal vectors too. In addition to easing (local and) translocal journeys, Ethiopians and Chinese shoe manufacturers meet, at a distance, through the prism of the object. Decisions about what can be made within a range of price-points and profit margins encounter decisions about what people can and want to wear on the journeys of everyday life, and about what they can, in the circumstances, afford to buy. Chinese shoes ground complex negotiations and decisions that reach far into Ethiopian lives.

Shoes expose household budgets and the negotiations they embed. They expose trade-offs between budget priorities, and between the competing claims of family members on collective resources. They probe the privacies of family life for its unarticulated workings. They reveal what is both socially mediated and intimate at the same time. Shoes reveal individual conceptions of aesthetics and style. They provide a means through which people engage with the imaginative processes in which lives and selves are co-created. Shoes reveal both personal lives and the social practices, including translocal[2] ones, constituting them. Shoes reveal striking differences between places, between people in the same place, and even people in the same household. They provide a visual log of social inequalities and of pragmatic decision-making. They cover the body-part most implicated in everyday journeys.

Converging Routes and Journeys

But we are racing ahead. The flip-flop trail has not yet reached feet. It has just entered the Mercato. At this point, only the shopkeeper knows whether or not they are contraband. Their separate supply chains, interconnecting routes and prices reflecting production costs and risks of the journey, are no longer decipherable. As one informant put it:

> He is telling me because I am not police. If the police come he will say it is a legal one. It is not possible to control this system. The legal one, which is the legal one, which is not? ... It is very hard to differentiate.... The trader is the only one who knows which is the legal one and which is the illegal one. For special customers the more expensive legal ones, for others the contraband ... one-time customers who buy and never come back ... but special customers get the good one, the strong [Ethiopian] one. (Kibralim)[3]

Government inspectors check the Mercato merchandise for contraband annually. But as the day of their arrival is known in advance, they find no flip-flops without official papers. Routes, risks and arrivals, the substance of the journeys erased by commentators who refer to them as the supply chain, translate into prices and qualities serving different types of customers. We will return to this later. This informant's comments provide the first intimation of local competition, and a third route to the market.

The Future is EVA

The third flip-flop route to the Mercato begins on the south-west edge of the city. Along this route travel flip-flops with 'made in Ethiopia' stamped into the soles. This is a badge of quality and addresses the local view that Ethiopian-made flip-flops are more robust, and therefore last longer than Chinese flip-flops, qualities that justify their more expensive price. As the same informant put it:

> This product is a Chinese product.... See the Chinese writing. But this one is an Ethiopian product. It is better.... This [Chinese flip-flop] is flexible but it will break: it is brittle.... It is 10 birr.... This [Ethiopian] one is stronger. The Ethiopian one is 5 birr more expensive.

Des, a neatly dressed 30-year-old Ethiopian shoe factory owner, wearing shiny leather shoes, explains what 'made in Ethiopia' actually means. His journey from market messenger to factory owner shows that the Mercato provides an informal job-training scheme as well as vital connections in the advancement of young men.

> My father was a shoe repairer, leather shoes: [in] a small kiosk. I did it [became a shoe manufacturer] by myself.... Fortunately my [urban] village is near the Mercato. That's why I know people working there as traders. I got the chance to get in. I was given messages to take to the Mercato traders. So that's how I got in. I am a good observer ... I became a salesman ... of flip-flops and plastic shoes. So I was observing so many things....
>
> I was a hard worker. I accumulate money. I deposit money. I opened accounts in different banks. So that money gives me the strength [capital] to open this factory....
>
> So then I started to visit factories, different Ethiopian factories, so I have the opportunity to speak to the experts of these machines.... Some Chinese worked in these factories so I talked with them and they told me that if I hired their expertise I could open a factory. So I did it....

The Chinese are the men who help the Ethiopians. Whenever you go to an Ethiopian factory the Chinese are the ones who install the main machines. They installed my machines. But they did not show me the detailed formula. If the machines break we call the Chinese. They are making money like this.... The Chinese are very hard-working men ... and clever.... That's why they are in this position.... They didn't give us the strong machines. I want to bring [in] the strong machines from China....

Plastic is very hot ... I have a big dream. I want to try new things, new styles, and to establish my organisation ... and compete with the Chinese and so win the market and become a big capitalist: in EVA, because there is higher demand for EVA.... I want my factory in EVA because ... you have to employ so many people to make leather products: there are the salaries of the employees and the manager has to have the skills. This [EVA] machine takes only two or three people to control it.... Plus the income of the Ethiopians: the majority are poor so the demand for EVA is higher than leather....

In Ethiopia there are people who never wore shoes in their lives. So this is a first step, first shoe. So with so little money they will shift to flip-flop [from more expensive if better-quality Ethiopian shoes]. So the next step is EVA.... No shoe then flip-flop ... *natalachana* [Amharic name for flip-flops].

In a production shed the size of a football pitch, three injection-mould machines, the latest Chinese technology for plastic shoe production, Des's workforce can make 4000 pairs of flip-flops in 24 hours. He buys discarded plastic shoes from villagers, who make a few coins by collecting them for resale. This scrap plastic includes flip-flop straps that have 'made in China' printed on them. Scrap and plastic granules are fed into the injection-moulding machine. The ten pairs of flip-flops that come out of the machine simultaneously, ready to be trimmed, are 'made in Ethiopia'. China clearly plays a leading part in making Ethiopian flip-flops. One man minds the machine. Standing next to him, a woman trims and packs them. Just as in China, different moulds are attached to the same machines to make different kinds of shoes as well as flip-flops.

Like the Chinese manufacturers from which he learned the business, Des employs a flexible workforce that expands and contracts with orders. In contrast to this large-scale EVA factory, his small factory-workshop near the Mercato can only make four-dozen pairs of leather shoes in a day. Des says:

> They [Chinese] control the market in EVA.... The Chinese have flexibility and more styles than the Ethiopians.... It is difficult to compete.
>
> Even the product, these EVA shoes are different than the Chinese ones. We use the same formulas but...

The scrap produced by *this* process is not recycled. There are machines that can do that but it is expensive to import them from China. The scrap is given to villagers who use it for fuel on their fires.

Des's story unpacks some of the complexities of working through Chinese technology, knowledge and raw materials. This version of 'made in Ethiopia' means that the flip-flops were made in a factory owned by an Ethiopian using Chinese technology, knowledge and raw materials. In the start-up period, Ethiopian factories were often run by Chinese workers who later handed over to the Ethiopian workforce they had trained.

'Made in Ethiopia' has other meanings too. Flip-flops exported from China as soles and straps to be assembled are also stamped 'made in Ethiopia'. There are forms of joint ownership, collaboration and co-production between Chinese investors or producers and fledgling Ethiopian manufacturers and entrepreneurs, too. These flip-flops are 'made in Ethiopia'. Around the industrial zone where Des's factory stands, Chinese-owned and (sometimes) Chinese-staffed factories make flip-flops. These are 'made in Ethiopia' too because, although they are made by Chinese workers, they are made on Ethiopian soil. The 'made in Ethiopia' tag has multiple meanings. It both marks Ethiopia's coming of age as a global manufacturer of shoes and flip-flops, and assimilates Chinese technical, financial and intellectual support. From Des's story, we might suspect that China exports its industrial vitality in ways that both hinder, and support, interlocking with Ethiopian commercial and industrial enterprise. Is this the story of the Chinese in Africa writ small?

Shoes: Big Issues/Small Places

Flip-flops are a 1990s addition to Ethiopian footwear from China and Kenya. Their popularity built on robust, homemade, sandals made from rubber tyres from the mid twentieth century on. This footwear side-product of motorised transport coexisted with an established leather shoe industry, in which local hides were turned into shoes and sandals in small-scale craft-based production units geared to local needs. Commercial production of leather shoes in Ethiopia dates from the 1930s[4] and was founded by Armenian shoe merchants, whose retail activities nurtured the native shoe makers operating around the Mercato. This resulted in a sizeable cluster of leather shoe manufacture in this part of the city. Historically, and in common with other Africans, Ethiopians made their own footwear from locally available materials when shoes were necessary, or they walked barefoot. Rural life was possible in bare feet in ways that urban life, with its underfoot hazards, was not. Urbanisation generated its own footwear requirements.

Today Chinese shoes compete with domestic production and drain the Ethiopian economy of foreign exchange for a product it can make itself. China is Ethiopia's most important trading partner and Ethiopia's Chinese imports cost it US$291 million in 2004 with US$96 million accounted for by textiles and footwear. Footwear alone cost US$14 million,[5] a figure that includes flip-flops and leather shoes, both of which are also made in Ethiopia. At this – nation-state balance of trade – level it seems that the vitality of Chinese export-led growth fosters competition in which China has a head start. In the first half-decade of the new millennium, Chinese shoe imports caused the Ethiopian shoe industry to downsize and informalise.

An estimated 400–500 informal, home-based, shoe production units resembling the home factories making Chinese flip-flops operate in the informal sector (outside of the taxation system). But instead of starting factories (as in China), home-based production in Ethiopia was a scaling down, rather than a route to larger and more profitable scales of production. Home shoe production uses manual methods, and this limits productivity and profitability. At a larger scale, there are estimated to be 75–100 semi-mechanised units employing 15–20 workers each, producing shoes for city shops and kiosks. At a larger scale still are an estimated 30–40 units of medium-scale production with 30–40 workers each, in better-equipped and more mechanised workshops that can retail in their own shops because their brands are better known. All scales of production are for local consumption not export,[6] and thus do nothing to address adverse terms of trade with China.

While limiting Ethiopia's shoe industry in the early part of the millennium, Chinese production also revitalised it, as Des describes, transforming it from 2004 onwards. Case studies and interviews by other researchers with Addis shoe makers,[7] show that a renewal began as peasant farmers from the commercially minded southern Gurage area served apprenticeships in Addis's shoe factories and then went on to start their own businesses. As fledgling handicraft and micro industries, the start-up costs were low and this opened it to new entrants. Downsizing and informalisation are dynamic processes: a route up to bigger scales of production as well as a route down. It seems that Chinese competition was a temporary setback that has also stimulated Ethiopian success.

Using the 'made in Ethiopia' tag, Ethiopian shoemakers are taking back the domestic market from China, building exports, visiting trade fairs overseas and studying design on the international scene. Ethiopia now exports to Italy, renowned for quality leather shoes, capitalising on its abundant supply of raw materials and skill. This success indicates high levels of entrepreneurial skill in navigating the local scene, making competent decisions about managing personnel, design, costing, marketing and so on,[8] despite the stultifying centralising tendencies of a post-Marxist government of a command economy in transition. The Chinese are skilled competitors, and if Ethiopian producers are outperforming them in some segments of shoe manufacture, despite the structural disadvantages built into the Ethiopian economy, then they are succeeding against the odds.

Ethiopia's long-term relationship with China pre-dates its significance as a market for Chinese exports. Their relationship was consolidated in the global dynamics of the twentieth-century alignment of communism and capitalism, in which China and the Soviet Union provided antagonistic models of communism. China consolidated its connections throughout the African continent in the post-independence period. The Marxist Derg modelled its strategies for the organisation of the peasantry on the Chinese approach.[9] China and Ethiopia developed formal economic and technical cooperation from 1971, but prior to this Ethiopia received soft loans, grants and technical assistance through aid. This relationship transformed along with China's economy, so that China is now a key investor in Ethiopia, as elsewhere in Africa, building roads and bridges and supporting infra-structural projects that are developing Ethiopian trade, easing circulation and boosting industrial growth, in addition to being a significant trading partner. The Chinese footprint in Ethiopia is extensive, historically deep and multi-dimensional.

To put this in its broader context, the Ethiopian shoe industry operates in what is still a precarious, centralised and overwhelmingly agricultural economy. As late as 2006, half of Ethiopia's GDP, 80 per cent of its (formal) employment and 60 per cent of its (formal) exports came from agriculture, with coffee its most profitable export crop. All land is owned by the government and leased.[10] It is slowly developing an enterprise culture in the aftermath of the Derg, who governed Ethiopia between 1974 and 1990. But the private sector is still weak and the government operates monopolies. The growth of mobile phones, for example, is limited by government provision of phone networks, which has sapped the vitality, and hampered the expansion of telecommunications, conditions repeated in other sectors.

This has implications for Ethiopians' lives. The unofficial youth unemployment rate is estimated at 70 per cent.[11] A generation of Ethiopian youth lacks opportunity, as is evident in the impetus to smuggling and other semi-illicit activities in the borderlands and urban hinterlands. Despite being an agricultural economy, food security remains a challenge. Feeding 80 million people, dealing with a high infant mortality rate,[12] an average life expectancy of under 50 years, and high rates of HIV[13] would challenge any government, particularly in a country where the population increases by 2 million a year.[14] The higher prices of Ethiopian-produced shoes place a heavy burden on low, and precarious, household budgets in a country where 80 per cent of people live on less than US$2 a day.[15] All but the cheaper styles of flip-flops are beyond the means of most Ethiopians. While these lessen the strain on household budgets in the short term, they need replacing more frequently. Such calculations form a part of everyday household spending decisions and, for most Ethiopians, they are balanced against basic needs for food and shelter. In this respect, shoes display local social conditions and the broader, regional, national and international circumstances in which local conditions are produced.

Ethiopia has simultaneously an ancient, timeless feel and a pressing contemporary international significance. Exempted from Africa's colonial domination, except for a brief period of Italian rule (1936–41), it counts time differently from the rest of the world using the Julian, not the Gregorian, calendar which the Christian world adopted in 1582.[16] Consequently it celebrated the millennium in 2007. A poster child for African development on account of its social programmes and efforts at democracy – until the 2005 elections, marred by mass killing in Addis Ababa – it is, as suggested earlier, on the front line in the 'war on terror'. This is because of suspected jihadist operations staged by its Somali neighbours, and because it is known to have collaborated in the CIA programmes of extraordinary rendition,[17] factors which add a sense of urgency to its contemporary significance. Ethiopia is geopolitically significant and is also a significant Chinese trading partner.

Navigating Globalisation from the Kiosk

A shift in scale. In passing through the Mercato, the flip-flop trail passes through Addisu's wholesale kiosk. Addisu is in his mid 40s. He owns a substantial wooden-hut kiosk structure in the core of the Mercato, piled with every available style of flip-flop. His story offers a window onto his life-journeys and the skill it takes to navigate them, allowing us to take a closer look at another dimension in the supply chain's human fabric. He shows that a successful market trader must be skilled in navigating the intersections between the local and the translocal routes along which flip-flops travel. Skills are, of course, always constituted within a matrix of social relationships.[18]

Addisu is a successful second-generation trader. His father made the transition from peasant farmer to trader in traditional Ethiopian clothes, later moving into shoes. Addisu's father was so successful that the business grew too big for him, especially as he grew older, and so Addisu stepped in. Leaving his job as an elementary school biology teacher, Addisu took over the challenges of the flip-flop shop and his father, aged 80, retired to his village 100 km beyond Addis to live on the proceeds of his success. Through his father, Addisu maintains his village-family connections in much the same way as migrant Chinese factory workers, visiting for New Year (12 September) and sending money, so that his father doesn't have to sell the family land. He says of his village connection: 'I am helping their belonging, their attachment, their love.' Such connections transform rural areas too and again support the view that the rural and the urban are not separate domains so much as transitional sites for remaking the other.[19]

Addisu walks to work, a journey of only 25 minutes from his home, where he lives with his wife, also an elementary school teacher. Their house is substantial. It has seven rooms housing five immediate family members, five extended family members and a servant. In his kiosk Addisu employs two (male) carriers for unloading when the trucks arrive and two (male) assistants to help behind the counter. He works from 7am to 7pm six days a week. Market traders divide their work. Mornings are for selling and afternoons are for dealing with the supply side distributing merchants.

Addisu takes a keen interest in the complications, complicities and challenges of the market within, and beyond, the Mercato. He understands the vulnerability of unofficial supply chains, and knows that they produce uncertain quantities of flip-flops at fluctuating prices, although he has no direct knowledge of what happens in the borderlands. More secure and predictable flip-flop supplies are expensive to source and less profitable to resell. Against uncertainties in supply and fluctuating prices, Addisu must estimate demand for a product that is less essential than food, and which varies throughout the year. With only limited storage space, he makes fine judgements about when to buy and stockpile against a mismatch between supply and demand. Dealing with the merchant suppliers is the most difficult part of his job. He says, without wanting to elaborate: 'I have different methods to control the suppliers.' He spreads the risk of short supply and stockpiles from different sources. While this makes it easier for him to meet demand, it also increases the number of suppliers with whom he must conduct what he regards as tricky negotiations.

Addisu sells locally made flip-flops as well as imports. The 'made in Ethiopia' supply is more reliable, but more expensive and less profitable as their price, like so many things in post-socialist Ethiopia, is government-controlled. The difference between the wholesale and retail price is only 50 cents, or half a birr a pair.[20] On a slow day he sells 60 pairs for a profit of only 300 birr and, exceptionally, selling 600 pairs would only make him 3000 birr. Chinese imports, especially contraband, are more profitable. When he can get these, Addisu shifts 200 to 250 one-dozen bundles a day, mostly to small traders operating village kiosks. His profits depend on the wholesale price, which varies. Assuming he makes only 1 birr on each pair and sells 200 bundles a day, he makes 2400 birr, multiples of the profits he makes on locally made flip-flops. His long-distance Chinese trade connects him with the activities of contrabandists he has never met.

This is how Addisu understands the commercial and social grammar of global markets.

> The Ethiopian plastic shoe is better quality but the Chinese shoe is very cheap. The traders are controlling the Chinese product, but … now China is exporting its technology, its machines.… I haven't imagined the Chinese experience. So it is difficult to imagine. There are some Chinese workers working in Ethiopian factories. They are

making money. Business is business … it's globalisation. The market, the market is free, so anyone can share anything, so you are competing with the world. The Chinese or anybody is competing with the world market. But if there is something they are trying to make, to balance the economics we [the Ethiopian government] have to control them. Sometimes they [the Chinese] come and ask me about the products. Is there something that has to be improved? They come to this shop.… Now the world is becoming a small village. Everyone in a village can work in the system of this country. I think some capitalists are making the system because they want to maximise their profits. But the majority, especially in Africa, the Third World countries, the poor countries, cannot make the money.… I am not sure about whether it is right, this system, or not, but for the time being the majority of the poor are mistreated, ejected out from this system.… It is very difficult for the poor to make money because the system is so hard and they can't penetrate the system. So 1000 birr is nothing nowadays. It's very hard to build a business, to make money. (Addisu)

In stocking his shop, Addisu must negotiate with big players in supply chains. He must make finely tuned calculations about risk and certainty, profit margins and demand for different types of flip-flops, based on his assessment of customers' needs and spending patterns. He must decide whether to buy officially imported, contraband or Ethiopian flip-flops. Traders exchange information on importing merchants' pricing and supplies, and they analyse it in order to establish the direction in which things are moving, and, make the calculations and predictions that underpin their commercial strategies on the basis of it. Are prices rising or falling? What is the state of the market? What is the state of the supply chain? What must they pay to secure supplies? How much are their customers willing to pay? What quantities do they need to stock? Assessing the local–global political and commercial present, and predicting the future, requires sophisticated skills and in-depth understanding of how a range of factors, within and beyond supply chains, actually works. With these skills, Addisu navigates the intersections between local and global scales of operation where distant worlds interpenetrate.

Addisu understands the logics of global supply chains. He understands the logics of nation-state regulation, and he grasps the uneven (global) playing field on which Africans must operate. He uses the term 'globalisation', and understands how its macro- and micro-dimensions reverberate through his business. He acknowledges the deep inequalities global markets routed through Ethiopia support. He understands the difficulties posed by Chinese competition, and how this impacts the circumstances of the poor. He says that he is neither rich nor poor, and that his future lies in moving up the supply chain into wholesale, where he expects to exert better control and make bigger profits. He knows that his future lies in his own hands, and beyond, with the merchants and with the system itself. The future is:

> Determined by the political and economic situation and social attitudes, but my plan, my dream is to grow and become a supplier, become the wholesaler controller.... I am researching what wholesalers are doing, the system. It takes money. It depends. There are different types of wholesalers ... big wholesalers, medium wholesalers or a small wholesaler ... you need a minimum amount of money ... (Addisu)

In Addisu's story we glimpse the skills and calculations it takes to shift flip-flops from global logistics chains to consumers' feet. The Mercato, its traders and their calculations, are crucial in these circulations of travelling objects. Flip-flops ground and transform a matrix of fluid geographies across boundaries and inaugurate new routes, on feet. Experts suggest that economic globalisation has stalled throughout Africa, and this weakens the capacity of the formal economy to generate jobs. Half of the population of sub-Saharan Africa live in poverty and, whether globalisation has stalled or not, Africa is linked to global economies in truncated ways.[21] Addisu's account of globalisation suggests that he understands this, and manoeuvres within it to secure private advantage.

Beyond Trading Posts

The Mercato provides Addisu with a complex set of navigational skills, and a particular vantage-point on globalisation. But markets are more than trading posts. Commercial intersection between sellers and buyers (and buyer-sellers) are the most obvious and visible layers of Mercato activity. But the social textures of commerce contain more. AbdouMaliq Simone suggests that 'African cities act as a platform for people to engage in processes and territories elsewhere'.[22] We witnessed in Addisu's calculations, some of the substance of this engagement, in the ways in which markets broker long-distance connections.

Through markets, Africans negotiate with China and the rest of the world. Indeed, some commentators suggest that market transactions are one of the ways in which the global South practises modernity.[23] Flip-flop journeys show some of the concrete practices through which Ethiopians engage with their own modernities, as well as with the modernities of elsewhere, through trading, market circulations and consumption. Ethiopians live on intimate terms with the objects they consume, just as Chinese factory workers live intimately with the same objects in production. In translocal circulation, these intimate proximities become impersonal. Chinese producers and Ethiopian traders never meet. They are connected instead through fleeting proximities with others: with goods handlers in logistics chains, and with interlocutors who broker connections face to face at crucial points along the trail. But these personal connections are few. Not only do Chinese flip-flop makers never meet the Ethiopians who trade and wear what they make, neither is curious about the other, as I discovered on the trail.

Other distant associations circulate the Mercato too. The Ethiopian Diaspora manifests its presence through periodic money-injection. Remittances from Washington, New York, California, the UK, Denmark and Sweden wash through the Mercato, reaching a peak at New Year, when money is sent 'home' in lieu of, or accompanying, family visits. Traders calculate the impact of remittances generating seasonal demand, in stocking decisions. Remittance monies are a more intimate interpenetration of distant worlds. These circulate through the everyday lives of Ethiopians in Europe, Scandinavia and North America, where they are siphoned from the daily expenditure of migrants, refugees and undocumented migrants and sent to family members to spend in the Mercato.

There are other social textures too, which show that the market exceeds its significance as a trading-post. The Mercato is a social hub, channelling local, proximate social ties and activities. People pass time there. It is a place for meeting and exchanging information. It is a place of possibility and opportunity. Lives are made and lived in the Mercato. A child scoops up an abandoned flip-flop lying on the street and wears it on his left foot, walking barefoot with his right, until he can find another to mismatch it with. Gathered flip-flops, paired in contrasting colours, designs and sizes provide children with footwear in the absence of other options. Childhoods are enacted here, later to be translated into the adult world of work and getting by. The Mercato is a place of entertainment. A cinema near its centre shows popular Hindi movies. Local films are a fledgling industry. People eat at hundreds of stalls where street food is cooked. The Mercato is a transport hub: a place of arrivals and departures. Villagers from outlying areas come to trade and to shop. Rural-to-urban migrants arrive, stay or move on. A constant rural exodus increased the population of Addis by 20 per cent between 1997 and 2007, further straining the city's creaking infrastructure.[24]

The Mercato provides job-training schemes as already noted. The flip-flop trail alone provides at least two types of job training. Des's route from errand boy to factory owner was routed through the Mercato. The Mercato provided Abash with an apprenticeship in contraband. Loading, unloading and running errands are routes into other opportunities – at least for boys. The Mercato is a place of opportunity, and social exposure. It channels aspiration and provides social advancement.

Markets are vital in the production and circulation of knowledge, producing opportunity and advantage.[25] Myriad social worlds intersect in urban markets, and move on in unpredictable directions. Information is disseminated and advantage is traded. The Mercato is a motor of urban vitality, a place where lives are elaborated in dialogue with emerging opportunities. Markets are not just, as global supply chain theorists would have it, places where supply chains and consumption intersect. They are crucial sites in making cities and the lives they sustain. This makes them an important focus in unravelling and understanding cities.

The City Beyond

The separation between residential and commercial space which organises cities in the global North, depends on the regulation of urban space through zoning, and through the streaming of production and commercial activity. None of this holds in Addis, with its population estimated at 3.5 million, comprising 78 ethnic groups.[26] In Addis work and life are minimally separated: life is work, and work is life. Commercial activities, largely informal and humble ways of getting by, thus compose the fabric of everyday life in Addis, providing subsistence, in the absence of formal employment, for those who must survive on their own skill, on the opportunities that arise and on the resources available. 'Desperate manoeuvres', 'endless circulation' and 'precariousness' describe the situation of urban Africans, who nonetheless manage to make lives in their cities; and make cities in the process, as platforms on to the world beyond.[27]

An important force in shaping Ethiopian lives, the Mercato also grounds the regulatory ambitions of city planners and the agents of municipal governance. This is no small task. There are 46 (formal and informal) markets in Addis.[28] Establishing markets centralises commerce. But this, in turn, creates further informal diffusion of market activity. Addis's subsidised public transport system is too expensive for its citizens to travel to formal markets. The sprawling of informal markets into all neighbourhoods, a source of income for the poor, is a consequence of the mismatch between public transport costs and incomes. Informal markets complicate commercial regulation for municipal authorities concerned with tax evasion, congestion and the encroachment of trading on road space. These activities beyond the reach of regulators shape the city. The Addis Ababa city authorities have plans to develop a network of formal secondary markets to soak up informal activity. This involves building some new markets that connect with freight terminals, and upgrading existing ones. They also plan to build a bridge and road connections between the Mercato and the new (Chinese-constructed) ring road, relocating storage and manufacturing from the area around the Mercato to the transport hub served by the ring road. The municipal government's aim is a gradual formalisation of trade, focusing informal trade in certain areas of the city to 'establish acceptable levels of informality of trade and production activities'[29] within the bigger structure of municipal governance.

Moving On

Addisu's last sale of the day is a bundle of a dozen flip-flops to a retail kiosk owner called Moapa. Leaving the Mercato with his bundle of flip-flops in a carrier bag, Moapa heads back to his kiosk, and the flip-flop trail moves on. As he walks, the Mercato fades into a densely populated zone of informal commercial activity and low-cost rental housing, occupied by the city's poorer citizens. Here, washing hangs across the street, and oil drums await new purposes as industrial-sized mixing bowls and building material. A woman in her early 40s makes *jeerah* in the main room of her two-roomed house. In a recycled oil drum, she mixes a grain called *tief*, ground into flour, with water, to make the sour pancakes she supplies to hotels and restaurants, feeding her children on the profits. Being an informal wife, she gets no support from the father of her children, who has another family to support. So she makes *jeerah* to make ends meet. There are so many kinds of informality in this city.

This route from the market leads on to the urban village of Tekele Hainmanot, less than a 30-minute walk from the core of the Mercato. It is also known as Gambo Safir, or the Pepsi factory area, so-called on account of the factory's location. The village is a settlement of small, low-rent housing units, made in cement. Moapa's kiosk, selling flip-flops and other household essentials, sits at the junction where the (main) Pepsi Factory Road opens onto the village, forming another junction on the flip-flop trail.

9
Urban Navigation in Flip-flops

Moapa's kiosk is set back, slightly off the Pepsi Factory Road on a stony V-shaped piece of land. The road at this point is at a slightly higher elevation than the surrounding landscape, and so the fabric of poorer residential Addis, in a mosaic of rusting corrugated iron roofs, atop simple concrete dwellings, comes into view and stretches into the distance. The narrow part of the V plunges into the 'village' of Tekele Hainmanot, and runs through it along an unmade road. Despite forming part of a seamless urban landscape, Tekele Hainmanot is a referred to as a village by those who live there, many of whom have migrated from rural villages. Village is a way of thinking about dense patches of residential-commercial urban life such as this. At its widest point next to the road, the V-shaped piece of land is both *of* the village and the way out of it.

Capitalising on the commercial potential of being on the edge of a number of possibilities, of supplying both the villagers and the passing traffic, Moapa's kiosk anchors a small cluster of informal commerce. Alemu, a 30-year-old 'general metal worker', as his business card declares him, repairs passing vehicles as well as other metal objects like door and window frames. He works outside, his equipment stored in a small shed. Sparks fly from his welder, oilcans and other motor-trade paraphernalia is scattered around the stony ground on which he works. Next to Alemu works an elderly man called Kebede, repairing shoes. Considered too old at 60 to continue to work in one of Addis' leather shoe factories, Kebede reworks scrap rubber from tyres and inner tubes as shoe repair materials. He says: 'Most of the time I have Chinese shoes and they are not good quality, but I mend them.' He does not repair *natalachana* (flip-flops). These are, he says, disposable shoes. This micro-cluster of commerce provides a good place for villagers to sit and talk, and a place for children to play. Folk sit on a concrete post lying on its side, or stand around in small groups, or just watch the world pass-by. Loud popular music blares from a tinny radio, mixed with the sound of the welding machine and the traffic.

Consumption Breakdown

Moapa's kiosk is 9 feet deep by 12 feet wide, with an orange plastic awning and metal shutters. It sells groceries, household items and Chinese flip-flops. It opens from seven in the morning until ten o'clock at night, seven days a week, only closing when he goes to the Mercato for new stock.

He says his life is all work: 'I am working for the village.' His busiest time is after 6pm, when people return from work and prepare their evening meals, although there is a steady trickle of unemployed, under-employed and casual workers around during the daytime too. Moapa only recently took over the kiosk, taking a step up into the world of self-employment after many years as a mobile trader. His old job involved driving his employer's truck to different parts of Ethiopia. He risked encounters with road robbers (land-based pirates) and traffic accidents, and rarely saw his family. Saving his wages, he accumulated enough to buy and stock the kiosk. He lives nearby, on the eastern border of the Mercato. His father, aged 73, was a trader too, working only 'half a kilo' away, as Ethiopians refer to distance.[1] Moapa's wife works in the business with him, and cares for their children aged 12, 10, 8 and 4. Comfortable but not well off, they live in a three-roomed house with a kitchen, sharing a communal bathroom with their neighbours.

Moapa retails on the micro-scale villagers require. His most popular items are unroasted coffee beans, grains, sugar, tiny bottles of oil and dried macaroni. He says these are goods which people buy to go with fresh vegetables from the market. They are sold in the tiniest of quantities, neatly folded in newspaper. Instant coffee comes in single-servings. Pre-packaged items – soap, laundry detergent, matches, flip-flops, refrigerated soft drinks, and biscuits – sell more slowly. He sells small luxuries too: nail polish, plastic footballs and sweets. Moapa trades in the gap between the scale on which goods are traded in the Mercato and the small household budgets of the area. He buys in sacks and dozens and breaks these down for those who can only afford a single cigarette or enough coffee beans for one 'coffee ceremony' with their neighbours. Moapa's kiosk links the grander scales of commerce in the Mercato and the people of Tekele Hainmanot, who live precariously on small budgets, and even smaller quantities of groceries.

Zema[2] bought her flip-flops for 10 birr and 50 cents at Moapa's kiosk. After the long journey of their making, their transportation across seas and borderlands, and their journey through the Mercato, flip-flops finally make it onto feet, and the section of the trail that constitutes their consumption. On Zema's feet as she navigates the city, rather than as an object of trading activity, flip-flop journeys on this section of the trail reveal the city in a different way from markets, as will become apparent. What follows is Addis from the vantage-point of Zema's feet.

A Life in Shoes and Three Movements

Zema is a sturdy diminutive widow in her late 60s with sad brown eyes, whose husband had died six months earlier from dysentery. She navigates Addis Ababa in flip-flops her son has repaired with a nail to keep the strap attached to the sole a little longer for her. Her circumstances have turned a disposable shoe into a shoe which must be repaired. Her life is composed in three movements: routine domestic journeys, city journeys and (rural–urban) migration journeys of the past. These journeys are unfolded as she narrates her life in shoes, and in her routine trips around Addis. In addition to her flip-flops, she has only one other pair of shoes. These are flat ballet-styled shoes in black plastic, neatly stitched along one side where they have split.

Journeys Past

Zema's migration from an outlying village to the city reveal shifting personal and political circumstances that echo the stories of her neighbours, who left farming for casual city employment too. Over the last ten years, rural-to-urban migration has increased the population of Addis to 3.5 or 4 million. The estimated 8 per cent annual growth rate[3] weighs heavily on the city's fragile infrastructure, so that the needs of its population for drinking water, electrical power and other basic amenities, remain inadequately met. Leaking water pipes, power cuts and phone service breakdowns are routine. Only one street in ten is paved.[4] As in China, rural and urban living intersects, and circulations between country and city are routine.[5] Zema's journey from the (rural) village where she was born to the (urban) village where she now lives, framed her subsequent journeys. Her migration is set in the time before Chinese plastic shoes – in the time of barefoot – in the late 1940s, when Zema was a child. Barefoot and Ethiopia's brief period of Italian colonisation coincide. The past is gathered, re-collected, into un-numbered sequences that mark time as political time, sequenced by changes in regime, implicitly acknowledging the shaping of people's lives by regimes. Zema says:

> My mother and father were together when the Italians came to conquer Ethiopia. So during that time they got married but I don't have the real information because I am not learned ... [literate] so I don't know how to locate the time. I don't remember if there were Italians in our

village. My father was a priest and a peasant and my mother was the wife of a priest. It was a respectable job. My father grew *teif*.... I came to Addis starting from Emperor Haile Selassie ... because I had a relative in Addis.

When I was in Showat, in the countryside in the northern part of Ethiopia, I walked barefoot, I had no shoes. I got shoes for the first time when I came to Addis and worked in construction. I used to wear this plastic shoe [black ballet slipper] on the construction site. And when I got home I changed into *natalachana* (flip-flops). I came to Addis when I was married. I married when I was 14 years old and I came to Addis when I was 19. When I first came to Addis Ababa I was a housewife. So life became very difficult for me and so I started to work. That was when I worked in construction and wore shoes.... I was working just helping my husband, but ... there was a big storm, which [caused a building site accident and] broke my leg. Because it's men's, boy's work. So then I left that work and worked in the house.

Urban migration, heavy construction work and shoes coincide in Zema's autobiography-in-shoes. Born in 1940, she was 19 in 1959 when she got her first pair of shoes. In 1965, when she was 25, her husband[6] gave her the shoes she prized most of all. She was devastated when they were stolen, a loss she vividly recalls.

When I was 25 my husband gave me some shoes in canvas like you were wearing yesterday [trainers] as a present. But a thief took them when I put them outside the house.... I don't know for certain but after I came to Addis Ababa, after a short period of time I started to wear flip-flops.

It was around 1994 when Chinese flip-flops arrived in Addis, to be incorporated into the journeys of Zema's everyday life.

Zema's daughter, Demaku, born in Addis Ababa, picks up the family story and her own shoe biography:

Before we were 5 years old we had no shoes, we were barefoot. In this [urban] village it was common. Nowadays there is technology so that is why you see children wearing shoes. But when we were 5 years old it was common to be barefoot. Our first shoes were rubber sandals like you can see in the market cut from a tyre...

When we were 10 years old we went to primary school. At that time there were no Ethiopian flip-flops so we were wearing Chinese ones. We don't know exactly where they came from but they came from outside Ethiopia. After that we shifted to black plastic [ballet slipper-styled] shoes.

Zema's son Mihret, a carpenter, develops the story. He can make tyre sandals but doesn't any longer because:

Flip-flop is better than this one because this is very hard to the sole of your foot. It's not comfortable although it is cheaper than the flip-flops. People who wear them are very poor.... The salvage people gave me this. This is casual dress for me. This is fabric. *Farengis* [white people] wear this kind of shoe, it's not Ethiopian.

He proudly displays his shoes, made in modern fabric with a big toe shape and thick rubber bottoms. Shoes display poverty, modernity and more besides. They are important makers and markers of social distinction, as well as a vital tool in navigating the journeys of urban life. The salvage he refers to sells discarded clothing and shoes, shipped from charity stores in the global North, and by this route providing him with the shoes that distinguish him from his neighbours.

Zema says of her current flip-flops:

I usually wear this *natalachana* all day. If the place is near or outside this village, but if I go to far remote areas, I will change into plastic shoes that cover the whole of my feet ... the sun makes it hot.... Because my leg was broken I can't wear this when I go to remote areas. I feel pain in my leg ...

Before this I had another pair [of flip-flops], which went for a long period of time ...

Medical circumstances justify household expenditure on her shoes, and her notion of remote is not far from home. To keep her feet warm, she sometimes wears her flip-flops with thick socks, making it difficult to keep them on. But even with only two choices, shoes must suit the journey, particularly the type of ground and the distance to be covered. It is thus in a pair of flip-flops repaired with a nail, and a pair of black plastic ballet slippers with a neatly sewn tear in the side, that Zema navigates the routine journeys of her everyday life around Addis.

Journeys around Home and Neighbourhood

Movement around her own and neighbours' houses account for most of Zema's journeys. Zema's house has two small dark rooms on the ground floor, a reception room at the front, and a kitchen, also her bedroom, at the back. A room above, accessed by a ladder from the back corner of her bedroom-kitchen, is where one of her sons and two unmarried daughters, each with a young child, sleep. Downstairs, the front part of the house is a lounge with a peeling veneer sideboard and upright chairs. This is a formal place for entertaining guests. Because it is early January – and the Ethiopian Orthodox Christmas is later – there is a Christmas tree with flashing coloured lights, and 'Merry Christmas' in shiny red and gold paper letters brightening the lace curtains, the pale blue painted walls and the tiled floor. A beautiful embroidered cloth covers the precious radio and tape player to protect them from dust. Framed photos of the Virgin Mary and Wayne Rooney, standing next to each other on the sideboard, reveal the family religious and footballing allegiances. Younger members of the household are Manchester United fans. They show detailed knowledge of the club's fortunes, the capacities of individual players, the match scores and the play-strategies.

With no window the backroom is dark. A back door leads from it to a small outside space and lights the room a little when opened. Outside at the back of the house are the toilet and a fire-pit for cooking. This back room contains Zema's bed, her clothes and cooking utensils. The potatoes and onions she sells on her stall outside of her front door are stored under the bed. In a green-painted wooden chest she stores her clothes. She sits in this small room on a stool, over a single gas ring, and prepares family meals. With an enormous knife, she chops onions on a board. The room also has a cupboard where food and kitchen pots are kept. There are yellow plastic containers of oil. Her makeshift domestic arrangements recall those of migrant factory workers in China. She says:

> We eat *shoorah* and *injirah*. Just on holidays we eat meat. I buy those vegetables from the Mercato [and resell what we don't eat]. We eat together. It's not fixed but we eat our breakfast around nine in the morning and we eat lunch at one in the afternoon and our supper at

nine in the evening. Sometimes we skip one of these meals. Two meals are common, morning and evening. Usually we eat bread with tea for breakfast…. It's not good. I don't have a good income or work and I can't eat three times a day. And, as you can see, I have only one room with my children, so that's very difficult. It's hell. It's not the same [life] as other villagers. And if you go out from this village there are people who are very rich, living their lives peacefully and, good economically. So there is a gap.

In this gap sits Zema's business, integral to her domestic arrangements and a source of longer city journeys. Her business consists in small piles of tomatoes, onions and potatoes, placed on a piece of cloth outside of her house. She buys them in the Mercato and resells them to neighbours who can't, or won't, walk there.

If the day is very good and nice I make between 5 and 10 birr profit. We can't say this is profit because I reinvest it in my day-to-day life. I make coffee ceremony and *shoorah* and I make *injirah* so I have not any further money, any additional money to be deposited. Especially if I do not sell the tomatoes in time, I will throw them away…. I have no refrigerator to keep goods for a longer period of time.

Her contribution to the household economy consists in providing some of the meals and her (reciprocal) coffee ceremony arrangements with neighbours. Zema's children are all casually employed; their resources are meagre and irregular, leaving little to extend to Zema. She says:

My daughters work as waitresses in different cafes. And the boys are working as brokers dealing in the Mercato area. So if they have a job it is good. They will get money. They will accumulate it and give it to me. They have occasional work, not everyday work …

Before, I was in charge of the whole thing in this house before my husband passed away. Me and my husband were in charge of it. But now they [her adult children] started to give me some money and I use it to make their food. Sometimes they give me some, but if they don't I have to cover this thing…. If I don't have money they will escape and they will spend their time fasting…. This is why I establish this business … but it is nothing…. I am ashamed to ask them for money because they are young and they need it.

In the words she chooses, and the silences she leaves between them, delicate matters in the circulations of money and food around Zema's household are hinted at, but not fully explained. In paying her for the time she spent with me, I was instructed to be careful not to do so within the sight of family or neighbours, hinting at obligations and complexities she chose not to explain.

Today is a feast day in celebration of the local saint and family and neighbours are gathered in Zema's front room. As this is a special day the coffee ceremony includes bread, ceremonially cut to Orthodox prayers 'In the name of the Father, the Son, the Spirit of God'.[7] Michael and I are included. A heady smell of incense burning and freshly roasted coffee fills the room. The floor is scattered with fragrant leaves and solemn religious music plays on the tape player. Coffee ceremonies are constrained by their cost as they have strong reciprocal elements. They establish, deepen and anchor, social connections demonstrating 'affection' and 'kindness'. Zema can only afford coffee ceremonies on special occasions, and her neighbours are in much the same position. Nigist, one of her neighbours, arrives dressed in her best clothes and greets everybody, her visit the sequel to the coffee ceremony held at her house the week before. Reciprocity is vital in the social economies of connection. Nigist's house is opposite Zema's, and the layout identical. She is a widow too with three daughters and five sons. Most of her sons are casually employed around the Mercato, although one is in prison serving a sentence for burglary. Her youngest daughter is still at school and attends the coffee ceremony in her green school uniform. The coffee ceremony on this day celebrates both the local saint, and Nigist's new fridge freezer, donated by an NGO (non-governmental organisation). This will enable her to sell ice to the village, augmenting what she earns by doing laundry.

The houses in which Zema and Nigist live belong to the local administrative sub-division of the Addis municipal government. They pay 20 birr a month in rent. But this must be paid annually, meaning that the rent must be carefully accumulated, although it is possible to get credit from the municipality if money is tight. The current (national) government retains the former Marxist ownership and regulation of land use. Ironically, this prices most of Addis' citizens out of housing at the same time as it stifles business development, because land cannot be used as security against loans. Large-scale low-cost housing construction to the east of the City, attempts to address the overwhelming problem of homelessness.[8] As both a city and a state, Addis is responsible for education, health care, policing and water supply. The city comprises ten sub-cities, further divided into 100 wards or *kebeles*. Most services are delivered on a municipal or even lower, neighbourhood *kebele*, scale. In this respect the city is decentralised. Municipalities elect their councils, which focus on housing and street cleaning, issues with which they clearly struggle.[9] This forms the administrative framework in which Zema, her family and her neighbours' journeys are cast, providing a significant strand in the social architecture of their lives.

City Journeys

City journeys involve changing shoes. Zema drags the black plastic ballet slippers from under her bed. She is going to the Mercato, a place she describes as 'very sophisticated' and a 'traffic area', both factors that make flip-flops inappropriate and uncomfortable footwear for this, and other journeys of a similar distance. Reflecting on the city journeys composing her life she says:

> It [Mercato] is close to my village but it is not comfortable to me, because it will take off [fall away] from my feet when I walk.... For the Mercato it takes two hours for me. To walk there [is 30 minutes] to come back [30 minutes]. It depends on the roads. If it is comfortable, I go for an hour, more than an hour, if the road is asphalt. It will be comfortable for an hour. It is better for me to walk on asphalt. I don't use a car or a taxi. I move on my foot. But I spend [most of] my time at home. If it is remote I use a bus....
>
> I go to the market and to church. I used to go every morning to church, early in the morning.... I go to ceremonies at the church today because it is a fasting day. The Ethiopian Orthodox Church fasts for two months in order to celebrate this Christmas and New Year. So I am fasting now and I go to church this afternoon at 12 and get home at 2.30. Today is the day of Tekele Hainmanot [the local saint the area is named after, so it is a time for] ... thanking God, giving prayer to God, singing for God.

In her black plastic ballet slippers, Zema navigates, on foot, the 30-minute back route to the Mercato in pursuit of tomatoes, onions and potatoes to sell on her stall. She makes straight for a section of the market that sells only the type of vegetables she needs, and which supports an interactive style of trading (bargaining). She buys 5 kilos of onions and bargains hard for the price she wants. She pays 10 birr. Then she starts negotiating at the potato stall. She stops and moves on to another area where she thinks they might be cheaper. The price is the same, at 2 birr and 30 cents a kilo, and she agrees to buy 5 kilos, slowly selecting the best ones. She checks she has the full 5 kilos from the trader, waits for her change, and rejects some of it, demanding notes in a better condition instead. Zema swings 10 kilos of onions and potatoes in an orange plastic bag onto her shoulder and weaves her way expertly through the crowds, like a fish moving through water. I struggle to keep up with her.

In common with other urban Ethiopians, Zema walks. On occasional journeys across the city, she takes the bus. Only at her husband's funeral did she ride in a car. Seventy per cent of Addis trips are made on foot, especially trips between work and home, some of which involve walking for more than an hour.[10] The mixes of bus and foot journeys depend on distance and cost. The state-owned Anbessa City Bus Service runs 530 buses, on 89 radial routes from three terminals, servicing the city and surrounding area. It shifts 1.2 million people a day round the city, at a flat rate fare fixed by city authorities.[11] Although bus fares are subsidised, subsidies are gradually being reduced in an effort to mix public and private funding and bus fares, as a consequence, are rising to levels many people find unaffordable, something which significantly impacts city circulation. There are 7500 minibuses and set-route taxis in the city, charging four times the bus fare on 106 constantly evolving routes.[12] This post-Derg (1992) transport deregulation is intended to allow small pockets of private enterprise. Private cars, many of them over 15 years old, in disrepair and cast-offs from the Gulf,[13] account for only a small proportion of city journeys. Pedestrians (and donkeys) are significant in the mix of street movement. Bicycles are ruled out by the rough condition of road surfaces. The government's campaign to banish donkeys from cities has been taken to the highways' billboards. Along with a picture of a man driving a laden donkey they bear the message 'How do you use your time?' suggesting that animal transport is antithetical to modern city life and conceptions of time.

The Other City

Zema's home neighbourhood and city journeys reveal the precarities of her life and the skill with which she navigates them; dabbling in petty commerce, and relying on her adult children, who themselves struggle to secure anything resembling continuous employment. Grating against a Marxist legacy,[14] private enterprise has yet to generate sufficient opportunity to sustain urban lives like these. Meanwhile, as Zema shows us, people make lives, somehow making their city work for them. Through informal practices and bricolage, gathering small piles of tomatoes, wearing plastic shoes, urban Africans make lives that are provisional, that exceed the city's ability to provide for them; offering an alternative to seeing African cities as failed[15] and strongly suggesting the resilience of their citizens.

Things are changing in Addis. Another city is slowly emerging, revealing the impact of the estimated 6–7 per cent annual growth of the last decade,[16] reconfiguring the city and, consequently, in small ways, the lives of its citizens. China has provided vital urban infrastructure, like the ring roads in Addis, under construction at the time of my first visit (in 2008), and well used by the time I returned (in 2013). While building roads has increased volumes of motorised traffic, most still navigate their city on foot. The most evident change is the scale of construction in the city, mostly by private developers in upscale detached housing and condos, but also some low-cost rental units built by, or on behalf of, the city authorities. Coffee and pastry shops are springing up all over the city, signalling rising disposable incomes, for some. The city is expanding on its northern and southern peripheries, as suburbs spread into the country.[17] Informal settlements have little protection from developers[18] and, while Tekele Hainmanot is still standing, and everyone is still living and trading in the same place as in my earlier visit, residents believe that this centrally placed piece of city land will be cleared in the near future, as Zema suggests.

> People are saying this area will be demolished … like the other side there are plans soon but we are waiting to hear.… They might give new houses and we will transfer and for those who own the house, if it is not rented by the *kebele*, will get compensation .… I am confident they will never let me out from this place without preparing another for us.… We cannot know [where] but we will be going where they locate us.… For that matter we don't know what they will do, but we will accept. All of my children were born here.… I have lived here … more than 50 years maybe 53 years.… [The neighbourhood] is the same: Everybody is still here.

Most significant in the emergence of the other Addis is the city authorities' ability to collect revenues to spend on improving the urban environment. This is up from 1 billion birr (2002) to 16 billion birr (2012) and these increases, as we will see later along the trail, impact on street cleaning and garbage disposal. Many of the problems of the old city remain. Unemployment is still estimated at 31 per cent, and the monthly income of those with employment is less than US$68. Combined with a high dependency ratio, of three dependants to each earner, life on these wages is a struggle. Around 26 per cent of houses have no toilet, meaning that rivers and ditches are used instead; 35 per cent of solid waste is not collected.[19] In some ways Addis in 2013 is a new city compared to how it was five years earlier. In other ways old problems remain, and the new prosperity is not well distributed. Some of it has trickled down to poorer neighbourhoods: the same simple houses have sprouted satellite dishes and acquired new furniture.

And what of the new Ethiopia? Since Deputy President Desalegn took over following the death of President Meles Zenawi in 2012, there has been no change in regime. Even though Zenawi's obituaries reference the repressiveness of the regime, including recent imprisonment of journalists, and the middle and educated classes' grumbling continues, repression appears to be the price of economic growth and political stability.[20] Meanwhile recent aid totalling £331 million from the UK and US$675 million underscores the enhanced political significance of Ethiopia in distant places. In UK politics, aid to Ethiopia is intended to address the drivers of migration into Europe, as well as an environment in which radicalism and fundamentalism prosper.[21] Both of these factors involve UK security and welfare concerns, and thus unfold another set of (major) global connections. There are others too. Recently, the Ethiopian government arranged with Indian corporations to allow agro-industrial projects in the south. This involved moving 1.5 million people from their land in a country that still relies on agriculture, and which has more than 34 million chronically hungry people.[22] Since 2008, Ethiopia has leased land amounting to the area of France to foreign companies, transactions 'backed by Western hedge and pension funds, speculators and universities'.[23] Alongside its flip-flop back roads, Ethiopia has some pretty impressive global super highways running through it.

Alongside the Addis etched by time, is the other Addis etched in the transformation of space. Near Zema's neighbourhood, is another version of the city her flip-flops do not navigate. Routes not taken are important too. This is the Addis of high-rise office and residential buildings, smart hotels, upscale restaurants, pizzerias and coffee shops. Malls, along with substantial new suburban housing, are sprouting in the Bole area to the south of the city near the international airport. As the diplomatic capital of Africa, Addis houses the headquarters of the African Union and the United Nations Economic Commission for Africa, and this drives demand for more international hotels, luxury resorts, spas and conference centres.

Better Shoes

The new Addis reverberates through people's lives. Returning in 2013 I find that the rough V-shaped area on the Pepsi Factory Road leading into Tekele Hainmanot supports exactly the same characters and commerce as five years earlier. But there are small traces of improvement. Alemu, the welder, is busier on account of the increased volumes of construction in the city, and this part of the Pepsi Factory Road is becoming a centre for the supply of metal construction materials. 'Where's my Arsenal t-shirt?' he asks, as I arrive. Moapa's kiosk is bigger and better stocked than before. Business has been brisk, more traffic passes along the main road, and some of the villagers have a bit more to spend. Kebede, the shoe repairer, is looking more prosperous and has, through rising family circumstances, accumulated the capital to stock dishes, pots and pans for sale. As I walk along the unpaved road in the village I spot Zema's pile of vegetables, still on a piece of cloth outside of her door. While her house looks much the same from the outside, apart from the addition of a satellite dish, the inside is transformed. It is crammed with a large sofa and comfy armchairs all in a tasteful shade of patterned gold, a fridge and TV. The furniture makes it impossible to move around her tiny front room. As she radiates the pride of improving circumstances, we go through her shoes.

She shows me the flat brown leather loafers I bought her five years ago from the market as a 'thank you' for her help with the research. She tells me that these are the shoes she wears to church. She has a similar pair in soft brown suede she says her elder daughter, Demaku, brought her from Beirut. Demaku also gave her pink plastic mule sandals with a large flower on the front, which she originally bought for herself and then didn't want. Zema wears these dainty shoes around the house sometimes. Her younger daughter bought her smart black leather lace-up shoes with a medium height heel from the Mercato. While these look smart and potentially serve more formal occasions, they also hurt her feet, so she rarely wears them. Around the house she wears a pair of old brown plastic sandals with a wide strap across the upper part of the foot that look like the sandals made in Ethiopia. Her life has not expanded, but a greater range of shoes services it. Zema no longer wears flip-flops. She has better shoes.

I track down Demaku. She is on the other side of the Pepsi Factory Road selling coffee from a piece of cloth on a side road. As she roasts the green beans on a metal plate over a small gas burner, then pounds them into a powder in her pestle and mortar and mixes it with hot water in a pot, she tells the story of her recent journeys, of how she navigated the road out of Addis, to Beirut. There are subtle changes in Demaku's appearance. Her dress style – jeans, blouse, track-top and pink plastic mules – is more contemporary. Her hair is cut short and funky with a deep red tint.

A very critical point in family economic situation [2009] led to Beirut: unable to do what you want to do, eat what you want to eat, wear what you want to wear, such things.... The first point is to get out of the country. I have a son and I want to raise him well. The very point that urged me to leave is the wage I get from my work is very small, very minimum, the money is very small, 80 birr a month as a waitress so how can I live with that money? ... It took me so long to save the 2000 and I used my tips.... So it makes me decide to go. While I was working at the café I used to save my money towards my own passport and the money for the agency.... I planned ahead.... After three months it was finalised and I gave him [the man at the agency] 2000 birr.... In total it cost 7000 birr. The agency took two months' salary, 5000 birr, for the transport one way, the visa and the passport.... My son stayed with my mum. It was very difficult but it was the only option that I had. There are lots who went there, as a last option.... It was my last option. I did not use a penny for myself but sent everything to my mum and child. As you saw there was nothing in our home but now we have a TV dish, sofa, electric cooking oven.... The physician advised an operation for this kidney problem. And if I get well without an operation [which she cannot afford] I will definitely go back.... Life has definitely improved since we last spoke.... My son is a very good student. Because I prioritised my mum I didn't send him to a good school, but now is the time to send him to the best school. I collect important books, I have bought everything for him, but sometimes he wants to watch movies rather than read books.... I am strict I push him not to do that.... To keep up his education and achieve more, to go to university and achieve a well-built life.... His name means 'there is nothing that he cannot do'.... It has some sort of freedom for maids getting out of their country that is why I chose to go there [Beirut]; there are other places to be a maid, Kuwait, Jeddah, Yemen, Bahrain, Dubai.... Beirut is cheaper to get to and it has better freedom.... You are free to move around the country you are not restricted to the household so you can spend your free time with your friends. In other countries this is impossible.... The men want to be with Ethiopian girls so this makes a politics between the women and the maid.... Numerous Ethiopian girls are pushed off balconies or have hot water thrown over them ...

Despite having never left the city before, Demaku navigates her way out of Addis and difficult family circumstances. She learns from other women who have made similar journeys, where to go among available options. She learns Arabic on the job. She learns the domestic routines and gender politics of Lebanese family life. She invests her money in 'stepping up my mum's economy', and then returns, intending to leave again in order to secure the future of the next generation. In these navigational skills and calculations, she acts much like a rural migrant worker in China, except that she acts transnationally. Learning the navigational skills appropriate to transnational migration as a domestic worker changes everything. On her return to Addis, she can no longer tolerate working for someone else. She sets up a small coffee business selling 43 cups a day at 3 birr, making her 129 birr minus costs: a considerable step up from the 80 birr a month she earned as a waitress. Impressed, other women have followed her example.

After Feet

Among the gathering fragilities and precarities of the flip-flop trail, here is another. The rising, if limited, tides of prosperity that wash through the city diminish the market for cheap Chinese flip-flops, rerouting the trail to places with denser precarities. The trail still serves Ethiopian families without a woman like Demaku, who is able to lift their circumstances by turning transnational Middle Eastern maid. And so the trail takes different routes through the same neighbourhood. It also runs through new ones. But the trail also, potentially, reroutes more dramatically, developing new geographies: shifting to markets in other countries where circumstances make everyday life still more precarious than it is in Addis. Flip-flop trails are circumstantially routed and mark the large and small precarities they serve with cheap shoes. The fact that the trail no longer passes through Zema's house indicates small, but significant, improvements and the social differentiations, in better shoes, which accompany them. But the trail only recently diverted from Zema's house. It still runs through her neighbourhood and others like it across the city. How does the trail move on from here? And what did Zema do with the flip-flops she was wearing in 2008?

'I throw them away ... in the house dirties ... and when I have money I will go and buy more. There is a skip and the government association takes it away', she says. Had they still been useable she would have sold them to the '*corales*', the men with carts who walk around neighbourhoods, offering to buy things that can be resold in the Mercato. No, the flip-flops were taken across the Pepsi Factory Road with the household rubbish. They were thrown into one of the blue and yellow skips provided by the municipality on a side street away from the traffic. Raised above the road and set back from it, the area around the skips has developed a small, plastic and cardboard, settlement of two or three dwellings: intimation of things to come. Zema tells me that the municipality moves the skips to Gebrekristos, to the city's rubbish dump. The trail moves on and I follow it for the last time, anticipating new plastic and social forms I cannot yet imagine.

10

Rubbish

Following Zema's directions, I take a taxi from Tekele Hainmanot and follow the route taken by the municipality's rubbish trucks, and the flatbed trucks carrying skips full of household rubbish, to the south-west edge of the city. Less than 11 km from the Addis of grand central avenues and four-star hotels, the city tapers. Turning off the main road and driving along an unmade track, following the directions of a local guide enlisted by the taxi driver, we find a small town called Gebrekristos. There is no sign of rubbish beyond the usual scatterings. Walking through the town, speaking with residents, it dawns on me that an unusually large number of people have the characteristic bodily disfigurations of leprosy. A conversation with one of the town's priests confirms that people are drawn here from all over Ethiopia by the famous leprosy hospital and the prospect of treatment. The journeys of medical migrants converge on Gebrekristos. This was another trail. Not the one I was looking for.

I am sure that the flip-flop trail goes to Koshe, the city's giant 50-year-old landfill site only 3 km away, an area, I later discover, that was, in the past, referred to as Gebrekristos. This misunderstanding with Zema is only the latest of the difficulties of translation which were typical of the trail. I struggled with my own navigational skills in reading those of others. More often than not I was lost in translation; or just lost. But I wonder about the associations drawn in Zema's directions, and their elision of discarded objects and people, both, perhaps, perceived as lacking a future. I wonder about the municipal logics in the siting of the leper hospital outside the city and next to the rubbish dump. I wonder if diversion and misunderstanding can sometimes pose useful questions.

My first sight of Koshe is from the highway. It runs alongside it, and away from the road as far as the eye can see: a giant, murky, grey-brown raised area of partially decomposed rubbish, with occasional bright specs of colour. As my hopes rise from having found it, by heart sinks as I try to take it in. The interpreter I have engaged for this mission through my contacts, a junior academic at Addis Ababa University, is not keen on going ahead. Leaving the taxi and crossing the highway by the bridge, I try to absorb the panoramic view afforded by this elevated viewpoint over the highway. This 36 hectare site – shrinking as the city attempts to regulate it – is patrolled from the air by large birds of prey, diving into the rubbish. Motley crews of wild dogs gambolling and snatching at the soft ground patrol it at ground level. Smoke rises in several places, adding a layer of haze to the murky colour scheme. Between the foraging dogs, the smoke, and aerial avian bombardment, some heavy machinery operates. Yellow bulldozers nose the heap and shift and level it; municipal rubbish trucks and flatbed trucks with skips arrive from all over the city and discharge their contents. Between the dogs, the birds and the machines there was something else, something I could only slowly take in: 200–300 people, dressed in the same murky hues as the rubbish dump, backs bent, hooks in hand, were working on its surface.

Feeling queasy I walk towards the end of the bridge. In order to reach the steps and the rubbish, I must walk past three young men using the vantage-point of the bridge for surveillance and information gathering. In an unspoken negotiation I don't understand, they take in my camera, and my shoulder bag containing digital recorders and money, and let me pass. This silent confrontation, between the comforts of my world and the difficulties of theirs, only further develops my anxieties. Descending the steps, I walk to the edge of the site where I am met by the site supervisor and his aides. They want a stamped authorisation of my visit from the relevant municipal department. What looks like a vast area, open to the surrounding countryside, is as closed to me as a Korean petrochemical plant. I turn back and head into the city to secure the relevant authorisation. While the taxi driver had waited, he refused to leave his car.

Rubbish as Social Archive

While I organise the paperwork, brief consideration of how to think about rubbish, garbage, trash or 'the house dirties', as Zema refers to it, frames its social relevance. Rubbish designates the objects, materials and substances that no longer have any use or value. They are separated from the things still in circulation and use, things that still form part of the material fabric of everyday life. Rubbish terminates the intimacies people develop with the objects and materials of their daily life. Because rubbish comprises dirt[1] – which is how Zema speaks of it – it is contained and removed from places where people might interact with it. It is removed from houses, from streets, from the city itself. Removed from human contact. Rubbish is consigned to places beyond sight and consideration, in special containers, in bins and skips, and in special places in the city. Often these are places outside of the city, like Koshe. Rubbish dismisses, it designates worthlessness; it places things beyond consideration. Rubbish need not be reckoned with. It can be ignored; it can be stepped over.

Or can it?[2] In a book called *Rubbish Theory*, rubbish is unfolded for its social significance and provisionally described as transient objects that decline in value.[3] In later consideration rubbish is acknowledged for its potential for re-emergence and re-absorption in everyday life in new forms through recycling.[4] It is described as lively, even in its decay into gases.[5] It is conceptualised as the fulcrum of a global business in waste management.[6] It is acknowledged for providing, in the tag 'rubbish society', a better way of thinking about the societies of the global North than 'consumer societies'.[7] Rubbish is redeemed and re-examined as 'matter unbound',[8] in the valorisation of transformations of material life, and of the people who carry out this work.[9] Rubbish is matter and rubbish matters. And so it is on the flip-flop trail. Rubbish is the end of the trail; it is where the logics of mass consumption and disposability lead. Rubbish is as much part of the trail as the factories in China, the petrochemical plants in Korea and the oil wells in the deserts of Kuwait. All of these places, as we have witnessed, lead to Koshe and the rubbish dumps in other cities all over the world.

One or two observations develop the social character of rubbish in the context of the flip-flop trail a bit further, hinting at its descriptive and analytic potential. The content of rubbish reveals material traces of the journeys composing people's lives. This works at household, neighbourhood and city scales. The content of Zema's rubbish contains the traces of short local journeys: plastic bags she no longer needs for her market trip, the flip-flops, socks beyond repair, all modest items sourced locally and cheaply, and made in China. When she eventually disposes of her furniture it will expose traces of her daughter's journeys between Addis and Beirut. The traces of money accumulated beyond what is locally possible in this household, in this neighbourhood. The contents of the rubbish collected from her neighbourhood in Tekele Hainmanot contains traces of the many journeys that cross it and the material lives these journeys compose.

The same holds for cities. The city dump contains the traces of more, and more diverse, journeys; it is an inventory, of a kind, of the city's material life. Addis in rubbish is not London or Moscow in rubbish. Rubbish provides a, crude and deeply flawed, account of cities, and their social, political and economic contexts. Rubbish displays social, material and income differences. This is particularly evident in circulations of objects and materials between people, and between neighbourhoods, as will become apparent when we take a closer look at Koshe. Some people's rubbish provides other people with the fabric of their everyday life, and, maybe, we shall see, this is the best way to think about Koshe – as a redistribution centre which indexes the differences between life-journeys, refracted through material cultures *at their point of disposal*. This grinds a most particular lens onto the city, but a lens none the less.

Not just the content, the handling of rubbish displays cities too, providing a critical focus on one of the crucial points at which urban informalities are reined in and formalised. How cities deal with their rubbish reveals them. And rubbish is a major challenge for municipal authorities in Addis, as we shall see when we explore some of the tensions of the dump. Addis is only able to collect two-thirds of the rubbish, distributed in collection points all over a city that is fast expanding, leaving the rest to private contractors and the age-old informal dumping practices on streets and in rivers. Thus rubbish provides a visual commentary on urban citizens' behaviour as well as the efficacy of municipal governance. In sum, rubbish exposes social content and fabrics of everyday life, and it exposes social contexts of different scales and social significance. For these reasons it warrants serious consideration. The handling of Addis's rubbish, rather than its content, is the focus of this chapter. Finally, rubbish is the third lens – following flip-flop circulations through market trading and journeys around the city on feet – that the flip-flop trail brings to the city, opening a further vantage-point onto the tangled routes and complexities that make Addis Ababa.

Rubbish Geographies

Getting myself into the rubbish is a story of municipal offices cluttered with old computers, fans, desks, officials and permissions. It is about writing a letter in Amharic explaining what I want to do and why. It is about negotiating an official stamp from the women in the office on the ground floor. It is about waiting until the electricity comes back on and we can Xerox my university ID. It is about listening to officials, who are concerned about my personal safety and the security of my possessions. There are phone calls to the landfill site and arrangements are made. Everybody is charming. I've come from London to take a look at the rubbish. Why? I am following a piece of plastic around the world. Really! First World problems! I go back to Koshe – which means 'dirty' in Amharic – and I hand over the necessary papers to the site supervisor, in his makeshift office, at the roadside of the dump.

Minutes later, I am scrambling after him, out onto the rubbish heap, navigating around the dogs which I fear, and the areas where it is soft underfoot and I sink up to my knees. My stomach is churning with fear and at the smell. My interpreter and I are using Olbas oil to mask the smell. We stop north of the main road, where it is firmer underfoot, in the area where the activity is concentrated. This is the area to which the municipal authorities and the site supervisor direct the trucks to dump their loads. A single white towelling slipper, with the Hilton Hotel logo on it, stands out in the grey-brown mush.

This area is a hive of activity that peaks to a frenetic pace with the arrival of new loads, and then falls away, leaving a more continuous stream of activity at a slower pace, and a legacy of dust and smoke that gets in everyone's eyes. As rubbish trucks turn off the main road onto the edge of the site, a group of five or six young men jump on the back and ride to the dumping area with it. This puts them at an advantage for grabbing the best items as the truck discharges its load onto the tip, but not without risk. The mechanism that crushes the rubbish occasionally catches a young man in its deadly and disfiguring grasp. As the young men jump off with the rubbish and begin picking items that catch the eye, the line of men and women, that has formed along both sides of the truck, spring into action, grabbing items and stashing them in woven plastic sacks. These are held tightly in one hand; in the other a homemade metal hook with a white handle, used to grab and dig into the grey-brown surface of the heap, is held. This hooked instrument earns the pickers – sometimes referred to as scavengers – the name 'scratchers'.[10] The moment of discharge unleashes a tense scramble for the most valuable items; a competition in which masculine physical strength prevails, and young, agile, women put up a good fight. Scratchers then go on searching, or rest until the next truck arrives, or regroup around the bulldozers unearthing new bounty. The social and material relationships of the dump demand skilled navigation.

From the vantage-point of the dump, the scratchers rework the geographies and hierarchies of the city. The tensest flurries of competitive scratching accompany the arrival of trucks from the most affluent areas, with the best rubbish. The Bole area, with its upscale detached housing, mall, hotels and the international airport, sends the most prized items, the cast-offs of affluence, including waste airline food in large green plastic bags, to the dump. Scratchers collect the food discarded by airline passengers for themselves, leaving a large pool of bright green plastic bags, which attracts a herd of goats. Rubbish from the central part of the city, from international hotels, the African Union HQ buildings and the embassies, is similarly sought after, and monopolised by the fittest young men. Scratchers recognise the sources of rubbish from the colours and types of trucks used by the different sub-cities and private contractors. And they recognise the drivers and their helpers, who regularly work the same areas. The discarded traces of the city's more affluent lives, especially foreign residents and visitors, most animate the dump. The rubbish from Tekele Hainmanot, in contrast, does not attract much attention. Rubbish logs social inequalities in cities and provides a minimal redress.

The dump has temporal rhythms. Scratchers know what time the trucks arrive from different parts of the city. From 8am through the morning is the busiest time. The dump is geared to municipal collection and transportation. By 5pm things are dying down as the trucks stop for the night, and the scratching continues with fewer scratchers at a slower pace. Bulldozers moving stuff around and digging into the surface of the dump also provide new scratching opportunities, and a lively crowd gathers around them. Scratching is a 24-hour activity, with people arriving after their working day is over. Night scratchers work throughout the night wearing torches attached to headbands. Scratching it seems is a (stigmatised) way of life as much as a way of getting by.

Within the urban geographies of affluence, materials establish another set of hierarchies. Scratchers search for anything they can use for themselves, or resell. Materials have a value in recycling, providing an afterlife for discarded objects. Metals, including nails, are the most valuable booty, and men dominate this, although a few women have ventured into metals too. Wood has value as firewood. Tourist clothes and shoes can be cashed in at the Mercato salvage section. Some scratchers just come to eat. But plastics are the most ubiquitous material on the dump, and among plastics, water bottles the scratchers refer to as 'highland', after a popular brand of bottled water, dominate, and in this niche women prevail. Scratchers specialise in particular materials, although they will also grab other items should they discover them serendipitously. Specialisms result from advice from experienced scratchers, from serendipity, or from knowledge of shifting recycling prices, gathered at the edge of the dump. Here materials are counted or weighed, and turned into cash, with the agents from factories using recycled materials. A pile of white dusty material arrives from the leather factory. The dogs take up residence. They are ejected by a group of men, who have decided that this is a good place to sit, while waiting for the next truck.

In their working clothes – they scrub up outside of work and look completely different – scratchers are dressed similarly and grimily, making them the same colour as the rubbish heap. Men wear trousers, shirts and tee shirts, baseball caps and sometimes hoodies to protect their heads from the sun. Women wear scarves and baseball caps, skirts, trousers, t-shirts and blouses. Some carry infants on their backs. All wear sturdy shoes, often trainers. The scratching population numbers 200–300, but expands after holidays with casual pickers. More women than men do it by a ratio of about 3 to 1, and, while people in their 20s and 30s predominate, ages range from teens to seniors. Most live in the villages around the dump in simple, rusted, corrugated iron dwellings, sometimes with satellite dishes. Rubbish has provided a source of local employment and subsistence for generations over its 50-year history, and is firmly embedded in local calculations of subsistence and accumulation. About 50 scratchers live in cardboard and plastic makeshift shelters off the edge of the dump, safely away from passing vehicles and next to a pen full of pigs. A woman – a rural migrant from the south who has lived in this makeshift settlement for 15 years – collects plastic carrier bags for recycling. She has an eye condition from living with the dust. The rubbish sustains rural arrivals, for whom it works as a gateway to the city, as well as long-term residents, whose rural routes have settled into the past, making them locals.

Closer examination of three rubbish biographies allows us to dig a bit deeper into the social forms rubbish sustains, and into the calculations undergirding it. This unfolds the significance of rubbish a little further, developing a way of thinking about rubbish and its relationship with the city a little more deeply.

Rubbish as Default

Amsalu, who is 38, began working on the dump 'by default', as he describes it, when he was 13. At that time he was a shepherd minding the family sheep. But a camp of Cubans, working nearby, provided his first scavenging opportunities and he later transferred to the dump, along with his shepherding skills. He says, 'I am a good shepherd. When the garbage arrives I search it.' When more formal opportunities ran through the neighbourhood, Amsalu availed himself of them. The Chinese employed him in the construction of the ring road and, when this was finished, he returned to the dump, his default. The only member of a large subsistence farming family to work the rubbish, Amsalu says he cannot afford to marry and lives with his parents. He was once one of the young men who specialised in metals – cans, stainless steel and wire – earning, he says, up to a 1000 birr a day. But now he is older and Koshe has changed. 'Now we search all day and cannot find anything.' The best rubbish is picked out of (some, unsecured) city collection points, and doesn't make it to the landfill. And, he says, there are many more scratchers. Once confined to locals, rural migrants from the south have increased the scratching population and hence the competition. In a move towards the formalisation of the dump and a hint of its future, the municipality employ him as a guard. He says:

> I get a salary as a guard of the compound. They hired me, and on my off times I can find things. I have a sense of belonging to the things that happen around this place so if something bad happens I will help out with that. Also organising where the trucks will dump things. I have spent 25 years here. The [municipal] government pays me 525 birr a month. I can sell up to 500 or a 1000 in [recycling] in three months. I oversee the machines. I try to normalise things when people are in disputes, as a human and as a senior person here, not as a guard. I speak to the people who can listen and understand me, but lots of people cannot understand me because of the language.
>
> If I get a very serious fight with blood running I will separate them and ask them not to do it again. But if they go beyond my capacity I leave them to do what they want. But often the cause of conflict is a language barrier ... when they communicate with each other they misunderstand. This is the starting point for the conflict most of the time.... Since we have the right to take what we want, we can stand where we like. We don't have a place to stand.... There is no opportunity beyond this for the time being ... so it is better to come here. Even the government don't leave us in peace; because we are jobless they might consider us disobedient guys so they will smash us and put us in prison.

Rubbish sustains long-term connection to this area, and offers subsistence between employment opportunities. Amsalu's story reveals the tensions and violence that erupts, as well as hinting at tensions with, and violence from, the authorities in their dealings with those who live off the dump. Amsalu's connections with the area, and his intimate knowledge of it, is useful to the municipality and he is drawn into the regulatory apparatus that is emerging around the rubbish.

Rubbish as a Platform for Future Journeys

Adina keeps her mobile phone in a plastic bag to keep out the dust; 20 years old, this is her second day at the Koshe dump. She moved here from her home and farming family, who live 180 km away. One of the migrants Amsalu complains of, the rubbish is on her route to elsewhere. A friend from her village supported the navigation of her journey to Koshe. New arrivals, as well as researchers, encounter access problems. She says:

> You have to know someone to work here or it is unthinkable to get the information.... People told me coming here and working has some sort of benefit, so I came. Yesterday I earned 120 birr, so it is good. I want to get abroad to the Arab countries so I am going to collect the money and use it for the visa and the passport.... I have my own passport, but I want a visa, so I came to take care of that. When the visa comes I will have to pay.... [She collects] Water bottles.... Until the visa comes I will be working here because I like it. Today I arrived at 7am. I will go at 6pm.... I think this [plastic] has the best price ... iron has the best price and plastic bags the least. I sell them to the people at the entrance.... I don't know the future. I will go to Dubai and after five years and collecting some money, I will come back. I want to open a shop. We are all doing the same job but we don't have a common understanding. I am a newcomer and most of them speak a different language than I know. I speak Amharic ...

Adina is navigating a route similar to Demeku's by different means. She has first to move to Addis in order to make the longer journey to the Middle East. Rubbish functions as a platform for transnational migration for young women living in villages in the Ethiopian countryside, it seems. Compared with Demaku, who worked as a waitress for 80 birr a month plus tips, Amsalu will fund her visa and passage to the Middle East much more quickly. Average daily earnings from plastic bottles are 100–200 birr a day. Men working in metals make much more. Rubbish is comparatively lucrative, if dirty work.

The Association, Ageing and Rubbish

Bathsheba, who is 54 and has been scratching Koshe rubbish for more than 28 years says:

> I have spent all of my life here. I don't have the opportunity to have another job and I have children so this is my only opportunity. I grew up here in a nearby village and I have always lived here since childhood. I have six children, five boys and a girl. The first is 28, which is when I started scratching.... My husband passed away ten years ago. I am with the Association. I think somehow it has changed. In their spare time people go and scratch. I scratch and by turn I pack bottles and others scratch. The big difference is we still work here but before they gave the wholesalers the bottles but now we sell directly to the factory so there is a big difference in the wages we get. They asked us, so when they asked us I agreed to join. It is very difficult, I have a kidney problem so I can't come here regularly these days, so coming a lot is unthinkable, but I can still get a good year [she refers to income]. I can't differentiate the life I had scratching and now: and things in Ethiopia are economically very difficult with prices going up. I start at 9 in the morning because there is a big fight there and it is very difficult for someone like me to fight so I come later. I finish at 6pm.

Bathsheba describes the difficulties of working the rubbish as an ageing widow. She finds the competition too much, and must combat physical frailty in order to get by. The Association she refers to is an initiative run by an NGO called True Concern for Community Development, which has some connection to the municipal authorities managing rubbish. This, too, is a move towards the formalisation of the rubbish dump and its workforce. Collective and cooperative, rather than competitive and individual practices work for Bathsheba and those in similar circumstances. Five associations have 20 members each and money from the bottles is shared equally, allowing the women to rotate between scratching, and the lighter work of sorting Bathsheba describes. The associations get more money per bottle – 10 birr instead of 3 – by selling directly to factories and cutting out the recycling dealers. Hence, Bathsheba can get by working fewer hours, and without the scrum with the rubbish trucks and bulldozers. The NGO struggled to establish this toehold in the rubbish. Men and boys refused to join, but mothers, anxious to feed their children, were easier converts to collective working. The man at the ministry admits that they need to formalise and incorporate this largely ungovernable population in planning the city's rubbish future. Big changes are coming to Koshe. He says: 'It's a way of life, they are resisting, and our office cannot penetrate them. We run schemes to retrain them ... they are not happy with this programme.'

Tensions and Futures

The ministry and its field agents say that the rubbish dump is a source of dangerous working practices by people who, like the rubbish they sort, are consigned to live beyond the limits of civic life. This places scratchers beyond consideration and out of sight like the rubbish they sort, while worrying about their well-being. The tension between these two positions runs through the ministry. A litany of accidents, deaths and disfigurements as scratchers take risks to recover value, are recited by the site supervisor:

Food comes from some place and a guy is going into the truck and he is injured and they take him to hospital but he died. Also someone else lost their legs in an encounter with a bulldozer. Two months ago a man who jumped in the truck dropped off when it broke. In recent accidents, two were women. The bulldozer operator has a lot to do to push the garbage. If they see something they want when the bulldozer moves the garbage they don't think about their life.

Koshe is also credited with a second source of dangerousness by municipal authorities. This is associated with crime and violence. In this place beyond the city borders, which the city, in spreading southwards has now caught up with, it is easy for criminals, murderers and fugitives from justice to conceal themselves among the rubbish and the scratchers. The dump is popularly associated with robbery and knife crime, making it a no-go area for most city dwellers. In living beyond formal systems of governance, this city suburb of rubbish is more like the Somali borderlands, patrolled by contrabandists and gunrunners, than a part of the city. There is a police station nearby, and policing and the justice system are slowly taking back the dump from a parallel system of authority, a mafia of five 'big men'. The big men regulate matters at the dump in their own way, conflicting with the regulatory efforts of the municipality and frustrating the NGO. They control access by scratchers in exchange for fees, making themselves wealthy in the process. Recently, some of them have been imprisoned, shifting the balance of power towards the authorities.

Incremental efforts by the city authorities in regulating the life-world of rubbish – controlling the dumping areas, setting up formalised cooperative working practices, turning locals into guards, employing a site supervisor, installing gas outlets for methane – anticipate the rubbish futures envisioned for the city. Once far away, a place outside of the city, outside systems of formal employment, taxation, law and municipal governance, Koshe is now on the edge of a city that has grown to meet it in what are fast becoming its upscale southern suburbs. A new development of large detached houses nearby anticipates this future. This incorporates the extended influence of developers, new housing for those in a position to benefit from rising prosperity, and the consequent shrinkage and rehabilitation of the site. These changes have far-reaching consequences in rerouting the scratchers.

According to the ministry, Addis's rubbish future involves setting up new sub-stations in half a dozen city locations, where scratchers can be trained as official sorters and recyclers selling directly to factories. But, given the tensions between the Koshe scratchers and the authorities, the distance from the city and connections settled scratchers have formed with the local area, this plan must envisage recruiting new scratchers, living around the sub-stations. In future, unrecyclable rubbish will be taken to a new landfill site on the north-east edge of the city, further away. Koshe will be fenced and closed. In collaboration with the British company, Cambridge Industries, the site will generate biomass electricity from the historic rubbish pile. The Koshe scratchers will be offered micro-finance, loans with which to start small businesses of their own, launching them on new journeys as entrepreneurs.

Given the recent experience of the NGO in formalising and regulating the scratchers' working practices, the micro-finance initiative is only going to work with women. Working with women – a priority in development projects – on a green initiative such as this, ticks all of the aid agencies' boxes. What about the men? The back-up plan, an official admits, is that 'force will be applied for sure if they don't move on; there are soldiers, but the city government is conscious, if you push them away ... they will be a headache for the city government'. A displaced and disenfranchised group of ex-scratchers, comprising those with criminal connections and a history of violence, this close to the capital? Banditry on the borders is one thing, but on the borders of the city it is another entirely. The municipal authorities are rightly nervous that they may create worse problems with their plan.

And what about the flip-flops in the landfill site in Koshe? Those that have some use left in them will be collected and used, or traded by the scratchers. Through their informal systems of commerce, they will be leveraged into further circuits of consumption. Perhaps they will walk around this area on the edge of the city, embarking on new journeys on other feet. But Zema's flip-flops were already broken and she must be frugal. Her circumstances do not allow her to throw them in the rubbish until there is absolutely no use or value left in them. Her flip-flops will sit in the landfill site, the man at the ministry says, for 100 years, because they are made of plastic, and do not easily decompose. If the municipality's plans for Koshe materialise, they will be turned into electricity, entering new lives in the city in a new form, serving everyday life in new ways. This might be the end of the trail. Or it might not.

11

Globalisation Revisited

What do the stories of the flip-flop trail tell us about globalisation? The flip-flop trail provides an empirical, ground-level account of the landscapes and lives in which people walk along a mesh of mutating translocal back roads. But what is its broader resonance for globalisation theory? Globalisation theorists raise grander and more sweeping lines of enquiry without the restrictions of empirical verification. They ask, what is globalisation? Is it taking new forms? How might the relationship between extended locales and nation-states be conceptualised? These are excellent questions. At least two of them resonate with the trail, as it probes the mutating forms and substance of translocality. The problem, and part of the reason why globalisation analysts talk *across* each other's concerns rather than *to* them, is that globalisation thinking is colonised by particular conceptions of theory.

It is these grand, abstract conceptions of theory that I want to dislodge. Offering instead, more modest and serviceable conceptions, suggesting new ways of thinking about globalisation, which draw on the insights of the trail. This shift in scale involves shifting my own thinking too, from a series of microcosmically small, detailed, empirical encounters, albeit with grander resonance, onto the higher ground of overview reflections. In the pages that remain, I want to revisit globalisation with an overview of the trail, gathering and developing some of the reflections scattered along it, like the pieces of brightly coloured rubbish that stand out from the heap, catching the eyes of the scratchers. This is social theory as scratching.

Theory

The boys on the bridge suggest the benefits of oversight from the vantage-point of higher ground, in their case, oversight of the rubbish dump and its approach roads. The first direction in my tentative, operational, definition of theory, is that theory is about reflection on multiple processes and the connections between them. Oversight of the entire trail, a step up in scales of reflection, proffers a position from which to think more deeply about its directions, its connections, its social fabrics, comparisons between different parts of the trail and, ultimately, the implications of this for how we think about globalisation.

My second direction of travel is that theory, as tentative forms of explanation, is always present, even in our most rudimentary thinking, whether we acknowledge it or not. It is imbricated in the selection, arrangement, investigation and narration of empirical detail. It was always embedded in the trail, as I acknowledged in my introduction. Theory, like photography, selects and frames. It can never be post-empirical; instead it provokes a dialogue between analysis and investigation, between reflection and discovery. Theory is about gathering the insights that come from the unloosening, as Lemert[1] calls it, that close examination entails. Consequently, theory always comes from a particular vantage-point, whether or not this is acknowledged. My version of globalisation is articulated from the flip-flop trail. I don't claim universality for it. I suggest instead that it provides an alternate vantage-point from other analyses, and one from which hitherto unacknowledged features of globalisation enter the frame.

My third direction of travel is that theory does not usefully encompass entire paradigms. Indeed this is impossible in conceptualising globalisation, as a number of scholars have noted in unravelling some of its plurality.[2] Rather than reaching for universals, the scope and ambition of theory should be appropriately modest and serviceable. Vered Amit[3] explores the benefits of mid-range concepts that are 'good to think with', that open up, rather than cap, enquiry, in place of overarching systems of thought. These three directions guide my thinking on theory in offering the journeys composing the flip-flop trail as empirical-analytic vantage-points from which to revisit our understanding of globalisation.

Beyond the Landing Places of Network Value

Globalisation has hitherto been viewed from a limited range of perspectives. The flip-flop trail tilts the angle of conception from the commanding heights of globalisation, from what I have at various points along the trail referred to as 'mainstream globalisation' or the 'global superhighways', to less hegemonic, less sensational, quieter, more mundane streams of global traffic and translocal connection.

Shifting the lens from high finance, media images, fast food chains and other high-profile vectors of global intersection, creates a conceptual space for other versions of globalisation in other places, to take shape. These are not better or more real than the insights of iconic-hegemonic versions, but they do reveal globalisation from different angles, exposing its less prominent features, and adding to what we know about it by other means. While globalisation theorists now admit its lesser-known geographies, the term *globalisation with Chinese characters* acknowledges the particularity of routes through China, they rarely focus their enquiries on them. Instead they rework the same, limited, empirical scenarios and territories, for deeper and ever more abstract truths. This challenge to the grip of hegemonic globalisation on the imagination of global theorists questions, for example, Castells' most excellent conception of globalisation for its focus on the key landing places of network value. My book shows that globalisation is more than this. It is more plural and open. It constantly reroutes trails and opens new ones. New trails, new routes, new configurations and articulations of social and material fabrics, form the mutating substance of globalisation.

The flip-flop trail discourages conceptual complacency. It shows that globalisation is always a work in progress. Only provisional assessments, pending further investigation of something so vast and diverse as globalisation, are appropriate. Further investigation of a diverse range of circumstances and vantage-points is urgently needed. In the interim, our theoretical pronouncements should be provisional and the limitations of their circumstances acknowledged, moderating claims to general truths. This is the first of the insights with implications for how we conceptualise globalisation, to come from the flip-flop trail.

Logics of Travel

The second of these insights is the consequences of shifting the framework of globalisation from objects (as commodities) to people, embarked on the journeys of everyday life. The flip-flop trail pursues globalisation from *inside* the logics of travel, unusually, foregrounding its mobile human substance. Journeys both embed the core logic of globalisation in movement *and* offer a way of investigating it empirically. The logics of travel foreground the everyday lives of people collaborating, in different ways, with the businesses of globalisation, with the macro as well as the micro landscapes that co-produce them. These living, moving, story-telling human fabrics graphically depict the substance of globalisation, and the landscapes on which its multiple possibilities are enacted. Their journeys reveal the skills with which people navigate and customise the trails they weave through their neighbourhoods. The benefit this brings to an understanding of globalisation will be unfolded further below.

Fragility and Precarity

The third insight on globalisation from the flip-flop trail challenges the robust, solid, enduring and thus, perhaps, apparently unchallengeable networked monolith presented in globalisation theory. The flip-flop trail instead exposes globalisation's fragility as an unstable, shifting and ad hoc tangle of translocal routes, which can, and do, as we observed on the trail, reroute in directions that cannot always be predicted. Flip-flop production is particularly fragile on account of its mobility. Low wages and easily learned technical skills make flip-flop production possible in thousands of locations. If flip-flops were people they would be experienced migrants living in transit. Dai Wei's reverie of Middle Eastern feet in the sand cannot be predicted from the logics of capital accumulation. The fragilities of life on the flip-flop trail consist in such random motilities as well as more systematic ones.

What is, perhaps, more surprising are the fragilities and precarities of the hegemonic forms of globalisation, developed around oil and petrochemicals. Viewed from the humanistic perspective of the flip-flop trail, life in Kuwait and Korea is precarious in its own ways, as we observed. On each of the platforms composing the trail, materials, objects and livelihoods can move in any number of directions. This is not to suggest that Kuwaiti, Korean, Chinese, Somali and Ethiopian fragilities are commensurable. They are not, as we could see. Fragilities take different forms and intensities in people's lives.

Globalisation's fragilities and instabilities weave their way through people's lives along the trail as incommensurable, personal insecurities and precarities. Precarity refers to the different ways in which risk is shifted from public and commercial bodies onto the personal circumstances of individual workers and their families. Precarities manifest themselves in being unable to eat three times a day, circumstances which Chinese producers and Ethiopian consumers share. They are manifested in risking imprisonment for evading import duties, in having to drive a taxi or dig clams in old age, and in fearing of invasion and violence. For much of the human substance of globalisation we witness on the trail, the fragile forms of stability available to them in a shifting, precarious world entail remaining poor, so that jobs are not relocated to still poorer places and people. People's navigational skills are attuned to the shifting precarities with which they coexist. They are skilled navigators, as we saw, of globalisation's precarities.

As a counterpoint to the stable networks, strengths and inevitabilities of classic globalisation theory, the flip-flop trail reveals, in the fabric of people's lives, another side to globalisation. This side is anything but consistent and stable. It is instead, an inchoate, ad hoc matrix of shifting, cross-cutting trails that are difficult to anticipate, and even more difficult to live. Globalisation produces fragile and precarious lives, even for those who live in its more privileged locations.

Globalisation on the Back Roads

Straying from the well-trodden superhighways of globalisation, departing from its hegemonic routes, taking the roads less known, striking out on new geographies, following an object without knowing where it is headed and generally wandering off the beaten track, furnishes new thinking on what globalisation is and how it works. What follows unravels the benefits of the back roads a bit further. The idea of back-road globalisation is intended to convey a sense of it as an alternative set of routes. I am not making a conceptual distinction between it and hegemonic versions of globalisation. On the contrary, as the flip-flop trail shows, the two closely intersect. Back roads depart from the main roads, with which they form significant junctions, they cross, and run alongside other main roads, forged by other steams of business animating other lives. Distinguishing back and main roads is thus a matter of descriptive convenience, signalling departure from hegemonic versions of globalisation, rather than a fundamental distinction. Back roads do not lack significance, or large scales of traffic as we have seen. They are back roads in carrying low-value goods and in not marking the landing places of network value, two factors which rule them out as vantage-points onto globalisation. Network value aside, the flip-flop trail reveals some of globalisation's macro-contours forming the social morphology of our time. Three revelations of the trail in particular display the benefits of these back roads.

They reveal significant streams of global migration. In the process they display the rhythms, scales of movement and volition driving these forms of human mobility. They expose the logics of rural-to-urban migrations and difference between points on the trail. These are in full swing across China, over in Korea, and scaled down in Ethiopia. They expose female transnational migration between Ethiopia and Kuwait.

Indeed, at the end of the flip-flop trail, further trails are generated from the rubbish dump to the Middle East. They expose another stream of movements too, in the traffic between Africa and China, which brings Chinese migrants to Africa, and Africans to China.

Second, these back roads reveal what is happening in China. As a global production centre in transition to becoming a major economic powerhouse, China is a twenty-first century force to be reckoned with. Accounts of globalisation should take this into account. These back roads unpack some of its small-scale factory production and the people whose lives it weaves. These back roads reveal China's (quasi-colonial?) relationship with Africa. This is important in rising (competition and) opportunity and (unevenly distributed) prosperity on this continent.

Third, these back roads reveal the current securitisation efforts and, sometimes, the military interventions of the twenty-first century, in borderland struggles with insurgents, jihadists, disaffected citizens and pirates. They expose the seizures and violence undermining the security and prosperity of the global North. In these moments local precarities are transformed and passed along, creating new routes to new places, in which they take new forms. Back roads through Somalia, Djibouti and Ethiopia vividly display the tensions in the (macro) geopolitics of the moment.

Journeys

The journeys composing the back roads of the trail portray the lives of an oil geologist, a team of Korean petrochemical workers, several Chinese flip-flop production workers, the rise of the bosses, an interlocutor in accessing global markets, two Ethiopian traders, a smuggler, an elderly Ethiopian woman and three rubbish scratchers. Their journeys reveal striking similarities between Ethiopians and Chinese in the hyper-local geographies of their journeys, in the purposes relating to them, and in the skills with which they navigate them. Journeys place everyone in the same frame. They enable comparisons between locations, and between lives in the same locations. Journeys display the contours of comparative (dis)advantage. They offer a means of grouping and differentiating people, avoiding the juggernauts of social categorisation, providing instead, as we observed, fine-grained portraits of lives and the circumstances of their living. Journeys reveal the scale on which lives are lived. They expose the hyper-local and the long-distance traveller, along with the rhythms of their routes. They reveal people's calculations and navigational skills, the capacities and circumstances that make their journeys possible.

Journeys reveal places. They expose the missing urban geographies of globalisation. They provide a series of lenses through which cities can be apprehended and analysed. They problematise the relationship between cities, as well as between cities and the routes composing them. Journeys, as I hope I have shown, provide sophisticated urban analytics, while placing the lives fabricating them at the centre of our concerns. Globalisation is increasingly lived in and through cities, in one way or another. In paying close attention to landscape we see the environmental impact of globalisation on the flip-flop trail, in the detritus on the oil and petrochemical landscapes in Kuwait and Korea, in the way discarded flip-flops sit in the landfill site on the edge of Addis, picked over by scratchers, and, perhaps, turned into biomass electricity.

It's All Local

Finally, in among the seething inchoate mobilities composing globalisation, its hyper-locality is declared. Globalisation is lived in houses and in neighbourhoods. It is lived through work. And it is lived in the social relationships of these restless groundings. What stretches these things beyond the local, what makes them global, is a chaotic patchwork of movement, on different scales, by different people, by objects like flip-flops, by materials like plastics, and by substances like food. The flip-flop trail shows that globalisation is made in little, hyper-local sections, all of them connected, in different ways to the next stage or platform on the trail. At no point, and this would seem to be crucial in thinking about globalisation, is an entire trail, or even large sections of it, revealed. Not even in the algorithms of logistics. Trails jolt uncertainly across the opaque intersections between neighbourhoods, locales and nation-states.

Globalisation is not what we think it is. As the flip-flop trail has shown, it is a loose patchwork of human and object journeys. It is an unstable, shifting, contingent mass of ad hoc-ery, with pockets of opportunity within overwhelming landscapes of precarity. Above all, globalisation needs to be re-examined for the opportunities for manoeuvre its instabilities might provide for the mass of people worldwide who struggle in their own ways to navigate it.

Notes

Date last accessed for URLs, unless otherwise stated, is March 2013.

1 Navigating the Territories of the Trail

1. 'Havaianas' with a diamond encrusted strap and feathers made from 18ct gold, and retailing at US$20,000, are among the more expensive flip-flops. See *Financial Times Weekend, How to Spend it Magazine*, 6 July 2008.
2. Edward Tenner (2003) *Our Own Devices*, New York: Knopf, Random House, p. 51.
3. See Tenner, *Our Own Devices*, for flip-flops' history.
4. Tim Ingold (2004:329) 'Culture on the Ground: The World Perceived Through Feet', *Material Culture* 9(3): 315–340, at p. 329.
5. Tim Ingold, (2000) *The Perception of the Environment*, London: Routledge, pp. 195–198.
6. See Daniel Miller (2005) 'Materiality: An Introduction', in Daniel Miller (ed.) *Materiality*, Durham, NC: Duke University Press; also Arjun Appadurai (ed.) (2005) *The Social Life of Things: Commodities in Cultural Perspective*, Cambridge: Cambridge University Press.
7. Michael Peter Smith (2005) 'Transnational Urbanism Revisited', *Journal of Ethnic and Migration Studies* 3(2): 235–244.
8. Igor Kopytoff (1986) 'The Cultural Biography of Things: Commoditization as Process', in Arjun Appadurai (ed.) *The Social Life of Things*, Cambridge: Cambridge University Press, pp. 64–91.
9. Daniel Miller (2008) *The Comfort of Things*, London: Polity.
10. Jane Bennett (2010) *Vibrant Matter: A Political Ecology of Things*, Durham, NC: Duke University Press. This develops further the argument of the anthropology of material objects that our lives are entangled with things, and belongs to the strand of enquiry that questions the boundaries between the human and the non-human. Bennett argues that matter has vital agency she calls 'thingly power' (p. xiii).
11. Craig Calhoun 'Possible Futures', Lecture at the ISA Conference, Gothenburg, 12 July 2010; also Ulrich Beck, 'Cosmopolitan Sociology: Outlines of a Paradigm Shift', Lecture at the ISA Conference, Gothenburg, 13 July 2010.
12. Katherine Boo coins this term in *Behind the Beautiful Forevers*, London: Random House, 2012, a wonderful book that blurs fiction and non-fiction genres and reveals sociology at it most readable and engaging.

13. Deborah Barndt (2008) *Tangled Routes: Women, Work and Globalization on the Tomato Trail*, Lanham, MD: Rowman and Littlefield. This is an excellent example of a trail story from an interdisciplinary and environmentally oriented perspective.

14. James Marriot and Mika Minio-Paluello (2012) *The Oil Road: Journeys from the Caspian Sea to the City of London*, London: Verso, is another excellent example of a trail story. The authors are more interested in tracing the political cartographies of oil than the lives oil touches, but their attention to place is inspiring.

15. Roy Moxham (2009) *A Brief History of Tea*, London: Running Press.

16. Mark Kurlansky (1999) *Cod: The Biography of a Fish that Changed the World*, London: Vintage Books.

17. Joe Bennett (2008) *Where Underpants Come From: From Checkout to Cotton Field – Travels Through the New China*, London: Simon and Schuster.

18. Alex Hughes and Suzanne Reimer (eds) (2004) *Geographies of Commodity Chains*, London: Routledge; Paul Ciccantell and David A. Smith (2009) 'Rethinking Global Commodity Chains: Integrating Extraction, Transport and Manufacturing', *International Journal of Comparative Sociology* 50(3–4): 361–384: Laura T. Reynolds (2002) 'Consumer/Producer Links in Fair Trade Coffee Networks', *Sociologia Ruralis* 42(4): 404–424.

19. Jessica Rothenberg-Aalami (2004) 'Coming Full Circle? Forging Missing Links along Nike's Integrated Production Networks', *Journal of Global Networks* 4(4): 335–354.

20. Gary Gereffi and Miguel Korzeniewicz (1994) *Commodity Chains and Global Capitalism*, London, Greenwood Publishing Group. Michael Peter Smith (2005) 'Transnational Urbanism Revisited', *Journal of Ethnic and Migration Studies* 31(2): 235–244.

21. James Clifford (1997) *Routes: Travel and Translation in the Late Twentieth Century*, Boston, MA: Harvard University Press; and Maurice Merleau-Ponty (2002) *The Primacy of Perception*, New York: Routledge; Zygmunt Bauman (2000) *Liquid Modernity*, Cambridge: Polity Press; John Urry (2010 [2000]) 'Mobile Sociology', *British Journal of Sociology – The BJS: Shaping Sociology over 60 Years*, 347–366, originally published in *British Journal of Sociology* 51(1): 185–203; Mimi Sheller and John Urry (2006) 'The New Mobilities Paradigm', *Environment and Planning A* 38(2): 207–226; Anne-Marie Mol and John Law (1994) 'Regions, Networks and Fluids: Anaemia and Social Topology', *Social Studies of Science* 24: 641–671; and Manuel Castells (1996) *The Rise of Network Society*, Malden, MA: Blackwell.

22. This book draws on some of the ideas of Michel de Certeau (1988) *The Practice of Everyday Life*, Berkeley: University of California Press, in which he outlines the importance of practices such as walking, the significance of everyday activities and draws attention to trajectories, 'the chorus of idle footsteps' (1988: 97) and the (Marxist) idea that everything is produced including

(urban/social) space. It is also indebted to Henri Lefebvre (2000) *Writing on Cities*, London: Blackwell, especially regarding rhythms, and the music of the city in routines of mobility.

23. Arjun Appadurai (ed.) (2005) *The Social Life of Things: Commodities in Cultural Perspective*, Cambridge: Cambridge University Press.
24. Ingold, *The Perception of the Environment*, p. 220.
25. Walter Benjamin (2002) *The Arcades Project*, Cambridge, MA: Harvard University Press Paperback.
26. Raja Shehadeh (2007) *Palestinian Walks: Notes on a Vanishing Landscape*, London: Profile Books.
27. Michel de Certeau (1988) *The Practice of Everyday Life*, Los Angeles: University of California Press, pp. 96–97.
28. Stuart Elden, Elizabeth Lebas and Elenore Kofman (eds) (2003) *Henri Lefebvre Key Writings*, London: Continuum, p. 208.
29. Doreen Massey (2005) *For Space*, London: Sage, p. 9.
30. This comes from Merleau-Ponty, *The Primacy of Perception*, developed by Ingold, *The Perception of the Environment*, p. 341; and Tim Ingold (2011) *Being Alive*, London; Routledge, p. 47, who suggests that in walking landscapes are woven into life, and lives are woven into landscapes. This book treats landscape and its surface as places for investigation of its fabric, its modes of fabrication and its (not hidden) depth. For discussion of landscape see also Denis Cosgrove and Steven Daniels (1988), cited in John Wylie (2007) *Landscape*, London: Routledge, p. 162, which provides lucid examples of this thinking. Also, Denis Cosgrove and Steven Daniels (1988) *Iconography of Landscape*, Cambridge: Cambridge University Press.
31. See Ingold, *Being Alive*.
32. Vincent Kaufman (2010) 'Mobile Social Science: Creating a Dialogue among Sociologies', *British Journal of Sociology – The BJS: Shaping Sociology over 60 Years*, pp. 367–372, at p. 368.
33. Doreen Massey (1999) 'Imagining Globalisation: Power Geometries of Time-Space', in Avtar Brah et al. (eds) *Global Futures*, London: Macmillan, pp. 27–44.
34. Ingold, *The Perception of the Environment*, p. 241; David Held, Anthony McGrew, David Goldblatt and Jonathan Perraton (2003) 'Rethinking Globalization', in David Held and Anthony McGrew (eds) *The Global Transformations Reader*, London: Polity.
35. Ingold, *The Perception of the Environment*, p. 228.
36. Michael Darroch (2010) 'Language in the City; Language of the City', in A. Boutros and W. Straw (eds) *Circulation and the City: Essays on Urban Culture*, Montreal: McGill-Queen's University Press, pp. 23–47.
37. This draws on Susan Leigh Foster's storying bodies in her (1996) *Choreography Narrative*, Bloomington: University of Indiana Press. I have developed these ideas about movement and comportment more fully in Caroline Knowles

(2000) *Bedlam on the Streets*, London: Routledge, and Caroline Knowles and Douglas Harper (2009) *Hong Kong: Migrant Lives, Landscapes and Journeys*, Chicago: University of Chicago Press.

38. Anthony Giddens (2002) *Runaway World: How Globalisation is Reshaping Our Lives*, London: Profile Books; David Held (ed.) (2004) *A Globalizing World? Culture, Economics, Politics*, London: Routledge; Held and McGrew, 'The Great Globalization Debate: An Introduction', in Held and McGrew *The Global Transformations Reader*, p. 3; Saskia Sassen (2007) *A Sociology of Globalization*, New York: W.W. Norton; Saskia Sassen (1998) *Globalization and its Discontents*, New York: The New Press.

39. David Held and Anthony McGrew, 'The Great Globalization Debate: An Introduction', p. 3.

40. Anthony Giddens (1990) *The Consequences of Modernity*, Stanford, CA: Stanford University Press, p. 64.

41. Doreen Massey (1993) 'Politics and Space/Time', in Michael Keith and Steve Pile (eds) *Place and the Politics of Identity*, London: Routledge, pp. 141–161.

42. See Manuel Castells (2001) 'Information Technology and Global Capitalism', in W. Hutton and A. Giddens (eds) *On the Edge: Living with Global Capitalism*, London: Vintage.

43. Manuel Castells (2010) 'Preface', in *The Rise of Network Society*, 2nd edn, Oxford: Wiley Blackwell, pp. 15–16.

44. Ulrich Beck (1992) *Risk Society*, London: Sage.

45. Manuel Castells (1999) *Information Technology, Globalisation and Social Development*, Geneva: UN Research Institute for Social Development (UNRISD).

46. Anna Lowenhaupt Tsing (2005) *Friction: An Ethnography of Global Connection*, Princeton, NJ: Princeton University Press.

47. Janet MacGaffey and Remy Bazenguissa-Ganga (2000) *Congo Paris: Transnational Traders on the Margins of the Law*, Oxford: James Currey.

48. Barndt, *Tangled Routes*.

49. Marriott and Minio-Paluello, *The Oil Road*.

50. Neil W. Adgar, P. Mick Lelley, Alexandra Winkells, Luong Quang Huy and Catherine Locke (2002) 'Migration, Remittances, Livelihood Trajectories, and Social Resilience', *AMBIO: A Journal of the Human Environment* 31(4): 358–366.

51. Colin McFarlane (2011) 'Assemblage and Critical Urbanism', *City* 15(2): pp. 204–224.

52. Adgar et al., 'Migration, Remittances, Livelihood Trajectories, and Social Resilience'.

53. Louise Waite (2009) 'A Place and Space for a Critical Geography of Precarity', *Geography Compass* 3(1): 412–433.

54. AbdouMaliq Simone (2011) 'The Surfacing of Urban Life', *City* 15(3–4), pp. 355–364, at p. 355.

55. Vered Amit (2010) 'Serendipities, Uncertainties and Improvisations in Movement and Migration', in Peter Collins and Anselina Gallinat (eds) *The Ethnographic Self as a Resource: Writing Memory into Ethnography*, Oxford: Berghahn.

56. Simone, 'The Surfacing of Urban Life'.

57. Vered Amit and John Mitchell (2010) 'Series Preface', in Ulf Hannerz, *Anthropology's World*, London: Pluto.

58. Michael Burawoy (2000) *Global Ethnography*, Berkeley: University of California Press; James Marcus (1995) 'Ethnography in/of the World System: The Emergence of Multi-sited Ethnography', *Annual Review of Anthropology* 24: 95–117; Ulf Hannerz (2010) *Anthropology's World*, London: Pluto, p. 74.

59. John Berger (1977) *Ways of Seeing*, London: Penguin.

60. In line with new urban agendas Saskia Sassen (2000) *Globalization and its Discontents*, New York: The New Press, p. 143, sees cities as open and cross-cut by multiple intersecting mobilities of people and objects. See also Ash Amin and Nigel Thrift (2000) *Reimagining Cities*, Cambridge: Polity.

2   Oil – Maps Beneath the Sand

1. This comes from the *Arab Times*, 5 June 2013: www.arabtimesonline.com/NewsDetails/tabid/96/smid/414/ArticleID/158913/reftab/96/t/Kuwait-has-1320-mosques/Default.aspx.

2. Unaccompanied women arriving at a Saudi airport not met by a male guardian stand the risk of being returned to their point of departure – not a good start to a research project. Being prohibited from driving a car would make it difficult to get around and access oil drilling in out-of-the-way desert locations. Even if I were prepared to wear a *burka* for the duration of my visit, these practical difficulties would make it difficult to research oil in what is effectively a gender apartheid state. Choosing research locations I focused on onshore drilling, given the additional practical difficulties of accessing offshore drilling.

3. These figures come from the US Energy Information Administration and relate to proven oil reserves in 2011, which map closely onto volumes of production and are as follows: Saudi 260 million barrels, Venezuela 211 million, Canada 175 million, Iran 137 million, Iraq 115 million and Kuwait 101 million (see: www.eia.gov/countries/cab.cfm?fips=ku).

4. See Daniel Yergin, 'America's Energy Is Once Again Changing the World', *Financial Times*, 17 November 2012.

5. See Adrian Atkinson (2007) 'Cities After Oil: What Future Is This Fast Approaching?', excerpted from his Introduction in *CITY* to his series *Cities After Oil* (2007): www.city-analysis.net/2011/02/13/cities-after-oil-what-future-is-this-fast-approaching/

6. The British Middle Eastern Chambers of Commerce offered to help me organise a trip to Basra through their contacts, which I declined on grounds of security.

7. See Jeremy Rifkin (2002) *The Hydrogen Economy*, Oxford: Polity, for an intelligent account of oil, the fossil fuel economy and what might happen when oil runs out.

8. See Michael Watts (undated) 'Oil City: Petro-landscapes and Sustainable Futures', pp. 96–97, africancitiesreader.org.za/reader/chapters/o16_oilcity.pdf, for a discussion of war and political calculation surrounding oil, as well as what he calls 'petro-urbanism' and 'hydrocarbon capitalism'.

9. Rig costs depend on drilling depth and in Kuwait range from US$21,000 to US$45,000 a day for the rig only. The other contractors needed to run a rig add to this, as well as catering and support services totalling US$1.5 million a day plus for a shallow well. Offshore drilling costs even more. I am indebted to the Head of Drilling Operations at KOC for these estimates.

10. At Howard Dixon House Museum in Kuwait City there is a copy of the agreement between Sheik Mubarak and the British Agent (dated 1899) to maintain the territorial integrity of Kuwait and secure, through British protection, the authority and lineage of Mubarak and his successors.

11. See Daniel Yergin (2012) *The Quest: Energy, Security and the Remaking of the Modern World*, London: Penguin, p. 287, for a lucid and comprehensive discussion of the global oil industry.

12. Bound copies of records relating to the British administration of the Kuwait Protectorate are on display at Howard Dixon House, now a museum in Kuwait City. Howard Dixon was the British Agent in Kuwait (1929–36) and records of his administration are in a series of green-bound books – Kuwait Political Agency Arabic Documents, vols 1–12, and a red-bound series Records of Kuwait 1889–1961 (vols 1–8). Tellingly vols 6–7 of the latter are titled 'Petroleum Affairs'. A letter from Ahmad Al-Jaber dated 31 December 1935 refers to Dixon's move from Kuwait City to Al Hammadi and assumption of his duties as the local representative for the KOC. Oil, KOC and the Kuwaiti nation-state were inseparable by the mid 1930s. Photographs around the walls of Dixon House of successive Emirs and British Agents in Al Hammadi support this connection.

13. US Energy Information Administration, www.eia.gov/countries/cab.cfm?fips=ku.

14. See Rifkin, *The Hydrogen Economy*, which discusses peak oil and what future scenarios after oil might consist of, and Yergin, *The Quest*.

15. Iraqi troops massing on the border with Kuwait from late July invaded in the early hours of 2 August 1990, a move that, if successful, would have made Iraq an oil superpower according to Yergin, *The Quest*, pp. 10–11. A UN-backed coalition mounted Operation Desert Storm on 17 January 1991, liberating

Kuwait City on 23 February and driving Iraqi troops – who left Kuwait's oil fields burning – back over Kuwait's northern border.

16. See: www.investopedia.com/articles/economics/08/determining-oil-prices.

17. Bassam Fattouh (2011) *An Anatomy of the Crude Oil Pricing System*, Oxford: Oxford Institute for Energy Studies.

18. See: www.opec.org/opec-web/en/2468.htm.

19. These figures are for 2012, see: www.cia.giv/library/publications/the-world-factbook/geos/ku.html.

20. Javier Blas, 'Energy: Corridor of Power', *Financial Times*, 4 October 2012, www.ft.com/cms/s/2/b4f57138-0ca7-11e2-b175-00144feabdc0.html#axzz2 XJVW9THn.

3   Choreographies of Petrochemistry

1. The term *chaebol* is often used to describe the big corporations composing corporate Korea, such as Samsung, Lotte and LG. These giant corporations grew through state support in the 1960s in the context of governments sufficiently authoritarian to develop the Korean economy through corporations. *Chaebol* also refers to the organisation of these corporations, which is hierarchical, paternalistic and bureaucratic. Although no longer supported financially by the government, the chaebols are now so well developed and entrenched that it is difficult for new entrepreneurs to break into this corporate scene. See Daniel Tudor (2012) *Korea: the Impossible Country*, Singapore: Tuttle Publishing.

2. Daesan's geography is its key attraction; it has deep water that can be navigated by large ships and tankers, and it is only '400km from China in a straight line' and hence its biggest market. See: 'Daesan in Seosan Takes a Leap Forward Towards the Goal of Becoming a World-class Petrochemical Complex', 21 August 2009, www.news148.ndsoftnews.com/news/article.

3. The Persian Gulf accounted for 75 per cent of Korea's 2010 oil imports. Saudi is its leading supplier (28 per cent), with Kuwait (12 per cent) and UAE (13 per cent) second. See: Energy Information Administration (2011) 'Country Analysis Briefs, South Korea', www.eia.gov/cabs/south_korea/full.html. Kuwait has developed a business partnership with Korean petrochemical industries, one of its key customers for crude oil.

4. Access, again was difficult, as petrochemical plants are as highly securitised as oil wells.

5. Naphtha passes through a cracking process where heavy molecules are broken down into lighter ones. The new products created, olefins and aromatics, are the building blocks of the petrochemical industry, from which the fabrics of the modern world, including numerous combinations making different types of plastics, are made. See: APPE flowchart, www.petrochemistry.net/from-crude-oil-to-petrochemicals.html.

6. 'How Plastics Are Made', Mindfully.org, 22 June 2008, www.mindfully.org/Plastic/How-Plastics-Made

7. See: www.elmhurst.edu/~chm/vchembook/325petrochem.html.

8. See: Energy Information Administration, 'Country Analysis Briefs, South Korea', www.eia.gov/cabs/south_korea/full.html, for a discussion of how petrochemicals shape the world in which we live. By 1900 there were synthetic rubbers undermining plantations; Bakelite was the first plastic (1907); solvents (1920) and polystyrene (1930s) followed, at first tentative and experimental. See: www.petrochemistry-net/what-is-petrochemistry.html.

9. There are no official estimates available of the proportion of the workforce who are women, so these figures come from anecdotal evidence I cannot check. Where gender is not seen as an issue there would be no reason to compile data on gender in the workforce.

10. BTI (Bertelsmann Stiftung's Transformation Index) (2012) 'South Korea Country Report', www.bti-project.de/fileadmin/inhdte/reports/2012/pdf.

11. BBC News, 19 December 2012, www.bbc.co.uk/news/world-asia20787271.

12. Korea's focus on children and prioritisation of education is contextualised by high literacy rates (98 per cent), falling birth rates and longer life expectancy. See: Library of Congress – Federal Research Division (2005) 'Country Profile: South Korea', May, http:lcweb2.loc.gov/frd/profiles/south-korea.

13. See Myung-Goo Kang (1998) 'Understanding Urban Problems in Korea: Continuity and Change', *Development and Society* 27(1): 99–120, for a fuller discussion of the shape of the Korean landscape under the influence of industry and chemicals.

14. BTI (Bertelsmann Stiftung's Transformation Index), 'South Korea Country Report'.

15. See Wendell Cox (2011) 'The Evolving Urban Form: Seoul', *New Geography* 17th February 2011 for a discussion of Seoul.

16. Data drawn from OECD (2012) 'Urban Policy Reviews, Korea', www.scribd.com/doc/112604664/OECD-Urban-Policy-Reviews-Korea.

17. OECD (2012) 'Urban Policy Reviews, Korea'.

18. BTI (Bertelsmann Stiftung's Transformation Index), 'South Korea Country Report'.

19. 'South Korean Economy', *Economy Watch*, 30 March 2010, www.economywatch.com/world_economy/south-korea.

20. Energy Information Administration, 'Country Analysis Briefs, South Korea'.

21. Energy Information Administration, 'Country Analysis Briefs, South Korea'.

22. Jung-yoon Choi. 'South Korea to Step Up Suicide Prevention Efforts', *Los Angeles Times*, 8 September 2011, http://articles.latimes.com/2011/sep/08/world/la-fg-south-korea-suicide-20110909.

23. S.Y. Kim, M.H. Kim, I. Kawachi and Y. Cho (2011) 'Comparative Epidemiology of Suicide in South Korea and Japan: Effect of Gender and Suicide Methods', *Crisis* 32(1): 5–14, www.ncbi.nlm.nih.gov/pubmed/21371965.

24. Jong Youl Lee (2000) 'The Practice of Urban Renewal in Seoul Korea: Mode, Governance and Sustainability', paper presented at the Second International Critical Geography Conference, Seoul, Korea, August; Myung-Goo Kang (1998) 'Understanding Urban Problems in Korea: Continuity and Change', *Development and Society* 27(1): 99–120.

25. *The Economist*, 21 November 2012.

26. See: 'LG Chem: Company Information from ICIS', www.icis.com/V2/companies/9145950/lg+chem.html.

4   Plastic City

1. Conceptualisation of the city as an expressive form comes from the work of Benjamin, Wittgenstein and Barthes, in which the city is a language spoken by its users in everyday practice. Michael Darroch, 'Language in the City, Language of the City', p. 26, discusses this. Rather than see the city as a language, in this book the city is a point of intersecting journeys of different kinds. These routine long- and short-haul journeys of different kinds fabricate the city. Thus what the city expresses are traces left by journeys past and present as well as the enactment of those journeys.

2. See: www.fuzhou.org (accessed December 2008).

3. The idea that cities have a footprint refers to their extension beyond their literal boundaries; see Ash Amin, Doreen Massey and Nigel Thrift (2000) *Cities for the Many not the Few*, Bristol: Polity Press.

4. See: www.fdz.com.cn/english.

5. Mette Thuno and Frank N. Pieke (2005) 'Institutionalising Recent Rural Emigration from China to Europe: New Transnational Villages in Fujian', *International Migration Review* 39(2): 485–514.

6. The Deng Xiaoping economic reforms stimulated transfers of foreign capital and expertise from the developed economies in the region realised in the special economic zones.

7. Joshua Cooper Ramo (2004) *The Beijing Consensus*, London: Foreign Policy Centre, p. 20.

8. Mihai Craciun (2001) 'Ideology: Shenzhen', in Chuihua Judy Chung, Jeffrey Inaba, Rem Koolhaas and Sze Tsung Leong (eds) *The Great Leap Forward*, Cambridge, MA: Harvard Design School, p. 111.

9. See: www.fuzhou.org (accessed December 2008).

10. Home Office (2006) *China: Country of Origin Information Report*, London: Home Office, December, p. 18.

11. Home Office, *China: Country of Origin Information Report*, p. 60.

12. Ramo, *The Beijing Consensus*, p. 11.

13. Home Office, *China: Country of Origin Information Report*, pp. 12–13.

14. Home Office, *China: Country of Origin Information Report*, pp. 12–13.

15. Li Xuju, one of its leaders in the People's Daily, cited in Ramo, *The Beijing Consensus*, pp. 11–12.

16. The Home Office, *China: Country of Origin Information Report*, p. 12 estimate concurs with that of the World Bank, which suggests that since 1979 China has lifted 300 million people out of poverty. See Ramo, *The Beijing Consensus*, pp. 11–12.

17. Ramo, *The Beijing Consensus*, pp. 23–24.

18. Home Office, *China: Country of Origin Information Report*, pp. 13–14.

19. Home Office (2006) *China: Country of Origin Information Report*, pp. 13–14.

20. Zhong Qingwu (1998) 'The Residential Identity Card', in Michael Dutton (ed.) *Streetlife China*, Cambridge: Cambridge University Press, pp. 94–97; and Gong Xikui (1998) 'Household Registration and the Caste-like Quality of Peasant Life', in Dutton (ed.) *Streetlife China*, pp. 81–86.

21. Michael Dutton (1998) 'Life on the Outside', in Dutton (ed.) *Streetlife China*, pp. 144–147; and Chen Baoliang (1998) 'To Be Defined a Liumang', in Dutton (ed.) *Streetlife China*, pp. 63–65.

22. Ramo, *The Beijing Consensus*, p. 8.

23. See: lifeofguangzhou.com (accessed January 2009).

24. See: www.rentalcartours.net.

25. In practice the delineation of rural and urban land is not clear-cut as much urbanisation involves the reclassification of 'counties into cities, townships into towns and encroachment of city into suburbs. Thus government enlarges the land area under its jurisdiction.' This refers to 'instant urbanization' (p. 293) and the 'lucrative business of city building' (p. 286); see Chiew Ping Yew (2012) 'Pseudo-urbanization? Competitive Government Behaviour and Urban Sprawl in China', *Journal of Contemporary China* 21(74): 281–298.

26. For discussion of Chinese land speculation and urban housing markets see Zhu, Jianhnan (2012) 'The Shadow of the Skyscrapers: Real Estate Corruption in China', *Journal of Contemporary China* 21(74): 243–260; Wooyeal Park and Kihyun Lee (2012) 'I Want to Be Expropriated!' The Politics of Xiaochaquanfang Land Development in Suburban China', *Journal of Contemporary China* 21(74): 261–279.

27. World Bank (2003) *Gini Coefficient Study*; also, Shankar Gopalakrishnan (2007) 'Negative Aspects of Special Economic Zones in China', *Economic and Political Weekly*, 28 April. Both cited in Ramo, *The Beijing Consensus*, p. 24.

28. Bhaskar Goswami (2007) 'Special Economic Zones: Lessons from China', 13 February, www.countercurrents.org (accessed January 2009).

29. 'Several Issues in Perfecting the Socialist Market Economy', from the 2003 Plenary session of the Party Congress, in Ramo, *The Beijing Consensus*, p. 21.

30. Geni Raitisga (2007) 'Business China', www.radio86.co.uk/explore-learn/businesschina.

31. Fulong Wu (2009) 'Neo-urbanism and the Making of the Chinese Market Transition', *City* 13(4): 418–431, argues that increases in home ownership (80 per cent in 2000) show the importance of cities in developing the contemporary Chinese political economy.

32. Craciun, 'Ideology: Shenzhen', p. 111.

33. Tatsuyuki Ota (2003) 'The Role of Special Economic Zones in China's Economic Development as Compared with Asian Export Processing Zones: 1979–1995', *Asia in Extensio*, www.iae.univ-potiers.fr.

34. Rem Koolhaas (2001) in Chuihua Judy Chung et al. (eds) *The Great Leap Forward*, the Chinese fieldwork project by his Harvard architecture students, pp. 27–8. See also Nancy Lin (2001) 'Architecture', in Chuihua Judy Chung et al. (eds) *The Great Leap Forward*, pp. 165–173.

35. www.fuzhou.org (accessed December 2008).

36. Li Peilin (2010) 'Sustainable Development Seen from China', paper presented at the International Sociological Association, Gothenburg. Li Peilin does not here make clear how he is using the term 'middle class'.

37. Max Weber's (1978 [1922]) notion of class, outlined in *Economy and Society: An Outline of Interpretive Sociology*, edited by G. Roth and C. Wittich, Berkeley: University of California Press, as clumps of occupations with similar life chances, is particularly useful. Wendy Bottero (2005) *Stratification: Social Division and Inequality*, London: Routledge, pp. 38–41, gives a clear account of this and can be used as a guide to the intricacies of class and social stratification. She points out that Weber uses the concept 'class situation' instead of social class. He sees classes as structural economic categories conferring similar life chances, by which he means differences in opportunity, lifestyle and general prospects. He defines class in relationship to property ownership and labour markets, as well as the circumstances to which these things give rise. This opens the possibility of a subtle range of class situations. While Weber himself sees class situations as loose, inherently unstable social groupings, and in the context of China they are most certainly quite fluid, it is important to add to his insights from more recent theories of class which foreground material social conditions and human agency. My book is particularly clear on the ways in which Chinese workers and factory owners actively and imaginatively create the social worlds in which they live: that biography is as significant as social structure in generating class, which is simultaneously an objective condition of economy and activated as a social and biographical project.

38. Social structure is also helpfully explained in Bottero's discussion of Weber (in *Stratification: Social Division and Inequality*, pp. 38–41). Social structure has three discrepant and overlapping dimensions – class, status and party – in which resources gained in one dimension, can be converted into the others. Status is about social prestige and is self-consciously articulated in lifestyle: buying a condo, wearing flip-flops to the bathroom rather than the market, etc. Party refers to the kinds of social and political power arising from

contacts and associations and is particularly relevant in China, as this chapter has demonstrated. The material, biographical, and hence social and human agency dimensions of this are clearly drawn in my book. It is people who animate structures and systems in creative and unpredictable ways.

39. Zhu Di and colleagues at the Chinese Academy of Social Sciences in Beijing, for example.

40. Alexandra Harney (2008) 'How Li Luyuan Became Middle Class', *Financial Times Magazine*, 5 April: 23–27, provides a graphic biographical portrait of a rural migrant factory worker in Shenzhen.

41. Li Zang (2001) *Strangers in the City: Reconfigurations of Space, Power and Social Networks within China's Floating Population*, Stanford, CA: Stanford University Press, pp. 3, 107.

42. See Stephan Feuchtwang and Wang Mingming (2001) *Grassroots Charisma: Four Local Leaders in China*, London: Routledge, pp. 59–60.

5   Plastic Village

1. On this part of the trail I worked with Singapore artist Michael Tan who photographed the landscape, the people and the factories. These photographs have been exhibited in a number of places, including at the National Museum of Singapore in 2008. Some of them are also exhibited on the website that comes with this project. Michael speaks Mandarin and so provided invaluable interpreter services on this part of the flip-flop trail. In earlier sections of the trail in China Dai Wei acted as interpreter.

2. The Village or the plastic village refers to a specific 'village' – as locals refer to it – which has a large concentration of plastic, and particularly flip-flop, factories. This was once a village on the southern outskirts of Fuzhou: here the land was owned by those who farmed it and who were, in various ways, compensated when it was appropriated for factory production. I will not name the village in order to protect those who generously gave their time in interviews and allowed us into their homes. We did not seek permission from the Chinese government for this research. While journalists cannot work without it academic researchers operate in a grey area where it seems possible to work under the radar of official notice rather than through a government minder, a circumstance that would make gathering this kind of material impossible or meaningless. The downside of this informality is that it sometimes made people uneasy about how their information might be used and whether they could get into trouble with the authorities for giving it. Anonymity is therefore not just an ethical requirement but essential in order to protect informants from any consequences arising from their participation in this research, and, of course, the anonymity of people is better protected in the context of the anonymity of places and factories.

3. Landscape is used as a verb in this context and so refers to the production of place.

4. See Zhang Quingu (1998) 'The Resident Identity Card and the Household Register', in Dutton, *Streetlife China*, pp. 94–97. Also Gong Xikui, 'Household Registration and the Caste-like Quality of Peasant Life', in Dutton, *Streetlife China*, pp. 81–86.

5. See Feuchtwang and Wang, *Grassroots Charisma*, pp. 34–38 for a discussion of these social processes in relation to another village in Fujian Province, set in a discussion about the Ancestor's Hall.

6. This story is corroborated by Rachel Murphy (2002) *How Migrant Labour is Changing Rural China*, Cambridge: Cambridge University Press, pp. 12–13. Murphy suggests this ban was in 1998, although the millennium celebration rekindled the demand for firecrackers and production began to return to villages in Jiangxi after 2000. Women assembled firecrackers at home and in small factories. She also points out that Jiangxi is a major exporter of labour with 20 per cent of its labour force currently working in other provinces (p. 35).

7. Stephan Feuchtwang (2004) 'Curves and the Urbanisation of MEIFA Village', in Stephan Feuchtwang (ed.) *Making Place: State Projects, Globalisation and Local Responses in China*, London: UCL Press, p.166.

8. Murphy, *How Migrant Labour is Changing Rural China*, pp. 25, 105–176.

9. Murphy, *How Migrant Labour is Changing Rural China*, pp. 25, 105–176.

10. Li Zang (2001) *Strangers in the City: Reconfigurations of Space, Power and Social Networks within China's Floating Population*, Stanford, CA: Stanford University Press, attests to deep regional divisions between migrant workers in city and factory areas.

11. Murphy, *How Migrant Labour is Changing Rural China*, p. 1.

12. Li Zang, *Strangers in the City*, p. 3.

13. Li Peilin (2010) Lecture in International Sociological Association session 'Globalization, Crisis and the Actor', using data from the Chinese Office of Central Rural Work Leading Group, Chinese People's Congress, 2 February 2009.

14. Feuchtwang and Wang (2001) *Grassroots Charisma*, pp. 38–40, chart the close association between the Village Gathering Hall and significant economic and political changes China-wide, as well as in the village they studied in another part of Fujian Province. They also point out that ritual is more than it seems. It involves the re-creation and extension of local religious cults, the reproduction of the household as a village socioeconomic institution, extensions of the household economy, the making of social relationships in the mobilisation of resources, and the creation of collective identities.

15. Feuchtwang, 'Curves and the Urbanisation of MEIFA Village', p. 166.

16. Tatsuyuki Ota, 'The Role of Special Economic Zones in China's Economic Development …'.

17. Frank Pieke, Pal Nyiri, Mette Thunø and Antonella Ceccagno, *At the Margins of the Chinese World System: The Fuzhou Diaspora in Europe*, ESRC Transnational Communities Programme, Research Briefing No. 4, www.transcom.ox.ac/wwwroot/pieke (accessed August 2007).

18. See: www.USinfo.state.gov/eap/archive-index/The-social-organisation-of-Chinese-human-smuggling (accessed August 2007) citing extracts from Ko-lin Chin (2001) *Global Human Smuggling: Comparative Perspectives*, Baltimore, MD: Johns Hopkins University Press.

19. See: www.fdz.com.cn/english.

6   Making Flip-flops

1. In the interests of protecting the anonymity of those who collaborated with this study the factories and their workers will not be identified so as to protect informants' security. All names are fakes. While half a dozen factories of different scales and types of production in the area were investigated as part of the research, The Factory was chosen for detailed study because it seemed typical of most types of production in the area, being of a medium size and with medium technology and because it (unusually) allowed me better access than others.

2. Murphy, *How Migrant Labour is Changing Rural China*, p. 2.

3. Murphy, *How Migrant Labour is Changing Rural China*, p. 33.

4. Home Office, *Country of Origin Information Report on China*, p. 11.

5. Home Office, *Country of Origin Information Report on China*, p. 12.

6. Murphy, *How Migrant Labour is Changing Rural China*, pp. 93–102.

7   Logistics, Borderlands and Uncertain Landings

1. White woven plastic sacks hold 100 pairs of flip-flops, a cardboard box only 60 for a similar volume in the container. Dai Wei says that packing for containers is important: clever packing reduces transport costs.

2. Access to the enclosed environments of seafaring as well as the guarded spaces of ports is complicated and could easily have taken over the trail in terms of the amount of time and permissions involved in getting into them. I therefore decided that, while these spaces are important, they could not receive the attention they deserve but need to be the subject of their own book.

3. See Mimi Sheller, and John Urry (2006) 'The New Mobilities Paradigm', *Environment and Planning A* 38(2): 207–226, and Anne-Marie Mol and John Law (1994) 'Regions, Networks and Fluids: Anaemia and Social Topology', *Social Studies of Science* 24: 641–671 for elaborated notions of flow.

4. World Bank (undated) 'The Evolution of Ports in a Competitive World', *World Bank Port Reform Toolkit, module 2*, www.worldbank.org.html/fpd/transport/portstoolkit (accessed February 2009).

5. World Bank, 'The Evolution of Ports in a Competitive World'.

6. This section draws on Wee Beng Geok, Yang Lishan and Ivy Buche (2005) *Pacific International Lines*, Nanyang Technological University Business School, AsiaCase.com – The Asian Business Case Centre, Singapore.

7. Chen, the founder of PIL, in Wee Beng Geok et al., *Pacific International Lines*, p. 6.

8. John Law (2001) *On the Methods of Long-distance Control: Vessels, Navigation, and the Portuguese Route to India*, Centre for Science Studies, Lancaster University, and John Law (2003) *Materialities, Spatialities, Globalities*, Centre for Science Studies, Lancaster University, www.comp.lancs.ac.uk/sociology/papers/Law.

9. Chen, the founder of PIL, in Wee Beng Geok et al., *Pacific International Lines*, p. 7.

10. Bin Wu and Jonathan Morris (2009) 'Riding the Waves of Globalization: The Boundaryless and Borderless Careers of Chinese Seafarers', *Economic and Industrial Democracy* 30(3).

11. See Seafarers International Research Centre, Cardiff University, SIRC Symposium, July 2007.

12. Roger Middleton, a Chatham House expert in this region, uses the following definition of piracy in his analysis, developed by the UN Convention on the Law of the Sea: 'illegal acts of violence or detention ... committed for private ends'. Roger Middleton (2008) 'Piracy in Somalia: Threatening Local Trade, Feeding Local Wars', Chatham House Briefing Paper, www.chathamhouse.org.uk/publications/papers, p. 3.

13. See: www.chathamhouse.org.uk/research/africacurrent_projects/armed_non_state_actors.

14. Middleton, 'Piracy in Somalia ...'.

15. BBC News (2008) 'Somali Pirates Living the High Life', 28 October, www.news.bbc.c.uk/1/hi/world/africa.

16. Middleton, 'Piracy in Somalia ...'.

17. Middleton, 'Piracy in Somalia ...'.

18. See: http://pviltd.com/pages.

19. See: www.icc-ccs.org.uk/piracy-reporting-centre/live-piracy-map.

20. See: www.cia.gov/library/publications/the-world-fact-book (accessed March 2013).

21. See: www.reuters.com/article/2013/03/01/us-djibouti-unrestidusbre9200TT 20130301 (accessed March 2013).

22. *The Guardian*, 27 January 2013, www.guardian.co.uk/word/somaliland.

23. Mark Tran writes for *The Guardian* on Somaliland, see *The Guardian*, 27 July 2011, for example.

24. *The Guardian*, 27 January 2013, www.guardian.co.uk/word/somaliland.

25. Mark Tran (2012) 'Inside Somaliland's Pirate Prison, the Jail that No Country Wants', *The Guardian*, 23 August, www.theguardian.com/world/2012/aug/23/inside-somaliland-prison-pirates.

26. See the United States index for example at: www.foreignpolicy.com/articles/2009/06/22/2009/failed_states_index. This, like other indices, takes a reading that includes numbers of refugees, grievances, uneven development, economic decline, human rights violations, security apparatus and a factionalised elite.

27. Sally Healy (2008) *Lost Opportunities in the Horn of Africa*, Chatham House Report, www.chathamhouse.org.uk/files/11681_0608hornafrica.pdf.

28. Roger Middleton, 'Piracy Symptom of Bigger Problem', BBC News Online, 15 April 2009, http://news.bbc.co.uk/1/hi/world/africa/8001183.stm.

29. Middleton, 'Piracy Symptom of Bigger Problem'.

30. Healy, *Lost Opportunities in the Horn of Africa*.

31. Middleton, 'Piracy Symptom of Bigger Problem'.

32. Middleton, 'Piracy Symptom of Bigger Problem'.

33. It has proved impossible to check this. No Chinese shippers admit to running a parallel global shipping operation and it is too dangerous to visit Somalia to interview traders who would have this information.

34. Janet Roitman (2005) *Fiscal Disobedience: An Anthropology of Economic Regulation in Central Africa*, Princeton, NJ: Princeton University Press, p. 8.

35. Roitman, *Fiscal Disobedience*, p. 154.

36. Roitman, *Fiscal Disobedience*, p. 155.

8   Markets

1. See: www.addisculturetourism.gov.et/en/tourism-addis-ababa-ethiopia-2/attractions-addis-ababa-ethiopia-2/mercato-addis-ababa-ethiopia-2.html.

2. See Priti Ramamurthy (2003) 'Transnational Feminist Research', *Cultural Anthropology* 18(4): 524–550, for a discussion of transnational movements of fabrics from the vantage-point of India.

3. Kibralim is a student and ex-contrabandist who worked for me as a market guide and interpreter while I was in Addis in 2008.

4. Tettushi Sonobe, John Akoten and Keijiro Otsuka (2006) *The Development of the Footwear Industry in Ethiopia: How Different Is It from the East Asian Experience?* Tokyo: Foundation for Advanced Studies on International Development, p. 4, www.fasid.or.jp/daigakuin/fa_gr/kojyu/discussion/2006-09-03.

5. Tegegne Gebre Egziabher (2006) 'The Developmental Impact of China and India on Ethiopia with Emphasis on Small-scale Footwear Production', paper presented at the Accelerated and Shared Growth in South Africa Conference, Johannesburg, August, p. 9.

6. Egziabher, 'The Developmental Impact of China and India on Ethiopia …', p. 14.
7. Sonobe et al., *The Development of the Footwear Industry in Ethiopia*, p. 4.
8. Sonobe et al., *The Development of the Footwear Industry in Ethiopia*, pp. 9–10.
9. Personal interview with Fecadu Gadamu, Professor of Sociology at the University of Addis Ababa and political activist.
10. *CIA World Fact Book*, https://www.cia.gov/library/publications/the-world-factbook/geos/et.html (accessed 10 December 2007).
11. Egziabher, 'The Developmental Impact of China and India on Ethiopia …', p. 14.
12. This is 91.9 per 1000 population; *CIA World Fact Book*.
13. *CIA World Fact Book*.
14. *The Economist* (2007) 'A Brittle Western Ally in the Horn of Africa', 1 November, http://www.economist.com/node/10062658 (accessed January 2014).
15. *The Economist*, 'A Brittle Western Ally in the Horn of Africa'.
16. *The Economist*, 'A Brittle Western Ally in the Horn of Africa'.
17. *The Economist*, 'A Brittle Western Ally in the Horn of Africa'.
18. Tim Ingold, *The Perception of the Environment*, p. 289.
19. AbdouMaliq Simone (2004) *For the City Yet to Come*, Durham, NC: Duke University Press, pp. 179–180, citing James Ferguson (1999) *Expectations of Modernity: Myths and Meanings of Urban Life on the Zambian Copperbelt*, Berkeley: University of California Press.
20. At January 2010 rates of exchange 10 birr is approximately US 80 cents, 15 is US$1.20.
21. Simone, *For the City Yet to Come*, pp. 184, 189.
22. AbdouMaliq Simone (2004) 'Critical Dimensions of Urban Life in South Africa', in Toyin Falola and Steven J. Salm (eds) *Globalization and Urbanization in Africa*. Asmara: Africa World Press.
23. Niko Besnier (2004) 'Consumption and Cosmopolitanism: Practicing Modernity at the Second Hand Market Place in Nuku'alofa, Tonga', *Anthropological Quarterly* 77(1): 7–45.
24. See Urban Planning and Development in Addis Ababa project, German Federal Ministry for Economic Co-operation and Development, www.gtz.de/en/praxis/6603 (accessed 5 December 2007).
25. Simone, *For the City Yet to Come*.
26. See: www.giz.de/Themen/en/dokumente/en-akzente-spezial-urban-management.pdf.
27. Simone, 'Critical Dimensions of Urban Life in South Africa'.
28. See: www.telecom.net/~aamp/Address ORAAMP, Addis Ababa City Government Office for the Revision of the Addis Ababa Master Plan (accessed 13 December 2007).

29. See: www.telecom.net/~aamp/Address ORAAMP, Addis Ababa City Government Office for the Revision of the Addis Ababa Master Plan (accessed 13 December 2007).

9   Urban Navigation in Flip-flops

1. Kilos are, of course, are a measure of weight, but are also commonly used to measure distance in Ethiopia and a reminder of people's past rural roots. Thus the suffix 'kilo' as in 'arat kilo', or 8 kilos, finds its way into street names where it refers to distances from the colonial historical centre of Addis under Ethiopia's brief history of Italian occupation in the 1930s.

2. Why Zema? In looking for a pair of feet supplied with flip-flops from Moapa's kiosk I consulted him on whom to choose. Among contending feet and flip-flops a fiercely insistent adult daughter, Demaku, re-routed me from a neighbour suggested by Moapa and promoted Zema's. The research on which this book is based is one of the opportunities to arise in these lives, and Demaku displays her skill in mobilising it to her family's advantage.

3. The Addis city mayor's office says the population of Addis is 4 million and that there is an 8 per cent growth rate (www.citymayors.com/mayors/addis-mayor, 28 September 2004, consulted 5 December 2007).

4. See Urban Planning and Development in Addis Ababa project, German Federal Ministry for Economic Co-operation and Development, www.gtz.de/en/praxis/6603 (accessed 5 December 2007).

5. Simone, *For the City Yet to Come*, pp. 179–180, citing Ferguson, *Expectations of Modernity*.

6. This is her second husband. Initially Zema did not reveal that she had been married twice, the first time at 14 in the village, the second time soon after she was 19 and she had left her first husband to migrate to the city, supported by a kinswoman.

7. Michael Tan, the Singapore artist who covered parts of the trail with me, was invited to cut the bread as an honoured male guest.

8. Garth Myers and Francis Owusu (2003) 'Cities of Sub-Saharan Africa', in Stanley Brun, Maureen Hays-Mitchell and Donald J. Ziegler (eds) *Cities of the World*, Lanham, MD: Rowman and Littlefield, p. 341.

9. See: www.citymayors.com/mayors/addis-mayor, dated 28 September 2004 (accessed 5 December 2007).

10. Matthew Asfaw (2007) 'Urban Mobility: Challenges and Prospects: The Case of Addis Ababa', www.bremen-initiative.de/lib/papers/addis. This data is for 1982 the most recent of this type of data available.

11. See: www.ppiaf.org/urban Bus Toolkit/assets/casestudies/summary (accessed 10 December 2007).

12. See: www.ppiaf.org/urban Bus Toolkit/assets/casestudies/summary.

13. See: www.capitalethiopia.com/archive/2007/may/week1/society (accessed 5 December 2007).

14. See: www.citymayors.com/mayors/addis-mayor.

15. Simone, *For the City yet to Come*, p. 209.

16. David Smith and Matthew Newsome (2012) 'Ethiopian PM Meles Zenawi's Death Sparks Fear of Turmoil', *The Guardian*, 21 August, www.theguardian.com/world/2012/aug/21/meles-zenawi-death-fears-turmoil.

17. See: www.amiando.com/eventResources/p/oJOQD6buh3xtNnr/Transportation-challenges-in-Addis.pdf.

18. UN Habitat Regional and Technical Co-operation Division (2008) *Ethiopia: Addis Ababa Urban Profile*. Nairobi: UN Habitat.

19. UN Habitat Regional and Technical Co-operation Division (2008) *Ethiopia*.

20. Smith and Newsome (2012) 'Ethiopian PM Meles Zenawi's death …'

21. DFID Operational Plan 2011–2015, updated June 2012, www.gov.uk/Doculaments/publications1/op/ethiopia-2011pdf.

22. Anuradha Mittal (2013) 'Indian Land Grabs in Ethiopia Show Dark Side of South–South Co-operation', *The Guardian*, 25 February, www.theguardian.com/global-development/poverty-matters/2013/feb/25/indian-land-grabs-ethiopia.

23. John Vidal (2013) 'Indian Investors are Forcing Ethiopians Off Their Land', *The Guardian*, 7 February, www.ethiomedia.com/addis/5624.html.

10   Rubbish

1. Mary Douglas famously designates dirt as matter out of place and establishes the symbolism of dirt in her *Purity and Danger: An Analysis of the Concepts of Pollution and Taboo*, London: Ark Paperbacks (1966).

2. My thanks to Francisco Calafate Faria, with whom it has been a pleasure to talk rubbish.

3. Michael Thompson (1979) *Rubbish Theory: The Creation and Destruction of Value*, Oxford: Oxford University Press.

4. Liz Parsons (2008) 'Thompson's Rubbish Theory: Exploring the Practices of Value Creation', *European Advances in Consumer Research* 8: 390–393; see also Kate Maclean (2013) 'Evo's Jumper: Identity and the Used Clothes Trade in "Post-Neoliberal" and "Pluri-Cultural" Bolivia', *Gender, Place and Culture* 1: 1–16, which empirically traces circulations of clothing from the global North to Bolivia and the ways in which they enter new lives.

5. Jane Bennett (2010) *Vibrant Matter: A Political Ecology of Things*, Durham, NC: Duke University Press.

6. Martin O'Brien (2008) 'Waste Management proves a Profitable Business', *Ecologist* , 7 August, http://www.theecologist.org/investigations/waste_and_recycling/269478/waste_management_proves_a_profitable_business.html (accessed January 2014).

7. Martin O'Brien (2007) *A Crisis of Waste? Understanding the Rubbish Society*, London: Routledge.

8. Rudi Colloredo-Mansfield (2003) 'Introduction: Matter Unbound', *Journal of Material Culture* 8(3): 245–254, Special Issue, which shows that waste has social significance and that it is important to consider disintegration, release and the circulation of matter.

9. Catherine Alexander and Joshu Reno (eds) (2012) *Economies of Recycling: The Global Transformation of Materials, Values and Social Relations*, London: Zed Books.

10. 'Scratchers' is one of the terms used by the officials at the ministry and it seems in the scheme of things one of the less derogatory ways of referring to these people.

11   *Globalisation Revisited*

1. Charles Lemert (2002) *Dark Thoughts: Race and the Eclipse of Society*, New York, London: Routledge.

2. Janet Abu-Lughod (2007) 'Globalization in Search of a Paradigm', in I. Rossi (ed.) *Frontiers of Globalization Research: Theoretical and Methodological Approaches*, New York: Springer, pp. 353–360.

3. Vered Amit with Sally Anderson, Virginia Caputo, John Postill, Deborah Reed-Danahay and Gabriela Vargas-Cetina (forthcoming) *Concepts of Sociality: An Anthropological Interrogation*, Oxford: Berghahn Books.

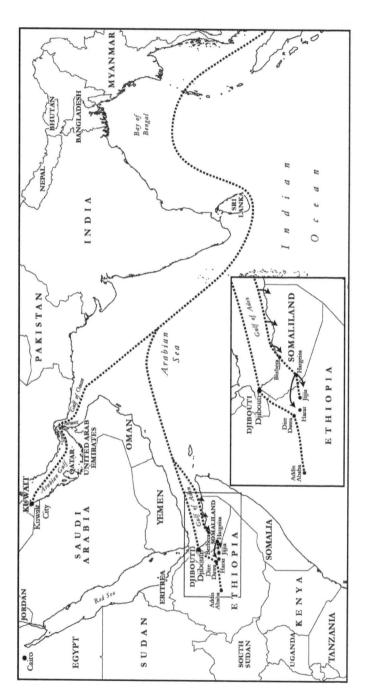

Map 1   The beginning and end of the trail

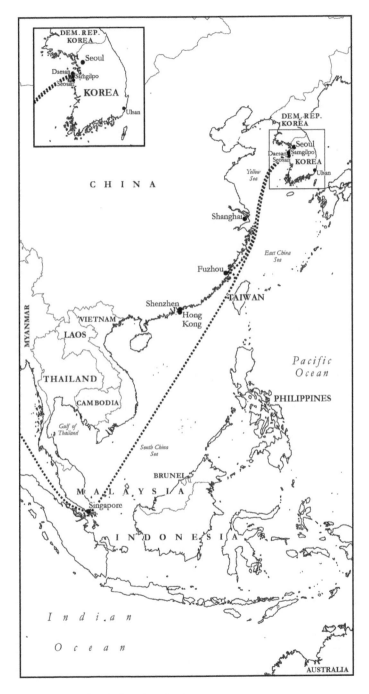

Map 2   Petrochemicals and production

Index